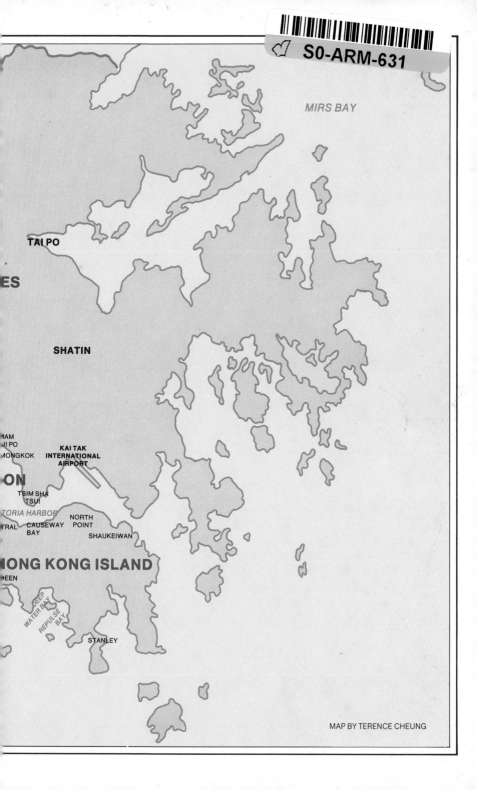

MIRS BAY

TAI PO

ES

SHATIN

IAM
JI PO
MONGKOK

KAI TAK
INTERNATIONAL
AIRPORT

ON

TSIM SHA
TSUI

TORIA HARBOR

RAL   CAUSEWAY   NORTH
       BAY   POINT

                    SHAUKEIWAN

HONG KONG ISLAND

EEN

DEEP
WATER BAY
REPULSE
BAY

STANLEY

MAP BY TERENCE CHEUNG

Living in Hong Kong

Eighth revised edition

*Note: While every care has been taken in preparing this book, no warranty
is given or implied as to the accuracy of any of the contents. While all
efforts were made to insure the accuracy of this information, details are
bound to change from time to time and, therefore, companies intending
to do business in Hong Kong should satisfy themselves on all matters.*

The American Chamber of Commerce in Hong Kong
Publications Department: 1030 Swire House, Central, Hong Kong
Mail: GPO Box 355 Hong Kong. Tel: 526 0165
Tlx: 83664 AMCC HX Fax: 810 1289
Cover Design by: Henry Steiner/Graphic Communication Ltd
Text Pages Design by: Cynthia Law
Printed in Hong Kong by: Gilman Business Machines
Cover photo by: Sunny Chan

The American Chamber of Commerce in Hong Kong

CONTENTS

Preface

The books publishing program of the American Chamber of Commerce in Hong Kong plays a unique role in the territory's English-language publishing world, as it continues to expand the base of business information available from the Chamber to its members and the public.

As I write, there are a dozen book titles now in print and three new titles in preparation, ranging from our most popular title and a Hong Kong best seller, *Living in Hong Kong*, to highly specialized industry titles like our, *Hong Kong Electronics Handbook/Directory* or *Who's Who in Hong Kong Communications*.

Barring firms which deal in books derived from expensive consultancies and proprietory information, with prices to match, there are few business book publishers in English, in Hong Kong. Only the UK firm, Longman's, and the two university presses here produce books for business readers in significant numbers.

Which means the Chamber has inadvertantly become one of the major business book publishers here, in terms of titles specifically on doing business in Hong Kong and China. We are also the only major American publisher in such local areas of interest.

The book publishing program has enabled us to break new ground where no Hong Kong/China information sources or regularly updated databases in book form previously existed: in electronics, communications, training services, staff recruitment, food and beverage distributors and markets, the presence of PRC firms in Hong Kong, establishing an office in Hong Kong, doing business in Guangdong province, and Chamber member or other American firms doing business in China.

But more than business intelligence is derived from our publishing program. We have also used a policy of copublishing whenever possible, so as to foster closer relations with like-minded organizations on business matters.

These copublishers have included overseas arms of the United States government, such as the Foreign Agricultural Service of the US Department of Agriculture and the Foreign Commercial Service of the US Department of Commerce. They have also included Hong Kong government agencies or those subvented by government, such as the Hong Kong Trade Development Council, the Hong Kong Departments of Labour and of Industry. In the private sector, we have worked with the Institute for International Education, America's oldest and largest student counselling organization, and with GTE, one of America's largest multinational publishers.

The program has also brought the Chamber's staff into closer working relationships with its members. Our books often carry donated chapters placing industries described in a Hong Kong context, written by locally experienced member specialists. Members of relevant committees are normally invited to advise and/or act as review readers before publication. Complimentary book copies are sent to committee chairmen, requesting they provide post-publication reviews for the improvement of future editions.

We are proud of the quality of our publications and eager to expand our catalog of useful titles in print. Please share your comments and criticisms with our publications manager and any ideas you may have for new subjects that might be usefully put into print.

Warren Williams, President (1991)
The American Chamber of Commerce in Hong Kong

Acknowledgements

The information in this eighth edition was willingly given by numerous individuals without whose enthusiastic support and help this book could not have been written. Acknowledgements must also go to the many people who put together the first seven editions of the book, their meticulous research has made updating editions a relatively easy task.

Many thanks to the following people and organizations: **Jachin Chan** (Hong Kong Bible Language Center) for his review of the 'Language' section; **Raylene Thompson** (Crown Pacific) for her work on 'Moving to Hong Kong'; **Lois Gochnauer** (US Consulate) for her work on 'Getting Settled'; **John Irvine** (Adventist Hospital), **Joseph Yip** (Wyatt), **Paula Saraga** and **Sister Joyce Smith** (Matilda Hospital) for their help on 'Living and Health'; **Diana Lyn Eilkin** (Promotional Marketing) for her help on 'Communications'; **Roy Ian Delbyck** and **Mattie Genovese** (Kingship Ltd) for their help on 'Legal Information'; **Jim Peterson** (Manufacturers Hanover) for has work on 'Financial Institutions'; **YY Tang** of the Hong Kong Insurance Council for her help in 'Insurance'; the **Hong Kong Department of Internal Revenue** for the latest information in 'Taxation'; **Kay Ng** (US Customs) for help on 'Leaving'.

Foreword

Since its first publication in 1973, *Living in Hong Kong* has become a standard newcomer's reference work among books about the territory and, we like to think, for good reason. Each edition is updated with the goal of providing a definitive source on all manner of needs. They range from things to know on your first reconnaissance here through finding a home, school and sports club when you've arrived, to preparing to leave for your next assignment.

In most cases we go directly to the people and organizations listed for updating, so the book's preparation takes about six months to complete. We are shy of achieving our goal of a new edition every two years (the edition prior to this was released in September 1989) — though we won't stop trying.

Since so much time elapses from conception to completion, we also design each chapter of the book with specific referrals to other more thorough or more often updated sources where relevant.

We hope thereby to serve as a sort of 'hotline' to other sources of help whenever we can't answer your question or can't be certain our answer will still be current when you need it.

Living in Hong Kong, like the American Chamber of Commerce here itself, is international in scope and outlook. It is meant to be of use to expatriates of all nationalities and so you will find things like information on Japanese and German schools as well as American and British, for instance. Although there are some 40 nationalities represented in Hong Kong, the non-Chinese population is tiny — less than two percent of almost six million people — which helps explain why it can be intimidating to newcomers. If this eighth edition of *Living in Hong Kong* helps make your arrival and settling in here more manageable, it will have served its purpose. If you find things missing or that might be covered more thoroughly please tell us, so we can pass on what you've learned to those who will follow, in our next edition.

Fred S Armentrout
Publications Manager & General Editor
The American Chamber of Commerce in Hong Kong

Chapter 1
BACKGROUND

Anyone who announces that he or she is going to live in Hong Kong is liable to receive a wealth of comment and advice from people who have visited here, who have lived here, or who know someone who has lived here. Some of this free advice may be helpful, but there is also a tendency for conflicting views and opinions to build up into such a kaleidoscopic muddle that no clear picture emerges and one still does not really know what to expect. Hong Kong can therefore hit you with a bang even after listening to everyone else's warnings and opinions on what the place is like, the climate, the people, and much else besides.

This chapter - indeed this book - is not intended to be comprehensive but rather to provide some introduction to the history of the place and to present-day conditions in Hong Kong. Fortunately, for those who can spare the time and have the inclination, there are now many guides to Hong Kong which give good descriptions and are usually overflowing with color illustrations. Hong Kong's natural beauty and its many unusual and colorful features make it, happily, one of the most over-photographed places in the world. Everything from spectacular aerial views to the most intimate street scene seems to have been recorded. It is well worthwhile to make time before arrival to look at such pictures and also to read as much as possible about Hong Kong, its background, and what it is like now. (see 'Further Reading')

Early History

Long before the British arrived in Hong Kong, there was a small population of farming and fishing communities in scattered villages. Evidence of very much earlier prehistoric habitation is being built up by modern archaeological diggings which are still proceeding. In the third century BC, however, the Guangdong province area was brought under the control of the Chinese emperor. At that time, Hong Kong was sparsely settled, as evidenced by excavated stone and bronze tools and pottery which appear to be some 2,500 years old. The Lei Cheng Uk Tomb in Kowloon dates from the Eastern Han Dynasty (first century AD), and in the New Territories the village of the Tang Clan has been populated since the eleventh century. Cantonese and Hakka probably arrived in the area during the Song Dynasty (960-1279 AD).

Contacts with the West

Although Arab traders reached China and had a community in Canton in the seventh century, and the Portuguese came to Macau in the sixteenth, Hong Kong only really became important (other than to the pirates for whom it was home base) in the 19th century, when Western traders with China needed a safe port to refit their ships and trade freely. Foreigners were then allowed into Canton only during the trading season and only in certain areas from which the local Chinese were excluded so that the 'barbarians' would not corrupt or contaminate Middle Kingdom. It was illegal for a foreigner to learn Chinese, to bring families to Canton (they remained in Macau), or to deal with anyone except the emperor's appointed representatives. The trade that was important enough to tolerate these conditions was import to China of opium and the export of silks, tea, porcelain, and a variety of Chinese products.

In 1799, China declared opium illegal. The emperor wished to halt the import of opium, but his representatives in Canton connived with British firms and firms of other Western countries to continue the lucrative trade. In 1839 the Chinese besieged the offices and dwellings - the much-illustrated 'factories' - of the foreigners at Canton, and boarded British ships to confiscate and burn opium. The English fled on board ships to the harbor of Hong Kong.

The Royal Navy retaliated, starting the First Opium War that ended in the Convention of Chuenpi, which, though apparently never signed or ratified, ceded Hong Kong Island to the British in perpetuity. Lord Palmerston, Queen Victoria's Foreign Secretary, wrote that Hong Kong (from the Chinese '*heung gong*' meaning 'fragrant harbor') was a 'barren island' and hardly a proper concession on the part of China. He wanted a commercial treaty and therefore once again found reason to attack China in a war that ended in the Treaty of Nanking in 1842. Five Chinese ports in addition to Hong Kong were opened for trade after this Second Opium War. In 1860, the Convention of Peking granted Kowloon (as far as Boundary Street) and Stonecutters Island in the harbor to the British in perpetuity. The New Territories, along with 235 islands, were leased in 1898; this lease expires on June 30, 1997, the date Hong Kong returns to China's sovereignty.

The island of Hong Kong covers 29 square miles, Kowloon has a little more than three square miles, and the New Territories, which include all the other islands, a land area of 365 square miles. Farms and small villages once occupied most of the New Territories but nowadays much of the space is taken up with industrial complexes and the 'new towns' such as Tai Po and Sha Tin. An extremely well-organised government housing project transformed these sleepy villages into enormous, modern cities in the decade between 1977 and 1987. Kowloon ranks among the areas of highest population density in the world. Kai Tak airport (soon to be replaced) crowds against residential and industrial areas; vehicular and pedestrian traffic is heavy. Nathan Road, from

Jordan Road to Star Ferry is known as the 'Golden Mile' and is lined with shops stocked with the consumer goods of the Eastern and Western worlds.

Government

Hong Kong has been a British colony since 1841, but the clock is ticking toward the expiration of its colonial treaties and the handing over of this capitalist enclave to Communist China. After two years of intense negotiations, Britain and China signed a joint declaration in December 1984 that paves the way for the transfer of the territory to China, in July 1997. The pact lays out a 'one-country, two-systems' philosophy: Hong Kong will become a special administrative region under the jurisdiction of Communist China, but for 50 years after 1997 it will be allowed to retain its current political, social, commercial, and legal systems, including the capitalist economic and trade systems that have made the territory an international center of finance and commerce.

The joint declaration's principles have been incorporated into a Basic Law that will govern Hong Kong after 1997. This law was drafted by China's National People's Congress, after receiving input from the Hong Kong public through a 180-member consultative committee of influential government, business, and community leaders. A Joint Liaison Group of Chinese and British officials has also been set up to tackle problems that might crop up during the transition to 1997. Hong Kong citizens were tense and anxious during the contentious negotiations between Britain and China over the territory's future. Some are skeptical of the agreement because of their deep-seated distrust of the Chinese Communists, an uneasiness born of their own experiences on the mainland. But a poll of the population soon after the pact was signed showed a majority found the agreement acceptable as a whole.

Still, the community has registered its concern over certain points, including possible interference by the Chinese government, Hong Kong residents being drafted into the Chinese military, the potential unacceptability by other countries of the new Hong Kong passport that will be issued, the preservation of their current rights and freedoms, the stationing of Chinese troops in the territory, the termination of transmissibility of British nationality for Hong Kong citizens, and the faithful implementation of the joint declaration.

Confidence in the territory's future, in general, is quite high although events following the June 4, 1989 massacre of demonstrators in Tiananmen Square have gravely darkened and confused matters at this writing. The business community and Hong Kong citizens are keenly reading between the lines of every statement being issued by China's leaders as their home gradually, but inevitably, changes hands.

Until that happens, Hong Kong is still a British Crown Colony, although the term 'colony' is officially avoided, and replaced with 'territory' in the interests of good relations with China. The Queen's appointed representative, the Governor, is the head of government and presides over two main policy-making bodies: the Executive and Legislative councils.

The Executive Council (Exco) meets weekly to advise the governor on financial matters and policy in a wide range of areas. Decisions are thus made by the 'Governor in Council'. The council is composed of four ex-officio members -- the Commander of British Forces, the Chief Secretary, the Attorney General, and the Financial Secretary -- and other members who are appointed by the Governor on the instructions of the Secretary of State. Executive Council official members are heads of government departments; unofficial members are community representatives nominated because of their particular knowledge and awareness of Hong Kong and its people. All have equal voting rights.

The Legislative Council (Legco) meets once a week on Wednesdays to enact legislation and oversee the spending of public funds. Before they become law, bills passed by Legco need the approval of the Governor, who is both a member and president of the council.

Legco, like Exco, was originally made up of appointed members but in 1985 the slow move toward democracy began with the council's first ever elections. Twelve members were elected by an electoral college -- a tightly restricted franchise which elected members for nine functional constituencies: commercial, industrial, financial, labor, social services, education, legal, medical, engineering and associated professions.

In September 1991, the government took another step towards democracy by dividing the seats even further. For the first time, 18 seats on the 60-member council were open to election under universal franchise. 21 seats were elected through functional constituencies and the remaining 21 seats were appointed. This move came three years later than planned after pressure from Beijing resulted in a slowing of the government's reform program.

Unofficial members of the Executive and Legislative councils also operate an office called UMELCO. This is not a government office; rather, it operates as a complaints bureau where the public can come to criticize and to seek advice and information.

Another group, the Urban Council, is supported by a percentage of land taxes (rates) and oversees street cleaning, refuse collection, food hygiene, environmental hygiene, liquor licensing, and recreational and cultural activities in the territory. It is composed of 30 members, 15 appointed and 15 elected, who meet monthly.

Public reactions to the government and the needs of the people are also voiced through a series of rural committees and district boards in 19 administrative districts.

Hong Kong law is a mixture of English Acts of Parliament (those enacted prior to April 5, 1843), Hong Kong ordinances, and the common law of both England and Hong Kong. The rights of the individual are safeguarded by the judiciary. The courts in Hong Kong include the Supreme Court -- consisting of the Court of Appeal and the High Court -- the district courts, and magistrates courts. In addition, the Coroners Court, the Tenancy Tribunal, the Labour Tribunal, the Lands Tribunal, and the Small Claims Tribunal have special responsibilities. Among the functions of the judiciary is the trial for all criminal cases and the determination for civil disputes, whether between individuals or between individuals and the government or with a department of the government.

Newcomers are reminded that when in doubt on legal matters, the prudent thing to do is consult one of the many competent local lawyers. AmCham can provide lists for your convenience.

Hong Kong Trade & Industry

Hong Kong's has been described by Nobel laureate economist Milton Friedman as the 'last laissez faire economy'. Hong Kong is a free enterprise economy which welcomes everyone to the marketplace with minimum restrictions, making it a 20th century intrepid in the tradition of its 19th century founding.

The manufacturing sector is the mainstay of Hong Kong's export-led economy, accounting for some 18.3 percent of the GDP and 28 percent of total employment. It is estimated that up to 90 percent of Hong Kong's manufacturing output is eventually exported. Light manufacturing, producing mainly consumer goods, predominates.

About 65 percent of the total industrial workforce is employed in the textiles, clothing, electronics, plastic products, toys, and watches and clocks industries. These industries together account for 73 percent of Hong Kong's total domestic exports.

Hong Kong is one of the top 11 traders in the world. Trade is normally in balance but in 1990 it showed a small deficit. Its largest trading partner, by far, is China, followed by the United States and Japan.

Hong Kong is almost entirely dependent on imported goods -- for manufacturing components, consumer goods and food. China provides almost 36 percent of Hong Kong's food imports -- mostly chicken, pork and vegetables -- while Japan and Taiwan lead the field in consumer goods and manufacturing components. With only six million consumers, Hong Kong is the world's 13th largest import economy. On a per capita basis, it ranks near the top.

Clothing is still the largest component of domestic exports. Other major export items are plastic toys and dolls, other plastic goods and jewelry. There is also a growing market for more sophisticated items such as electrical machinery, watches and clocks, telecommunications and sound recording apparatus as well as office machines and automatic data-processing equipment.

The United States is the largest market, importing 29 percent of Hong Kong's total exports. China is next with 21 percent, followed by Germany and Britain.

Re-exports showed a very significant increase in 1990 accounting for 65 percent of the combined total of domestic exports and re-exports. Once again China leads the way both as a port of origin of re-exported goods and as an importer of goods re-exported through Hong Kong.

The fact that imports are restriction-free, differentiates the territory from other Asian markets who aggressively export but assiduously block imports.

As a result of its economic philosophy and bottom-line results, Hong Kong continues to be an attractive location for overseas investments with the United States, Japan and the PRC accounting for three-quarters of all foreign investment.

People and Customs

Population . Before 1841 there were only a few thousand farmers and fishermen living on Hong Kong Island, but the new town expanded so rapidly that a housing shortage developed almost immediately for Westerners and for the immigrants from China and Macau. A growing population has been a problem ever since. The first houses were constructed along the northern shore of Hong Kong Island. The 19th century shoreline was at Queen's Road and much of what is now Central District began to be reclaimed from the harbor in 1904. Early settlers suffered malaria, typhoons and crime but persevered. The population in 1851 was nearly 33,000 (31,500 of whom were Chinese, with the remainder being as many Indians as British). By 1899 it was 200,000 and in 1931, 879,000. It declined dramatically during World War Two. When the Japanese occupation ended on August 30, 1945, the population was 600,000 but rose to 1.8 million by 1947.

As the Kuomintang began to retreat before the Communists in China, a huge influx of people arrived in Hong Kong from the mainland, approximately 750,000 in 1949-50 alone. By 1971, there were 3.9 million people in Hong Kong, and by the end of 1990 the population was almost 5.86 million.

In 1990, 21.5 percent of the population was under 15, compared to 25.5 percent ten years ago. About 98 percent of Hong Kong's people are Chinese; 59.3 percent of them were born in Hong Kong. Cantonese make up the greatest proportion of the Chinese population. There are also Hakkas, who live mostly in the New Territories; Hoklos, who are boat-dwellers but have settled on the islands; Tankas, the majority of Hong Kong's boat people and fisherfolk; and also people from the various provinces of mainland China.

The two percent of Hong Kong's population that is not Chinese comprise a truly international community. The largest group of non-Chinese are the 70,000 Filipinos (95 percent of whom are domestic helpers). They're followed by the Americans, British, Indians, Australians, Canadians, Malaysians, Thais, Portuguese, Japanese and Pakistanis. There are smaller communities of French, Germans, Dutch, Koreans, Indonesians, and Singaporeans.

Emigration continues to be a cause for concern in government and business circles. In 1990, 62,000 persons emigrated compared to approximately 20,000 in 1980. Most of the new emigrants are young professionals worried about Hong Kong's future. Last year, the government took steps to slow down the so-called 'brain drain' by asking Britain to do something to encourage people to stay. The result was an amendment to Britain's Nationality Act which would allow 50,000 heads of household to acquire British citizenship without having to fulfil the three-year residency requirement. This gesture was poorly received by the public, many of whom would prefer to emigrate to Australia, Canada and the United States -- the three most popular destinations for would-be emigrants.

Culture Shock. To help new residents understand more about this diverse population and its way of life, the Community Advice Bureau offers a series of orientation evenings in the Spring and Fall called 'Discovering Hong Kong' to new residents of Hong Kong. The Hong Kong Management Association also provides courses for expatriate business people who may be dealing with Chinese staff for the first time. But everyone who comes to Hong Kong must in one way or another learn a good deal about how the Chinese live and work, their culture, attitudes, and philosophy. 'Face' is spoken of, as is 'filial devotion'. The newcomer comes to learn about these and other aspects of Chinese cultural inheritance.

There are numerous contradictions that confront one new to the Orient. Some things, like Chinese books, may seem back to front, and tolerance of strange customs and habits is needed.

One example is that while love and respect for one's family is highly revered in Hong Kong, as in China, public behavior on the part of Hong Kong Chinese might often seem rude to Westerners. You might find much selfish pushing in bus queues. Rushing into an elevator or the underground subway before anyone can get out is very much a part of Hong Kong's go-getting pace.

A concern for health is manifest in the refusal to drink any water not boiled, although Hong Kong's water is said to be entirely acceptable. It also is considered unclean to carry a used handkerchief or tissue. On the other hand, spitting is quite common here, if much reduced.

One always tries to give and save 'face', yet you may very well be asked by a total stranger who admires something you're wearing, 'How much did you pay for it?' This is not intentionally rude, but a matter of not sharing a Western notion of courteous discourse. These and myriad other seemingly contradictory experiences give clues to the differing concepts of manners between East and West and to various aspects of the cultural thought-patterns of a people whose civilization has existed for thousands of years.

Certainly some of the problems for the foreigner in Hong Kong are purely language-related. It is often difficult enough to understand one's countrymen, let alone someone whose first language is different than your own. One cannot always translate a thought into another culture's language. The Chinese are a proud people who for centuries attempted to keep their borders closed, to refuse to admit 'barbarians' to their Middle Kingdom. Newcomers should read, listen, be patient, and attempt to understand that the difficulties they face in understanding the Chinese are no less tough than the problems the Chinese have in understanding them.

Language

Hong Kong has two official languages, English and Cantonese. Cantonese is a dialect spoken by most southern Chinese from Canton (Guangzhou) and some of the surrounding Guangdong province. Many dialects are spoken in China, but everyone can read Chinese characters. The characters have varying sounds and tones in each dialect, and the problems Chinese have in understanding those from different areas are a great deal harder than, for example, any problems a London Cockney would have in deciphering the utterances of a South Carolina belle. This leads to some peculiar situations. A man may be Mr Ng in Guangzhou, but when he travels to Peking,the character is read and pronounced 'Wu'. When Mr Wong moves from Hong Kong to Fukien he becomes Mr Wee, and in Beijing he is Mr Huang.

Chinese dictionaries and telephone books must organize their contents without the aid of an alphabet. But each character contains one of 214 'radicals' or basic elements and also consists of a certain number of strokes. Characters can therefore be 'alphabetized' by determining the radical and looking under it or, and more usually, by arranging them by the order and the numbers of strokes. You may soon begin to recognize some characters, as the street and direction signs are bilingual. But it requires the knowledge of about 1,500 characters, and special study of colloquial newspaper style, to read newspapers. A number system has been worked out so that cables can be sent in four-figure units to represent characters.

One difficulty that some Westerners have on coming to Hong Kong is pronouncing the romanized place and street names. The problem is that the most widely accepted romanization was done by an early missionary, and the forms do not always easily equate with what one expects. This has caused a number of peculiar and common errors. Some mispronunciations of Chinese place-names in Hong Kong have become established in this way. Tsim Sha

10

Tsui in Kowloon is perhaps the best, or worst, example. Local Chinese residents have assumed that these mispronunciations were the correct 'English pronunciation', when in fact they only arose from misguided efforts to say the name in correct Chinese, while using a poor phonetic romanization. Their continued use has thus become perpetuated by considerate Chinese residents, purposely mispronouncing Chinese under the mistaken impression that they are helping the foreigner to understand!

The People's Republic of China is making Mandarin, or Putonghua (the language of Beijing), the national language. Simplified or abbreviated characters are also used in China but have not yet been generally adopted in Hong Kong. The *pin yin* romanization system is gradually replacing older systems for Mandarin, but it is not used on the island of Taiwan. It is also one of the four official languages of Singapore. Most Chinese people in Hong Kong are from the Canton area, and when the Hong Kong government years ago responded to demands that Chinese become the second official language — for use in the courts and government proceedings — Cantonese was the language chosen.

Learning Cantonese. Cantonese is a tonal language and difficult to learn. The nine or more tones are particularly hard for Westerners. There are the usual stories of a man who invited a guest to sit down and actually said 'get out'. The word *gai*, depending upon pronunciation, can mean chicken, street, or prostitute and six or more things as well. At an elementary level, one tries to learn not to raise one's voice at the end of a question and to listen for the tones.

It is, however, rewarding to try to learn at least some Cantonese. There are many schools and private tutors available in town — listed in the Yellow Pages under 'Tuition' — and some companies will pay for families to take lessons. It will help you in many ways. Not only will an understanding of Cantonese help you communicate on a most basic level, but it is a way of showing that you care enough about the Chinese residents here to try to meet them halfway. And you won't find a more appreciative audience. Many expatriates, even some non-Cantonese Chinese, find that they can function easily enough in Hong Kong without going to the trouble of understanding Cantonese. In fact, many live here for 10 or 15 years without knowing more than a handful of Cantonese words. However, it's probably true to say that it is impossible to get the most out of a foreign country where you do not speak the language.

In Cantonese, a question is asked: 'Are you going, not going to movies?' and the answer is 'going' or 'not going'. Or 'Would you like, not like to do it?' Answer: 'like' or 'not like'. There is a more or less all-purpose 'no' (*mo-ah*), which really means 'not have'. *Hai* means 'is' or 'are' (it is the entire verb 'to be'). Therefore, offering an option — even in an English question — can help when talking to a Chinese person.

There are few tenses in Cantonese. Simple past, present, and future are made clear by saying when; today I go, yesterday I go, or tomorrow I go. Therefore, Cantonese often have trouble with our tenses. Not having a singular and plural form for nouns,things are bought or talked of in terms of 'pieces'. These are words called 'classifiers' (which translate as 'piece' or 'pieces'). The classifier changes for different kinds, sizes, or shapes of objects, but the most common one is *goh*. This means one buys not three books, but three pieces of book. A dining set may include four pieces of chair. At a flower stall one wants six pieces of rose. As you pay for a couple to board the ferry you can pay *leung goh*, which indicates that you are paying fares for 'two pieces' (of ticket or people). It is very useful to ask your (Chinese) *amah* or your friends to tell the name of your street and number and the name of your block of flats in Cantonese. Streets in Central and Tsim Sha Tsui and the names of the major office buildings are easy to learn and helpful in taxis. You can check the names of theaters in Cantonese, but be warned that the Chinese name for a film is often not a direct translation of the English title.

The traditional Chinese family is both extended and close. Filial piety is the great virtue, but respect is also due to all family members and elders. Everyone has a title of sorts. Most *amahs* are called *Ah* ..., the prefix being a friendly and somewhat honorary title that precedes part of the given name. One calls fellow office workers '*Ah* ...', but one may not say this to someone older. An elderly *amah* named Fung is addressed by a younger person as *Fung-sum*, the *sum* being a dignified form of 'auntie'. When an apartment building has a series of elderly caretakers or watchmen, they can all be called *Ah Bahk*, which is a respectful title, meaning old man or uncle. In traditional style, the first character of a name in Chinese is the surname. The next two characters are the given names. A few surnames, such as Au-yeung have two characters, and some given names are of only one character. Foreigners in Hong Kong often use all three characters to give a sound similar to their surname. This, of course, leaves nothing for the given name, but is yet another of the accepted oddities of Hong Kong. Visiting cards are widely used and the Chinese name and address is often given on one side and the foreign name on the other. Many Chinese acquire a Christian name (usually in school); others treasure their Chinese name, which is usually in the traditional order of surname first. Ng Ho Yee would be a member of the Ng family. Her friends would call her Ho Yee, and she may also be called Margaret Ng. Women will often continue to use their own family name (maiden name) after they are married, or in addition to their married surname.

There are two ways to say thank you in Cantonese: *Mm goi* is an all-purpose thanks for services, to the waiter who brings your bill, the doorman who opens a car door, to your husband when he holds your coat. It also serves as a polite 'Excuse me'. *Daw tse* expresses gratitude for a gift.

Amah, though not an English-sounding word, is possibly from Anglo-Indian rather than the Cantonese for mother. Domestic servants in Chinese are, both singular and plural, *gung-yun* (work-person). In Cantonese, one returns or comes back to work, school, and home. If you call an office at 9.15 am and hear that Mr Jones has not come back, it may be that he has not yet arrived. Think how fortunate that is when you are late to work and the boss calls! One last problem in understanding Cantonese or pidgin English is in reference to money — Cantonese do not say 20 cents or 50 cents. *Ho ji* or *ho* is a 10 cent piece, and you may hear 'two 10 cents' for 20 cents. The word for dollar — *mun* — is often replaced by the classifier *goh*. Therefore, *say goh say* is four pieces of dollar and four (10 cents), or \$4.40 (*say* means the number four).

Cantonese is a challenge but well worth the effort, both because it is the most widely spoken language in Hong Kong and because of the insight it provides into the Chinese way of thinking.

Climate

Hong Kong lies 100 miles south of the Tropic of Cancer and has a tropical monsoon climate. Although the winter is not severe, there are definite seasons. A long summer from mid-April to September is hot, humid, and very rainy; about 80 percent of the annual rainfall of 87 inches (2210 mm)occurs during these months. October to December are mild, sunny months, cooler and dry. January through March is the coldest period, with temperatures averaging 15C (59 F). In June and July, the hottest months, the average temperature is 28C (82F).

Typhoons may be expected from May to November. Typhoon is the local name for a hurricane, from the Chinese *(dai fung)* words meaning 'big wind'. Tropical storms are named in alphabetical order of their appearance. These storms, if they pass close to Hong Kong, bring heavy rains, high tides, and strong winds.

Typhoon and monsoon warning signals are forecast via visual signals in the harbor, and regularly broadcast on radio and television. You can obtain copies of the signals and their meanings issued by the Royal Observatory, from the Government Publications Office located in the General Post Office Building.

Typhoon Signals. The strong monsoon signal is a black ball.

Number 1 is a standby signal and means a tropical cyclone centered within 400 kilometers may affect Hong Kong.

Number 3 is a strong wind signal that gives approximately 12 hours' notice of strong winds with sustained speeds of 22-23 knots and gusts exceeding 60 knots. As soon as this signal is raised, all schools, kindergartens and colleges are closed.

Number 8 signals sustained wind speeds of 34-63 knots with gusts of 100 knots. When this signal is raised all law courts, offices, banks and stock exchanges are closed bringing commercial life to a standstill. Public transport stops as soon as is practical -- ferries are usually the first to stop as sea conditions are generally bad. All precautions should be taken at this point: typhoon shutters should be put up, any loose structures should be tied down. Stay indoors, away from windows and glass doors.

Number 9 means winds of 48-63 knots. Stay indoors. The typhoon is likely to be very close to Hong Kong.

Number 10 means winds in excess of 63 knots with gusts that may exceed 140 knots. If the eye of the typhoon passes over Hong Kong, there will be a temporary lull which may last anything from a few minutes to an hour. Do not go out during this lull; once the eye has passed over, hurricane force winds will resume -- from the opposite direction.

Precaution. Most expatriates live in reasonably substantial housing and even in a full typhoon are quite safe indoors. Nevertheless windows can be broken and should be taped. Air conditioners have been known to blow into rooms or be sucked out of windows. If windows leak, mopping-up operations can occupy a family for hours. Children should not be allowed near windows, beds should be removed from under windows, and curtains closed to prevent broken glass from flying into the room. If you have never experienced a severe typhoon before, do not be tempted to take risks and go outdoors while signals are up. Flying shop signs or loose scaffolding can be lethal, as can downed power lines in water.

14

Typhoons are potentially dangerous, and insurance is available to cover any damage to personal property. Many leases place responsibility for repairing typhoon damage on the tenant. See the 'Insurance' section in Chapter 4, 'Living and Health', for more information. If you remain indoors there should be little reason for concern about personal injury.

Food

It is sometimes hard to believe that an environment as apparently urban as Hong Kong's would produce any agricultural products. However, Hong Kong farmers, primarily living in the New Territories, produce 33 percent of the fresh vegetables that the territory's population eats, 37 percent of the live poultry, and 16 percent of the live pigs, while its fishermen catch 15 percent of the freshwater fish eaten in Hong Kong and 80 percent of marine fish and shell-fish. The rest of Hong Kong's food comes from all over the world, much of it from China and other nearby Asian countries.

Every kind of food can be eaten in the plentiful and excellent restaurants of Hong Kong. There is Chinese food from the provinces of Canton, Peking, Shanghai, Chiu Chow, and Szechuan - with or without music and floor shows. Other cuisines available include Japanese, Korean, Thai, Vietnamese, Malay, Indian, Hungarian, British, Australian, Russian, Italian, Swiss, Jewish, Filipino, Mexican, and French. There is a choice of Continental *haute cuisine* or American hamburgers. Imported to Hong Kong come the delicacies of the world: avocadoes, jellied eels, smoked salmon, and Kobe beef. From Hong Kong there is excellent seafood. Chinese food is as varied as Western food. There are regional specialties and differences in preparation, spices, and even the foodstuffs themselves.

In Chinese restaurants the usual rule is to order as many different dishes as there are persons at the table, plus one. The Chinese will also choose dishes that contrast color and textures. Dishes are placed in the center of the table and each guest helps himself with his own chopsticks (except at banquets, when a waiter may serve from the central dishes). Small pieces of food are taken and put into an individual dish or bowl of rice. There is usually another small bowl or plate for bones, etc. If food is spilled on the tablecloth, no notice is taken. Paper napkins are often supplied, and small hot and cold towels will be handed out before, during, and at the end of the meal.

Soup usually comes at the end of a meal, but before the rice, except at banquets when several soups may be served between other courses. Fruit signals the end of any large banquet. Most banquets consist of 8 to 12 or more courses; cold dishes (appetizers) are followed by 4 to 6 main courses, soup, rice and/or noodles, and dessert, which usually includes a sweet almond or bean soup. Tables are round, usually set for 12 people. At banquets and weddings, brandy or whiskey served in water glasses precedes and accompanies the meal. Soft drinks, beer, and tea are also served. Drinking water, wine and coffee are rare. The Chinese drink brandy and beer, usually very moderately. There is often a bottle of whiskey provided for Westerners.

Ordinary domestic meals are different in that the rice is the main staple and the separate dishes are all on the table at the same time and pieces are taken to flavor the mouthfuls of plain rice. The result is a better balanced and more satisfying kind of meal. Foreigners who do not like rice never really appreciate Chinese food in this way, and either find the dishes too rich on their own or not satisfying.

Cantonese food (southern China) is the style often served in restaurants in the US and UK, although Szechuan has rapidly gained in popularity. Cantonese cuisine is subtle, delicate, not highly spiced. Steamed or stir-fried to preserve texture, it is not greasy. Specialties include shark's fin soup, seafood, roast pork, chicken, abalone, and vegetables.

Peking (northern) food is perhaps less oily. Specialties include beggar's chicken, Peking duck, and in winter, a hot-pot of boiling broth into which each diner puts bits of food to cook - much like fondue. Wheat is used more than rice for a wide variety of noodles, steamed breads, and dumplings.

Szechuan (western) food is oily and very spicy, with sauces of chillies and hot peppers laced with garlic.

Shanghainese (eastern) food is also rich, salty, and spicy, with much ginger and heavy soy sauce used. Steamed crabs, drunken chicken, and braised eel are specialities.

Hakka, Chiu Chow, and other regional variations are also represented in the restaurants of Hong Kong.

Dim sum is served in many restaurants in the morning and at lunch time. These small delicacies are steamed or batter-fried dumplings of meat, fish, or poultry bits, wrapped in various envelopes of pastry. They are served on trays or roll carts full of baskets, each containing three or four small buns or dumplings, and you select which of them you want. There is no menu as such for them. The waiters call out the names of the dim sum, and you can peek into the baskets as they are carried or wheeled past your table. Your bill is totaled by counting the number of plates and baskets on your table.

Dim sum is a favorite way for the Chinese to eat breakfast, and many large restaurants begin to serve at 7 am or before. On Sunday dim sum is available from breakfast through dinner time, and is a fine Sunday brunch idea.

Chinese housewives and cooks use only fresh foods, and these are all cooked quickly to keep the flavor and nutritional content intact, after careful cutting and preparation. Chinese food, like every kind of cuisine, can be very simple or extremely elaborate.

Hong Kong's hotels have a variety of restaurants. Coffee shops, grills, and elegant Chinese and Continental dining rooms, many of which are regularly patronized by local residents.

Restaurants are very crowded between 12.30 and 2 pm, particularly in the business districts of Central and Tsim Sha Tsui. Reservations are needed. In some dim sum restaurants, these may be unobtainable after 11 am. Most guidebooks list at least some of the better-known restaurants.

After a slow start, Hong Kong has now taken to 'fast food' in a big way. many chains of 'take-away' or cafeteria-type restaurants cater to a growing demand. These include McDonald's, Pizza Hut, Spaghetti House, and Kentucky Fried Chicken. There are also chains of deli's, sandwich bars and health food outlets springing up everywhere.

For anyone interested in learning more about Hong Kong cuisines or specific restaurants, there are many excellent guides to be found in the local bookstores. In addition, the Hong Kong Tourist Assn provides free or very inexpensive booklets on various food-related topics.

Holidays and Festivals

There are 17 public holidays in Hong Kong each year (10 of which are statutory paid holidays). They are a mixture of Chinese and British holidays, some of which are interesting for the foreign resident; 11 of them have religious significance.

The most important festival, and the only time of year when all shops and businesses are closed in Hong Kong, is the three-day Chinese Lunar New Year. It is the start of the lunar calendar; its date varies yearly on the Western calendar from late January to early February. The house is cleaned, all debts are paid, respects are paid to the Kitchen God and the shrines of ancestors. Gifts are exchanged, and everyone must have a new suit of clothes. Huge banquets are consumed at home, and the children will receive *lai see*, or 'lucky money', in bright red envelopes stamped in gold with characters for luck and happiness. Tradition has it that at Chinese New Year the month's wages are doubled. Flowers, especially peach blossoms, kumquat trees, and narcissus, are found in every home. Everyone says *kung hei fat choy*, which is roughly 'Happy New Year' and literally 'Good wishes, good fortune'. Chinese like to wish each other 'prosperity', and it sometimes looks curious in translation, such as on a greeting card — red with gold characters — especially if there is an English translation: 'Congratulations on Being Rich'.

Lai see is customarily given to newspaper boys, delivery people from stores and dry cleaners, building caretakers, etc. This corresponds to the Western custom of Christmas tips. You can buy the red envelopes from hawkers and stationers shops, or get them from your bank. Larger gifts, which could be interpreted as bribes, may now attract the attention of the Independent Commission Against Corruption (ICAC).

The night before Chinese New Year, there are huge flower fairs in Choi Hung Chuen on Kowloon side and Victoria Park in Causeway Bay. Hawkers and New Territories gardeners apply to the government for licenses and stall allotments. They sell thousands of potted plants, fresh flowers, and tree branches during the four days they remain open. Flowers are also imported from Taiwan, Malaysia, and Japan. In the New Territories, many flower farms cultivate trees and plants, which bring great good luck, especially if they bloom on New Year's Day. The fairs are a wonderful experience if you love crowds. The first afternoon is most quiet, but the last evening, which lasts all night, is the most crowded, and some prices come down toward the end. When you go it's a good idea to have contingency plans for meeting up when you lose each other. It is exciting: family groups, people haggling over prices, brilliant lights, food, sweets and ice cream hawkers, children carrying loads of flowers bigger than they are, grandmothers holding firmly to the tiny hands of youngsters who look fragile among the throngs.

During Chinese New Year, shops will close, including food stores and markets, so stock up in advance. Barber shops and beauty parlors charge double during the week prior to the holiday, and movie theaters raise their prices. Your Chinese *amah* (even if she's just had a long holiday during your home leave) will have at least four days to a week off. Several hundred thousand people will use the facilities of the Kowloon-Canton Railway to visit their families in neighboring provinces of China. Many residents also use the long holiday for trips further afield to various parts of Asia. If you plan to travel at this time of year, you will need to book at least six months ahead.

The Ching Ming Festival is on April 5. This is an important holiday, particularly for the older and more traditional people in the Chinese community. Graves of ancestors are cleaned; food and wine are left for the spirits. Incense and paper are burned to reach the dead, and this holiday makes time for a visit to the cemeteries, to communicate with the dead and to ensure that they are satisfied with their descendants.

On the ninth day of the ninth moon, Chung Yeung, the other major festival of the dead, is celebrated as it has been for 1,900 years. During the Han Dynasty, in a kind of Chinese Noah's Ark fable, it is said that a man following the advice of a sage took his family to a high place. On returning, they found floods and sickness had destroyed everything. On this holiday, everyone visits mountain tops to ward off future disasters, and the overloaded Peak Tram has endless waiting lines. Graves of ancestors are also visited, swept, and honored. Many thousands of people go by train to the New Territories during this holiday to visit cemeteries.

The Tin Hau Festival on the twenty-third day of the third moon pays tribute to the most popular patron saint of fisherfolk — the Goddess of Heaven. She is variously credited with being the daughter of a high official who helped distressed seamen, and the daughter of a Fukienese fisherman who dreamed of danger and warned her parents in advance. In Hong Kong, thousands of boat people and tourists go to Joss House Bay where a large temple is dedicated to her. Lion dances and parades are held and there are prayers for good fishing in the future. You can go by special Hong Kong Yaumati Ferries to see the celebrations, or by private boat if you have one.

The Dragon Boat Festival (Tuen Ng) is held on the Double Fifth (the fifth day of the fifth moon). This holiday is said by some to be in honor of Chu Yuan, a minister of the Emperor in the fourth century BC, who drowned himself to protest against corruption in government. His friends threw cakes into the water to divert the fish, and used paddles to create waves to scare them away. Two of the rites repeated annually are the making and eating of buns, and

Dragon Boat races (symbolic of the paddles beating the water and rescue attempts). Long, narrow boats with dragon heads and tails seat 6 to 20 rowers. Gongs or drums beat loudly, flags fly, and the races are furious. They are held at Taipo, Stanley, Aberdeen, Cheung Chau and other places. You can take tours to see them or go by private launch if you have access to one. You can also see some of the action from the beach at Stanley. Some secondary schools recruit Dragon Boat teams, as do the various British military units and the local fishing population. It has now become an international event with many fine overseas teams participating in an international Dragon Boat Race.

The Cheung Chau Bun Festival (Ta Chiu) is a four-day festival celebrated in May on Cheung Chau. The biggest public features are a huge parade, Chinese opera, and the bun towers. On the sixth day of the fourth moon Ta Chiu begins in order to placate the spirits who, it is said, caused storms and plagues to befall Cheung Chau many years ago. Taoist priests advise a four-day abstention from meat, and a huge banquet is prepared for the spirits. Three towers — 50 to 60 feet tall — are built and completely covered with large buns. On the second day of the festival there is a parade with lion dances, colorful flags, small orchestras, and dancers. Incredible floats are paraded in which small children invisibly wired and fantastically dressed seem to balance on one foot on top of whirling balls, swords, or on the outstretched hand of another child. On the evening of the third night, after the spirits have had their feast, the villagers used to climb the towers to snatch the buns, but this practice was stopped for reasons of safety and security. The buns can still be eaten if you wish and are distributed rather than being fought over as before. You can also buy them in Hong Kong bakeries.

The Mid-Autumn Festival, or Moon Cake Festival, is held on the fifteenth night of the eighth moon. It is an occasion for parties, with everyone eating moon cakes to commemorate an uprising in 14th century China against the Mongolians who ruled China in the Yuan dynasty. Plans for the revolt were sent on paper baked inside small cakes. Considered a great delicacy, these cakes consist of a paste of ground sesame and lotus seeds, and in some cases a salted egg yolk, covered by pastry. All bakeries in Hong Kong produce a wide variety of these cakes and display them in their glass cases. Another source says the moon cakes represent the gifts which, during the reign of the Emperor Tai Tsung (976-999 AD), mandarins below third grade were required to give to their superiors. Another feature of this festival is the colorful lantern procession, and you will see shops full of paper lanterns in bright colors and many shapes. People carrying lanterns go to high places to see the moon rise, and, after dark, families and groups of children walk in the streets and parks waving lanterns lighted with small candles.

The Feast of Hungry Ghosts (Yue Lan) on the fourteenth day of the seventh moon commemorates the period when spirits of the dead are released to roam the world. Paper money is burned; food, fruit, and wine are offered to appease the ghosts. It is the functional equivalent of All Souls' Day or Halloween in the West.

Western holidays in Hong Kong include the Queen's Birthday, celebrated on June 21. Christmas and Boxing Day (December 26) are observed, the latter being a British holiday that has been explained variously as the day unwanted Christmas gifts are boxed for the poor, or the day gift boxes are opened. January 1, Good Friday, Easter Sunday and Monday are also observed as holidays, as are several summer Mondays.

Liberation Day (the last Monday in August) celebrates the end of the Japanese occupation of Hong Kong on August 30, 1945.

Calendar of general holidays and festivals

Dates of Lunar festivals vary each year, and only the months are indicated.

New Year's Day .... January 1
Chinese Lunar New Year (three days) ..... January or February
Good Friday.. March or April
Day after Good Friday............................... March or April
Easter Monday.. March or April
Ching Ming Festival................................... April 5
Tuen Ng (Dragon Boat) Festival............... May or June
Birthday of Her Majesty the Queen.......... June 21
First weekday in July................................. July
First Monday in August............................. August
Liberation Day,.. August (Last Monday)
Day after Mid-Autumn Festival ....September or October
Chung Yeung Festival................................October
Christmas Day..December 25
Boxing Day... December 26 or 27
(First weekday after Christmas)

Religions

Many Chinese people have difficulty responding to the Western question 'What is your religion?' or 'Do you believe in God?'

There are three major traditional ethical and ceremonial systems that only roughly correspond to Western ideas of religion: Confucianism, Buddhism, and Taoism. Most Chinese subscribe to more than one, and they are not mutually exclusive. There is a pantheon of deities, earth gods, kitchen gods, and patron saints for professions, events, and aspects of daily life shared by the official religious organizations — many of which are inherited directly from rural animism with no connection to a recognized religion whatsoever.

Ancestor worship is the fundamental basis of Chinese society and religion. Not precisely worship in the Western sense, the obligation is closer to respect or veneration. There are specific and complex duties laid down for sons toward their fathers, and after death ancestors maintain the same relationships they had with their family as in their lifetimes. Even after death the conduct of each family member affects the others. Religious festivals are set aside to pay homage to ancestors and to invoke their blessings. Relatives' remains are interred in propitious locations to ensure continued good fortune for the family. Nearly every home and shop in Hong Kong has a small decorated ancestral altar at which candles (nowadays a red electric bulb) and incense are burnt and food laid out.

There is no one day for worship. People go to temples as they feel the need. Holidays honoring patron saints, various spirits, and other gods are celebrated by the entire family. Some temples (and there are estimated to be more than 350 Buddhist and Taoist temples here) feature fortune tellers and are much-frequented for this purpose alone, combined with an equally important visit to a geomancer. In fact, many people will make use of whatever traditional practice or religion suits the occasion or problem. The Chinese almanac, *Tong Sing*, is also almost a 'Bible' for daily living and is very widely consulted whenever any change is contemplated. It forms a traditional blend of superstition and belief, which is still greatly respected. Some older temples are now overshadowed by the surrounding high-rise buildings in areas that were once villages. Other large monasteries on the outlying islands are well worth visiting as they are located in beautiful spots. Po Lin, a Buddhist monastery on Lantau above Silvermine Bay, is most popular.

A few words about each of the main codes or religions:

Confucius lived from about 551-475 BC. A great and respected sage, he defined a social code of humanity and love, and specified the duties and obligations that were the roads to harmonious living. While promoting belief in the gods, the Confucian code is a secular eithical system and not what Westerners would call religion. It is concerned with moral and social standards and practices, and with food, music, and all art forms. In 136 BC, Confucianism was declared the state doctrine, and in 124BC, a 'university' was built, centered on a classics department devoted to Confucius. Eventually all officials in China were selected from those who passed examinations in the Confucian classics. Mencius (371-289 BC) was perhaps the greatest Confucian scholar. He is said to have studied under Confucius' grandson.

Taoism is a magical and mystical religious force, with much secrecy in rites and organization. Taoist priests supervise worship, officiate at burials and marriages, organize some festivals, and form a religious hierarchy knowledgeable of the pantheon of gods and goddesses, dragons, and other spirits who guard the world.

Buddhism was brought to China from India in the first century BC and is responsible for the development of much art and architecture which Westerners usually think of as purely Chinese. The Indian stupa (tomb) was transformed into the pagoda as a sanctuary for relics of the Buddha Gautama, who lived from circa 563 to 483 BC. Pagodas of stone, bronze, and even porcelain were built. The Emperor Yung Lo built one (in 1413) of bricks individually gabled with porcelain which was nine stories tall. Buddha taught compassion for all living things and, as he saw no one code of laws for all life, directed all men to seek their own roads to truth. After his death his ideas was codified and the religion accepted many divinities and lesser gods.

Each of these religious forces can accept the others. They partake of many similar beliefs: there are some people of each (or all) of the religions who do not eat beef, who believe in the power of ghosts to haunt office and apartment buildings, and in the accuracy of fortune tellers and geomancers. There are temples in Hong Kong dedicated to many different gods. Often you will see in holes in the walls of buildings, on the pavement beside doorways, or on large rocks a few incense sticks, bits of fruit, sweets, and the ashes of burned paper offerings. These are tiny temples, dedicated to earth gods who watch over family or neighborhood.

You may see the shops that make paper money and copies of other things one uses in life, including full-size paper replicas of cars. You may see the ritual burning of these objects in order to send them on their way to the dead. These burned offerings are attempts to guarantee ease and comfort in the afterlife.

Hong Kong also has a Christian community estimated at half a million, including Roman Catholics and Protestants of many denominations, a Jewish community of about a thousand members, some 50,000 Muslims -- half of whom are Chinese, and small Sikh and Zoroastrian congregations. Whatever your god or your belief, you will find followers and places of worship.

Establishing
an Office
in Hong Kong

The American
Chamber of
Commerce
in Hong Kong

8th Edition

Establishing An Office in Hong Kong

The 1991-92 edition of its annual service book, *Establishing an Office in Hong Kong,* has been published by the American Chamber of Commerce in Hong Kong. The eighth edition of the book features Hong Kong-context reviews of business services as varied as freight forwarding, law and architectural consulting.

What's a shelf company? Where do you get one? What does it cost to move an expatriate employee to Hong Kong? What is the tax structure? Is there temporary accommodation, and what does it cost? These are among the questions the 122-page book answers.

As a first-reference book for newcomers, the text material is divided into 28 brief chapters intended to raise the right questions and offer the best references for further information.

There are 12 maps in the book, covering Hong Kong's world trade flows; hotel locations in Hong Kong and Macau; commercial districts for Hong Kong Island and Tsimshatsui; key industrial areas, including those in the New Territories; residential areas on both the island and peninsula; and Mass Transit Railway Routes.

Useful listings include contact information on about 75 important Hong Kong business organizations, US State and Port Authority representatives, Foreign Trade Commissions, Hong Kong's banks and foreign law firms.

Establishing an Office in Hong Kong is available from AmCham and at business district bookstores. Member price HK$165/US$28. Non-member price HK$195/US$32. Postage inclusive.

Chapter 2
MOVING TO HONG KONG

CRAFT **ARRIVALS**

flight 班機	from 来自	scheduled 預定時間	status 情況
TG 610	BANGKOK	12.45	
Q 8	SINGAPORE	13.00	
L 731	TOKYO	13.00	
808.	KUALALUMPUR	13.05	
751-	NAGOYA	13.10	
827.	TAIPEI	13.15	
401	KAOHSIUNG	13.15	
900	MANILA	13.20	
503	OSAKA	13.30	
874	JAKARTA	13.50	

PHOTO COURTESY OF HONG KONG TOURIST ASSOCIATION

If you plan to live in Hong Kong, or are even considering it, there is certain essential information you'll need before packing your bags: What visas are you and your family required to have? What clothing and other items will have to be brought here? How will they be sent? What about pets?

The answers are all here, so relax and read on.

Immigration and Visa Information

It is essential that you lay the legal groundwork back home before you come to work in Hong Kong. In order to enter Hong Kong for purposes of employment, or to establish a business, you must obtain an employment visa issued by the Hong Kong Immigration Department. In addition, your accompanying family members must obtain dependent visas. The employment and dependent visas must be obtained through a British embassy or British consular or diplomatic office prior to your arrival here. An employment visa is normally granted to US passport holders for six months; the dependent visas are normally valid for the same period. Chapter 6, 'Legal Information', offers a detailed explanation of the process and requirements of obtaining visas for you and your family.

Preparations for Moving

It's never easy knowing just what items to take with you when you move across town or to another state, let alone a place exotic as Hong Kong. Along with a friendly neighbor who might lend a hand, your biggest asset by far will be advance preparation. Such planning will do much to prevent panic.

It might be best to begin by taking note of those things you do not want to bring with you or which, if you have a weight allowance, simply cannot go. Plants and flammable items should not be shipped. (Check with your local Hong Kong consulate to find out which items are forbidden entry here.) It might be best not to take opened liquor bottles, although your mover may be able to seal them. Firearms and drugs are absolutely prohibited from entering Hong Kong. Frozen and perishable foods should not be shipped. Important paper is -- such as passports, documents, savings account bankbooks, insurance policies, money -- should not be shipped. Rather, they should be put in a safe place where they will not accidentally wind up in a wooden crate.

Since it may be several months until you see your packed goods again, consider taking those items (clothing, toiletries, books, small games, toys, etc.) that you will want while either traveling or staying in a hotel or apartment. Keep in mind changing seasons, too; you might move in summer but not see your shipment until winter. Some families bring a coffeepot for use in a hotel, but bear in mind that the voltage in Hong Kong is 200 at 50 cycles, and shavers and other items should be adaptable. A can opener, a knife, and other small kitchen utensils are useful. Even though hotels provide room service, it is often pleasant -- especially with children -- to be able to buy food in a store to keep in a hotel room, which more often than not will have a refrigerator.

Things to do before you leave:

(1)   Inform the post office of your move and give them the forwarding address or your new business address if you have not found a flat before arrival.

(2)   Advise friends and business firms of your change of address.

(3)   Arrange to close or change addresses of charge accounts. You   m a y wish to keep accounts open with major department stores if you think you would like to write to them for catalogs or purchase.

(4)   Collect and photocopy medical and dental records for each family member.

(5)   Collect and photocopy children's school records and credentials.

(6)   Resign, sell, or convert to absentee any club memberships.

(7)   Check personal insurance policies, particularly with regard to coverage in foreign locations.

(8)   Return library books or any borrowed items, and collect what you have lent out.

(9)   Keep utilities and telephone operating through moving day.
Collect any deposits from utilities services (as well as your landlord).

(10)   If you are shipping your refrigerator, disconnect it, defrost it, wipe it dry, and allow it to air with the door open at least 24 hours before the movers' arrival. Silica gel or other desiccants packed inside will help keep it smelling fresh.

11)   Mildew can be a problem during shipping and storage. Fungi that cause mildew grow on almost anything: leather, wool, cotton, paper, and wood. Mildew can discolor and rot clothing, shoes, gloves, etc. You may find it extremely difficult to avoid getting at least a little bit of mildew on your personal articles. However, prior to shipping and storage, the best preventive steps for you are to take care to clean all garments and carpets and to use silica gel, activated alumina, or calcium chloride -- all moisture-absorbing chemicals. Placed in cloth bags among clothes and other articles, they will help keep things dry.

Mothballs placed among shoes, books, and athletic equipment will also help to kill fungi.

(12)	Stereo systems and other electrical items that operate on 60-cycle current need to be changed over to 50 cycle, if they are not already supplied with a switch for this purpose. You can do this before leaving, although it may be less expensive to have it done in Hong Kong.

(13)	Ask the mover for 'standing wardrobes' if you want clothing shipped on hangers. Be certain as well that the clothes are securely hung in your standing wardrobe. Packing clothes flat will reduce volume and shipping costs, but apparel will need considerable pressing after several weeks in cartons.

(14)	Find new homes for small pets (turtles, tropical fish,birds, etc) that you do not want to take. But check in advance with the mover about shipping your cat or dog. International packing firms normally provide this service.

(15)	Check with your attorney to be certain that in the event of your death your estate can be settled where you choose. (See also Chapter 6, 'Legal Information')

(16)	Check also with your attorney to determine your address for driver's license.

(17)	Determine your address in order to maintain your US driver's license.

(18)	Make an inventory of items being shipped.

(19)	Make a separate list of any items you plan to keep in storage.

(20)	Keep a record of all expenses connected with the move.

When contacting movers—and you may wish to call several for estimates—select those with experience in international packing and forwarding. Ask them which firms they list as clients, as this may indicate how experienced and skillful they are in the complicated business of shipments overseas.

You may want to insure your goods while they're in transit, particularly if they have a high replacement cost. Estimate the value of your personal goods before deciding how much insurance coverage you need. It's probably best to insure the whole lot together as you might have problems collecting a full refund if you've only insured a few items—even if one of those is damaged. Remember to consider your clothing, shoes, antiques, paintings, silverware, and other items of high value. A copy of this list should be attached to the insurance certificate provided by your mover. Ask how long it will take for your shipment to arrive. It sometimes takes several weeks or months to locate and furnish an apartment in Hong Kong, so check where (and at what charge) your goods will be stored if you cannot accept them on your arrival. Ask for the name of the Hong Kong agent of your moving company, the address, and the telephone number.

What to Bring

American, British, and European residents of Hong Kong can easily maintain their living standards here. Hong Kong imports goods from around the world, and the shops are full of necessities and luxuries in abundance. Suitable clothing, furniture, appliances, audio and video equipment, toys, etc, are all available. Nonetheless, occasional items, certain brands, and large sizes of shoes, clothing, and undergarments can be difficult to obtain. It is always difficult to tell what someone might consider a 'basic necessity', but Hong Kong has at least some of everything.

One important consideration in planning what to bring is whether or not you will have to live in a hotel or 'leave flat' for several months while awaiting furniture shipments and locating housing. It is therefore advisable to bring sufficient clothing for this period, and favorite toys and games for children. If you have young children who are growing fast, bring along (rather than ship) the things they will be needing in the next few months. It is disheartening to have to buy things in Hong Kong that you already own—if only you could get your shipment here, or out of storage.

Appliances

You will need kitchen appliances, although these can all be purchased in Hong Kong. Refrigerator, stove (called a 'cooker' in Hong Kong), washer, and dryer are normally not supplied in rented 'unfurnished' flats except where companies maintain fully furnished units for their employees. Electric current is 200 volts, 50 cycles. Electric stoves can be tricky as many buildings do not have wiring for them and it is sometimes easier to consider using a gas stove, except that American gas stoves should be checked for suitability to use on the local town gas. Toasters, blenders, coffeepots, mixers, etc, are all available here, although at prices higher than in their country of manufacture. Refrigerators, washing machines, vacuum cleaners, coffeepots, and toasters can be used with transformer, if wired for 110 volts. The size of the transformer depends upon the size of the machine and the wattage/amps needed by it, which is usually shown on a small label on the base. Never use a transformer of lower wattage. Appliances need transformers of roughly these sizes:

Small hand mixer	200W
Blender	1000W
Coffeepot	1000W
Toaster	1000W
Iron	1500W
Hair dryer	1000W

A transformer in the kitchen for 110-volt appliances need not be an inconvenience at all, but some people say that transformers are a pain to lug around. It certainly seems more sensible to bring appliances and transform them than to purchase all-new 200-volt equipment if you are going to be here for only a few years. If you decide to bring newly purchased equipment, you should find out which brands are available here in case maintenance should ever be necessary. On the other hand, the classified ads of the local English-language newspapers as well as supermarket bulletin boards are good places to find offers of used appliances at reduced prices. There are also numerous dealers for new and used equipment and service counters for these items, which can also be rented. See also chapter 11, 'Shopping'.

It is also worth noting that changes in electric current do affect the performance of such apllicances as electric knives (they jiggle more slowly) but generally do not hurt the equipment. Clocks and clock radios cannot be converted from 60 to 50 cycles (or the reverse). New models are often adaptable, so that you can buy them here to be used on either 110 or 200 volts, and 50 or 60 cycles.

Air conditioners are a necessity in Hong Kong's long, hot, humid summer. In Hong Kong, heating from reverse- cycle air conditioners is adequate, but if temperatures fall to an exceptionally low level, supplementary heating may be required. Running a 60-cycle unit on 50 cycles is not advisable.

Babies' and children's needs

Clothing and diapers, medications, toys, furniture, books, games and equipment are all available. Apart from places such as Mothercare, Watson's, Manning's and the major department stores, there are two huge Toys 'R' Us stores which stock mostly American brandname goods. Their baby cribs are definitely the biggest in town. They also have a wide range of other baby equipment, diapers, party favors, bicycles, clothes -- and of course, toys.

Fisher Price, Kiddicraft, Little Tikes etc are readily available although more expensive than in UK or the US. The same goes for good shoes which are generally imported from the States or Europe. Shoes available locally are not as sturdy and are usually made in a standard width. Hong Kong is a large producer of shoes and it is relatively easy to have them made-to-measure.

Clothes are mostly available at the two extremes of the market -- with very little in the middle. They are either functional, hard-wearing, basic clothes -- hardly the height of fashion -- found in markets or local shops, or they are designer-label ensembles which cost a fortune. Toys 'R' Us and Mothercare fall somewhere in the middle although the latter leans toward the top end of the market. Real bargains are found in the few factory outlet shops which specialize in children's clothes. Here you can find Western brandname clothes which, for whatever reason, have not been exported.

You will probably not have a yard, so swings and other outdoor play equipment are not practical. It is never cold enough for snow suits; however, heavy sweaters and jackets are needed and can be bought in Hong Kong.

Books

Reference books, encyclopedias, and British and US fiction and nonfiction are available but are more expensive than in their country of origin (at least 15 percent over list price). Some families order books from abroad. A copy of the Sears Catalog could be a useful addition to your library.

Clothing

Women's underwear, clothing, and shoes in large sizes are really the only items hard to locate here. But all shoes can be custom-made in Hong Kong, and the Happy Valley shoe stores are quite reasonable, particularly for women's shoes.

Cooking utensils

Good utensils are generally available, although at prices higher than in the US or UK. There is some good-quality plastic ware (Rubber Maid, for example) and many locally made items. Most families bring what they have and are accustomed to, but Teflon, Le Cruset, Royal Worcester, and Corning Ware can all be purchased here. Smaller items (can openers, etc) are also readily available.

Cosmetics

Revlon, Mary Quant, Max Factor, Estee Lauder, and other brands are readily available. They are more expensive than in the country of origin. If you are particular about lipstick and rouge, it might be wise to bring an extra supply so that you can have the time to determine what is and is not here. Perfume is cheaper than in the United States or Europe. Hair-care items of many brands are available.

Food

You will be able to find a wide range of food items here in Hong Kong: spices, powdered baby formula, French cheeses, imported beers, delicatessen items, even Campbell's soup. In other words, don't bring any food products unless you are on a special diet requiring highly unusual items. There are some canned dietetic foods and biscuits, and health-food shops have supplies of a wide variety of organic products. Supermarkets also carry toilet paper and tissues (American brands are somewhat expensive; local brands cheaper and acceptable), wax paper, plastic bags and wrap, detergents, household cleaners, and polishes.

Furniture

Unless your company provides a furnished flat, you might find it worthwhile bringing your furniture. And even if basic furnishings are provided, you will nonetheless want linens, china, crystal, kitchen utensils, bedding and towels, pictures, books, and favorite objects. You can buy all these things here, but local prices may surprise anyone who thinks Hong Kong is cheap. If you have them, bring them.

Light fixtures

These are usually not provided, but there is a fair selection available here. Bayonet-type (plug-in) and screw-in bulbs are both available. Bring your lamps. A three-pronged plug and 200-volt bulbs are all that are needed for conversion. Three-way bulbs are difficult to find here, but they do exist.

Medicines and drugstore items

Non-prescription remedies and articles for first aid and personal hygiene are all available at local drugstores, such as Watson's or Manning's. Prescription drugs can also be made up. See also Chapter 4, 'Living and Health.'

Musical instruments

Renting or buying a piano here is probably much preferable to bringing your own. The extreme variations in humidity, however, mean that you will need to tune your instrument fairly often. Guitars, accordians, flutes, stringed instruments, etc, may also be purchased here. Bring your own if you have them.

Records, tapes, compact discs

Availability, rather than cost, is the main problem in buying audio 'software' here. If it's a recently recorded item, Hong Kong will have it. If it's that obscure jazz recording you heard 15 years ago, you've got real problems. Bring any records, tapes, or CDs you're certain you couldn't find here.

Stereos, tape players, and compact disc players

Tape recorders and record players can be converted from 50 to 60 cycles, and back. You can do this prior to shipping your stereo equipment, or in a number of reputable shops here. Newer equipment, including CD players, is also probably adaptable to either 100 or 200 volts. If not, you can run 110-volt components on a transformer. There is a wide variety of all brands of stereo equipment available, particularly from Japan.

TVs and VCRs

Do not bring your TV unless you are coming from the UK or Europe, which are also on the equivalent of the Hong Kong TV standard of 625 lines, 50 cycles, operating at 200 volts and the PAL color system. A slight adjustment might need to be made in order to tune in to local stations. Sets with screens as large as 26 inches are available in a wide selection and may also be rented from several companies. Unless you have a special adapter on your bought-in-America VCR—and, likewise, on your TV—you will not be able to use it in Hong Kong.

Moving

Get a baby-sitter to watch the children, take the bulbs out of your lamps, and sit down while you still have something to sit on. It is usually best not to interfere with the movers as they probably are much more experienced and skilled in packing than are you. Besides, they will often refuse responsibility for breakage of items they do not pack. Clothing may be left in drawers, pictures on walls, and all other objects in their customary places.

Packing and loading for the average family takes three to four days. It is a good idea to plan to remain at least two days past the scheduled completion date because rain or other unforeseeable circumstances can cause delays.

Shipping

Below are listed the approximate shipping times from a number of countries to Hong Kong. These are approximate ocean transit times only. To these times must be added the days required for packing, transport to the terminal, customs clearance, and delivery. Be prepared for delays. The ocean transit time will also vary, depending on the shipping line and whether or not there is direct routing. Frequency of sailings is another matter to consider, and your goods may have to wait in storage. The packer should advise you of the available shipping dates so that the goods can be packed and shipped without delay. If goods arrive before you have located a flat, the storage fee is around $3.50 per cubic foot. This price varies slightly from company to company so it is good to shop around.

US West Coast	4-5 weeks
US East Coast	6 weeks
England and Europe	4 weeks
Indonesia	2 weeks
Japan	1 week
Philippines	5 days
Singapore	5 days
Taiwan	3-4 days
Thailand	1 week

Customs Clearance

Customs clearance is usually a simple procedure, since very few items have duties imposed on them in Hong Kong. Drugs are firearms are strictly prohibited. This includes all guns, even antiques and some replicas. Duty for revenue purposes is imposed on liquor, cigarettes, and tobacco, methyl alcohol, some hydrocarbon oils, non-alcoholic beverages, and cosmetics.

There is a fee imposed on automobiles of 90 percent CIF (cost of car, insurance and freight) on basic private cars (those valued under $30,000), 105 percent on semi-luxury cars ($30,000 to $60,000) and 120 percent on luxury cars (over $60,000). This is not technically a duty but a first registration tax. In addition, there is an annual license fee ranging from $3,815 to $11,215 depending on the cubic capacity. The cost of gas is now about $7.00 per liter. The import and first registration of a car is something to evaluate very carefully. You might reasonably decide not to bring a car, and even not to have one at all on Hong Kong's crowded roads. There is an excellent public transport system which is often as convenient and as fast as having your own car.

It should be noted that electronic equipment and scientific instruments and apparatuses, including computers, computer peripherals, integrated circuits, printed circuit boards, and disc drives, are generally considered by the Hong Kong Trade Department to be strategic commodities. As such, they cannot be imported into Hong Kong unless an import license is granted by the Director of Trade.

Pets

You may bring your domestic pet (cat, dog or bird) to Hong Kong but there are certain facts to be aware of before you decide to uproot the family dog/cat.

Animals entering Hong Kong from Category 1 countries (any country geo-graphically isolated, ie an island) are not required to go through a period of quarantine, but will be required to when they return to their country of origin. Category 1 countries are the United Kingdom, Australia and New Zealand (there are others).

Category 2 countries are defined as approved countries with a high standard of public health. The United States and most West European countries fall into this niche. Category 2 countries require one month's quarantine on arrival but a minimum of six months when returning home.

Category 3 countries encompass the rest. This usually refers to third-world countries and most Asian countries. Animals from this category must be quarantined for 6 months.

All quarantine is at the owner's expense and can prove expensive. There are government-run quarantine clinics and one private. The owner has a choice and local vets advise owners to view kennels first.

Because of its close proximity to China, Hong Kong is prone to outbreaks of rabies. In 1989, Hong Kong was declared rabies-free after completing two full years without a reported case of the disease but this could change at any time. Because of this unpredictablity, strict quarantine laws apply. Incoming pets are required to spend one to six months in quarantine in Hong Kong and outgoing pets must all spend a minimum of six months in quarantine. All dogs must be licensed and innoculated against rabies every year. This service is free.

The Hong Kong government produces a booklet giving full details of all requirements for bringing an animal into the territory. You can write to the following address for a copy:

The Agriculture and Fisheries Department
393 Canton Road
Government Offices
12th Floor
Kowloon
Tel 368 8111

There are many pet shops in Hong Kong if you must keep a pet. However, given the limited space and the fact that most flats have no yard, it is advisable not to inflict the trauma of a move and new surroundings, plus the high risk of disease, on the family pet. It is also advisable to think twice about buying an animal in Hong Kong. Most pet shops here practise minimum hygiene and many cats and dogs are terminally ill from birth. There are reputable pet shops around, but it is best to consult a vet in Hong Kong before buying any animal.

Chapter 3
GETTING SETTLED

PHOTO BY ALAN MOORES

H ong Kong is without a doubt one of the most exciting and interesting cities in the world. It has the pace of New York, the industriousness of Tokyo, the glamor of Paris and the scenic beauty of San Francisco. But Hong Kong is truly unique unto itself, and the newcomer will find much that is different from 'home' in the cultural, economic, political and geographical sense. Yet what makes this city so interesting also makes it a little intimidating to the newcomer. Living in Hong Kong can be a memorable experience for an expatriate family provided they are prepared to face, with an open and flexible mind, the problems they inevitably will meet here.

One thing that should be understood from the start is that no matter how frustrating life may seem here, there's always someone who's been through it before and who can help the newcomer sort it out. More on that later.

One of the first things you'll actually want to do after your arrival is simply to make your way around the city. Maps and street guides should be obtained and consulted.They can save a lot of time as well as making your surroundings seem less strange. If you don't already have these guides when you arrive, make a visit to a bookstore, the Government Publications Centre in the General Post Office near the Star Ferry, or even to some of the street stands. There are several maps, street guides and general guidebooks available for Hong Kong, Kowloon, Macau and China. Take time to make sure you understand the general geographical layout — such simple things as the fact that Hong Kong is an island and Kowloon is the tip of the peninsula facing it, and which direction is north, where the Star Ferry and MTR cross the harbor, and where is the airport. A trip up to the Peak can help make a lot of this clearer as well.

Don't be shy about obtaining tourist information, because much of the free literature available to tourists can be just as handy -- even handier -- to the new resident, who has the time to take advantage of all that Hong Kong can offer. The offices of the Hong Kong Tourist Association, in Jardine House, offer excellent publications and advice, both for free.

There are also organizations that provide services, advice, introductory courses, and other information for the newly arrived. They often have up-to-date information sheets. Some property companies also produce excellent booklets for their clients, with general information and a shopping guide, which has many useful addresses and telephone numbers. Some sources:

(1)   The American Women's Association (527 2961) runs a *foon ying* (welcome) program geared to the social aspects of getting settled. The

program is open to AWA members only -- joining is a very simple process.

(2)   The Community Advice Bureau (524 5444) gives excellent up-to-date, free information on almost any subject. Staffed by a team of experienced volunteers, the office is in the St John's Cathedral New Hall, 8 Garden Road and is open Monday through Friday from 9.30am to 4.00pm. The CAB, in conjunction with the YWCA, run a very popular "Discovering Hong Kong" program on Monday evenings in May and November, complete with speakers, films, and refreshments.

(3)   The Women's Corona Society with its headquarters in the United Kingdom, is an international organization of women to help those who are moving from one country to another and to provide friendship and help. They have coffee mornings at 10.00am every Monday morning at the China Fleet Club in Wanchai. For more information write to GPO Box 8151.

(4)   The YWCA in MacDonnell Road (522 3101) runs an informal course on Monday mornings called "At Home in Hong Kong", to assist newcomers in making friends and finding out about the city. In addition, an informative newsletter to members gives details of many other courses and activities.

There are a number of other national groups such as the Australian Assn, the New Zealand Assn, Canadian Club, all of which, through coffee mornings and other activities, can be valuable in making contacts and providing advice. National consulates and commissions in Hong Kong can generally provide the contact for such organizations.

American Consulate Registration and Services

If you're an American expatriate, one of your first orders of business will be to register with the American Consulate in Hong Kong, which provides a variety of services for US citizens residing in or passing through the city. Examples: replacement of lost or expired passports, notarial services, registration and documentation of births of American-citizen children born in Hong Kong, and some provision of general protection in cases of arrest, serious illness, or destitution.

To enable the Consulate General to supply these services, it is recommended that every American resident in Hong Kong register with the Passport Unit. This is an easy process that may be done by any member of the family in a few minutes. Bring along the passports of all family members.

Any other information on what an American should know or do to regularize his or her status upon arrival in Hong Kong can be obtained by calling the Special Consular Services Unit of the Consulate General. Tel 523 9011.

If you are an American citizen whose passport is due to expire here in Hong Kong, it may be brought to the Consulate and a new one can be issued. If an American citizen dies in Hong Kong, the death should be reported to the US Consulate General, which will report it to the Department of State, advise on local funeral parlors, and, in the absence of an immediate relative or legal representative in the consular district, arrange for shipment of the remains to the US. In the latter case, US Consular Officers can take possession and dispose of personal estates located in the consular district. Reports on the death of an American citizen abroad are issued by the Consulate General. Call the American Consular Services Unit. Tel 523 9011, ext 323, 211 or 225.

Other Foreign Nationals

The consulates or commissions of other nations will advise their citizens of the services they offer and any regulations to which the citizens must conform. Should the passport of any foreign national expire while he or she resides in Hong Kong, the consulate or diplomatic office of their nation should be consulted regarding procedures for renewal or reissue.

Identity Cards

You should also be aware that all residents of Hong Kong are required by law to register for an Identity Card within 30 days of their arrival, with the Hong Kong Registration of Persons Office - in Hong Kong, or the New Territories. The only exceptions are persons in transit, tourists whose stay is limited to several days, or business people whose stay is for a few weeks. Children from 11 to 17 years old must also register for juvenile identity cards.Within one month of reaching age 18, young people should apply for adult identity cards. For more on identity cards, 'Legal Information'.

Survival and Adjustment

Even after making the most careful preparations for the move to Hong Kong, and overcoming all the problems of travel, accommodation, registering with the proper authorities, and settling in to a new environment, you might go through periods of doubt.

If you do have difficulties in settling, it is helpful to realize that you are not alone, that other people have felt the same, and that you can learn to analyze and overcome these various states of anxiety. For guidance on this matter, Dr Mildred McCoy, formerly Senior Lecturer in the Department of Psychology at the University of Hong Kong, has contributed an analysis of the several situations that can occur. This helpful and thoughtful approach should be read and re-read by anyone who finds difficulties in adjusting to the move to Hong Kong:

Adjusting to Hong Kong

Many people look forward to a life abroad as an opportunity for personal growth. They hope to learn more about another culture, acquire new skills, meet new people, experience a new lifestyle, or simply broaden their horizons. But the challenges of a new location occasionally escalate into crises. The task is to manage and prepare for stress and to maintain sufficient stimulation for growth, but avoid being debilitated or sent cowering by too much. Just as no one ventures to cross the Antarctic, climb Mount Everest, or step onto the moon without months of intensive preparation, so too a move to a new environment and culture requires thoughtful as well as practical preparation. For distant or unusual adventures, the expected daily activities are practiced under the rigors of realistically duplicated expedition conditions. We recognize the value of such preparation. It makes good sense! Accurate information in advance and being able to picture oneself successfully managing under new conditions reduces the unpredictability of the future. Normal anxieties and frustrations of challenging experiences are tempered by psychological preparation.

As an expatriate in Hong Kong, in addition to having knowledge about the new situation in which you find yourself, you also will find it helpful to recognize in advance the stages that are normal in coping with the stresses of adjustment and your own personal growth. And it is important to accept that process will have its painful moments. Anxiety, loneliness, frustration, anger, bewilderment, and indecision are all very normal reactions for an expatriate from time to time. They are part of the personal growth cycle in response to the challenges of a new setting.

What can be expected as the normal stages of adjustment to Hong Kong? There

41

is indeed a typical progression, although how long anyone spends in a particular stage is influenced by many things, such as how much they interact with Hong Kong's people and institutions, the degree of permanence envisaged for the stay, the amount of previous contact with people of different cultures, a person's openness to new and different ideas, and the similarity of roles between home and here.

The Work of Worry

The first stage of a move to Hong Kong begins not when the moving van arrives or upon disembarking at Kai Tak, but rather at the moment the idea is broached. The period prior to the actual move is far more significant than is often realized. It can be cut too short or be too dragged out, although there is no one ideal time for every family or individual. This is a time of decision making, hence of information gathering and assessment of personal suitability for the assignment and of whether dependents can be expected to thrive in the new circumstances. This period constitutes a psychological preparation for change -- what has been called 'the work of worry.' Very often the negative aspects of the move have been excessively minimized during the decision phase. This leads to a feeling after arrival of having been foolish or rash or of having been duped, and this causes unnecessary extra stress.

Pre-Move Emotions

In addition to assessing the appropriateness of the work, a second task of the pre-move phase is for all members of your family to begin dealing with the negative feelings associated with the move. Grandparents are being left behind and will miss important milestones in the lives of grandchildren. Spouses may resign from jobs, leave educational opportunities, or abandon -- at least temporarily -- carefully nurtured, prestigious roles in the community. Peer acceptance and belonging to an identifiable social group figure heavily in the self-esteem of teenagers, which a move will place in jeopardy. Younger children often fear anything foreign. They generalize from scraps of ugly TV news or negative fictional portrayals and may have many misconceptions about the people or place to which they will be going.

These personal disruptions may be judged worthwhile on balance, but the result is still a mix of positive and negative emotions. This is normal in such a complex situation, and recognizing feelings is the first step in dealing with them constructively, rather than letting them disrupt and distort the future. We often try to 'manage' negative feelings by not paying attention to them - our own as well as those of people around us. Or we may feel guilty for not being happy when logic says we should be. The feelings of different members of the family whose circumstances all vary may be justified or they may be totally illogical. In any case, their existence is the starting point. The most constructive approach is to accept them as reality so that they can be dealt with overtly even if everyone cannot be made completely happy or reassured about the outcome of the move. Optimism is a wonderful human capacity when it is grounded in a realistic appraisal of resources at hand to cope with the problems of the future.

In the pre-move period, then, before you ever arrive in Hong Kong, there are two major adjustment tasks to be worked on side by side with organizing physical details of the move. One is the 'work-of-worry' the development of coping strategies in advance of all the demands of the new setting. The other is in at least starting to deal with any negative feelings that are associated with the move: the uprooting, the extra burdens, the loss of identity. It isn't that there won't be positive feelings too. Most people are generally positive and look forward to good prospects in Hong Kong, rather than worry excessively about the problems that will be their lot in life here.

Arrival

Arrival in Hong Kong seems to be a mixed bag of feelings, impressions and ideas. For some, everything new is interesting and exciting. A certain euphoria carries the day, although if the truth were known, there is too much to take in at first glance. Whether one takes a few timid steps down Queen's Road Central or immediately ventures into a local market, only a fraction of the experience is taken in. This is because every newcomer is, in effect, wearing a set of lenses that were prescribed for another time and place.

It takes time and experience really to understand and appreciate Hong Kong. The usual first stage of adjustment to a new culture is characterized by interest, possibly even excitement. Although at first, differences may be captivating, a newcomer is more attentive to the similarities with the old culture than to the difference in the new setting. The Asian decor of a hotel room is interesting so long as the bed is comfortable and the telephone and plumbing work. It is very reassuring to find familiar foods on menus, advertisements for familiar products and people who understand your language. This establishes the self-confidence necessary to venture forth, and sample the abounding new experiences. Hong Kong is a particularly interesting place in the early days after arrival. You can observe so much of the life and work of the people while just strolling along the streets because of the dense living conditions and generally hospitable climate.

Growing Awareness

The second stage of adjustment arises almost imperceptibly out of that early fascination. As awareness of the many and pervasive differences grows, one begins to feel overwhelmed. Perhaps bewilderment or a nervous tension is experienced as a result of there being almost too much new to make sense. In this period, which may begin within a couple weeks after arrival or be postponed for several months, depending upon personal factors, there is a growing feeling of alienation and a sense of isolation, either physical or psychological. Inadequacy, loneliness, and isolation can combine and contribute to depression which almost everyone experiences to some degree, at one time or another, as part of the normal adjustment cycle.

After the 'high' of the first stage, the second stage seems to be 'low'. Typically, the effects of the second stage come and go rather than being a sustained episode. They may be manifest as a loss of purposiveness, or experienced as generalized confusion and difficulty in carrying out tasks. Sometimes, withdrawal is the response when a person feels surrounded and overwhelmed by noise, dirt, and too many people. These responses signal a growing awareness of the changes required to master new circumstances adequately, to live successfully in the dynamic hustle of Hong Kong.

In this stage of adjustment, each family member expends extra energy mastering newness. Family members become more interdependent. There are fewer safety valves for interpersonal tensions and many more demands. A family needs to marshal all its sources of strength and patience and be sensitive to each individual's uncertainty and need for an extra measure of support.

Turning Point

After a first stage of excitement and delight in the new and interesting, and a second stage of increasing awareness of all the changes that life in Hong Kong will demand, a third stage of development unfolds. This is really the beginning of personal development, although the growth is still fragile and easily nipped in the bud. Nevertheless, prospects are encouraging. The first changes are mirrored in greater self-awareness and greater awareness of one's own culture.

We find we have underestimated the difficulty of changing ourselves. In this stage, the core of our former identity is challenged. Hostility toward the challengers -- Hong Kong and its thriving people -- is a typical reaction to such a threat. This is the stage where we defend what we know and value, criticize their opposites, and reject different ways of doing things and other value systems.

The most familiar symptom of this stage is an irritated criticism of local people, their manners and their institutions. Griping is often the main mode of conversation wherever and whenever recent expatriates gather. The carping may be ugly and no doubt should be discreet, but it has healthy aspects. It signals an increasing awareness of the 'real' Hong Kong. This accurate awareness is necessary for acceptance, which may seem most improbable at the time. But it represents progress. We come to realize that every culture has worked out its own way of achieving the good life, and there are many versions of it that we might appreciate. Hong Kong has problems, but it accommodates a remarkable diversity and works well, with a minimum sense of coercion. Persistence through this negative stage allows an appreciation of Hong Kong and its people to emerge.

A somewhat opposite problem is often voiced by expatriates. They have difficulties in getting to know Hong Kong people outside their own natural groups. The kernel of truth in that complaint is that it is hard to break into any established society. Many personal credentials do not transfer readily. Likewise, social interactions are governed by subtle rules that may be difficult to distinguish and unsatisfying to conform to due to the rules one has lived by unconsciously for so long. The resulting difficulties and frustration may lead the individual to withdraw emotionally, thus abandoning the goals of the broadening experience.

Feeling at Home

Persistence is required and rewarded. The envisaged growth finally emerges in a fourth stage of relaxed mastery of the new environment. Pleasure in new insights, freedom from defensiveness, and greater personal flexibility accompany the development of appropriate coping skill. Among the fruits of development will be more tolerance, increased self-sufficiency and greater objectivity with regard to one's own culture as well as Hong Kong's. Finally, pleasure derived from an informed appreciation of the new selves predominates.

This progression through stages can be expected during any typical expatriate's sojourn in Hong Kong. Each of the stages is linked to internal developments, the changes in self image that are expected as a result of the challenges of forging a new life-style. The transition is a process. The demarcation between stages is neither clear nor irreversible. Personal experiences will contribute to some shifting back and forth from day to day. Furthermore, the predicted growth is not inevitable. It can be stunted by insulating oneself from new experiences, failing to make a serious commitment to face the inherent difficulties, or being so rigid that the need for adaptation cannot surface in consciousness. Growth and adjustment will also not occur if stresses are overwhelming. But, in the midst of some future 'lesson' about how Hong Kong manages to be itself, perhaps a wry grin of recognition that 'this is a normal stage of adjustment' will replace discouragement and despair.

Housing - An Overview

If you are an expatriate living in Hong Kong in either a company owned/rented flat then your housing problems are non-existent, you will be provided with - in most cases - a spacious flat, no doubt in a relatively convenient location.

However, if you do not have this support from your company or employer - and increasingly this is the case - you will find yourself faced with the dilemma of finding suitable accommodation at an affordable price - welcome to Hong Kong!

Hong Kong has always been faced with housing problems. The government attempts to improve housing conditions date back to the last century. During World War II, much property decayed or was destroyed. This was compounded by a massive influx of refugees from China in 1949-50, following the revolution. Together, these two factors created a huge problem for the government of the day. In addition, a huge fire at the Shek Kip Mei squatter village on Christmas Day, 1953, added a further 50,000 to the growing list of homeless.

In fact, this signaled the government's first major involvement in public housing, with the construction of huge, multi-story 'resettlement blocks'. The early blocks offered minimal standard accommodation to refugees, the homeless and other qualified groups.

Over the years, these blocks have been improved upon and although still meeting only the basic requirements, the housing project is seen as a huge success.

In the late 1970s, a new scheme was launched which has been equally successful. The Home Ownership Scheme (HOS) is aimed at the lower middle income groups who wish to own their own flats. Almost 45 percent of owners come from public housing -- therefore freeing up property for others lower down the ladder. The scheme allows eligible buyers interest-free loans to purchase purpose-built HOS property.

Almost three million people live in government subsidized accommodation -- whether it is public housing or home ownership scheme buildings. Another 2.6 million live in private housing with only a small percentage actually owning their own property. This accommodation ranges from small, 300 to 400 square foot units, to luxury flats which average 2,500 to 3,500 square feet.

Hotels

You may find yourself in a hotel not only immediately after you land in Hong Kong but also -- because shipments of household furniture can take several weeks to arrive - for as long as three months. While there are obvious discomforts implicit in this arrangement (especially if small children accompany parents), there are also some advantages. This period can be useful for learning about neighborhoods and local schools, for finding out about shops, for discovering tourist attractions that the children may also enjoy, and for generally getting to know your way around Hong Kong.

In many cases the choice of hotel, whether in Hong Kong or Kowloon, will be made by your employer. However, if you have a family - and a choice - you will want a hotel that has good family accommodations. In the selection of a hotel, consideration should also be given to its distance from the office, from the children's school, from recreational facilities, and from shops. Reservations should be made as early in advance as possible, especially if you are coming during the peak tourist and conference months of April-May and October-November. Room rates are not quoted in this book because they change quite often and because of the diversity of accommodations required by families moving to Hong Kong. Also, many hotels provide corporate and long-term discounts of varying amounts. A detailed guide to long-stay hotel rentals is published annually in AmCham's book, *Establishing An Office In Hong Kong*.

Hotel guests should know that the housekeeping department of the hotel might be able to provide additional items such as power adapters, certain household appliances (such as irons or hair dryers), and furniture for babies. They may also be able to advise you on how to ensure that delicate clothing is not damaged through the hotel laundry system. Emergency medical services and babysitting can be arranged through all the major hotels. Tipping in hotels is discretionary as most include a service charge -- usually 10 percent on rooms, meals and other charges. However, depending on the service provided, tips are always welcomed and may assist in ensuring recognition if regular use of the facilities is intended. When patronizing the hotel shopping arcades, guests should note that prices for 'residents' can be less than those quoted for 'tourists'. New arrivals should therefore point out that they are living in Hong Kong.

Some families find it useful to engage part-time '*amahs*' during their hotel stay to help with the children, and this can be less expensive than using hotel babysitting services. This arrangement can also serve as a trial period and if both the employee and the employer are satisfied, the *amah* can move with the family when permanent accommodations are found.

Such domestic helpers are most often contract workers from the Philippines. There are advertisements from specialized agencies in the daily papers and on supermarket notice boards. Start looking early for an *amah* as it can take six to eight weeks to arrange.

Depending on the requirements and family situation of the new arrivals, some hotels have certain advantages over others. Long-term hotels or 'service apartments' can be a boon for those anticipating a lengthy search for an apartment. The former offer larger rooms and suites with very basic self-catering facilities while the latter offer regular apartments which are cleaned and otherwise maintained by the building's staff and are available on a month to month basis.

'Normal' hotels such as the Hilton, Mandarin and Furama Kempinski are centrally located and can be handy for some schools and most offices. The Hong Kong Tourist Association issues a free leaflet. 'Hotels in Hong Kong' which lists hotels, guests houses and hostels in Hong Kong and Macau.

Leave Flats

Since many expatriates in Hong Kong have relatively long home leave, ranging from four weeks each year to several months every few years, they often sublet their flats. These 'leave flats' can often provide a more comfortable and spacious alternative to a hotel for families awaiting furniture shipments and looking for permanent housing.

All of these flats are fully furnished, with telephones and other necessities. Often they include an *amah* (maid) and sometimes the use of a car or even a boat. As such, they can provide a more normal family life and are a good introduction to living in Hong Kong. They are a good way of learning about shopping for the necessities at local supermarkets and market-places.

Leave flats are more readily available in the summer months when most people take their home leaves, but a reasonable choice of flats at various locations and for various durations is available almost any time of the year. The best way to obtain a leave flat is through the *South China Morning Post* classified advertisements - where leave flats are listed under a separate heading - or from advertisements in supermarkets.

Generally, leave flats are rented on an all-inclusive basis - that is, the rental cost also includes the *amah* and utilities. A security deposit of one month's rent is normally required to cover breakages and losses incurred during the period the leave flat is let. It is recommended that the tenants from whom the leave flat is being sublet put away valuables and fragile items. Kitchen closets and cupboards should also be cleared. Those who take a leave flat may also be requested to look after pets, for example. This should be clarified - along with rules on children - when inspecting and selecting a leave flat.

Permanent Housing

One of the most difficult transitions Westerners - particularly Americans - must make in coming here is adapting to the idea of living in a Hong Kong-style apartment. While there are a few lucky expatriates who are able to live in a low-rise building (three or four stories high) and maybe have the luxury of a garden, most end up sacrificing their house and garden back home for an unimaginative flat with (perhaps) a balcony in a high-rise block.

In selecting an apartment (here called a 'flat'), the family must develop a checklist of advantages and disadvantages of the flat itself and its location. This is important as it is rare to find a family that is perfectly happy with initial housing conditions.

These are some of the issues your family will probably weigh in deciding on a flat:

How much can we afford to pay? Do we want to live in the tranquil New Territories, or near the action of Hong Kong Island and Kowloon? We want to be near other Westerners, but what would we miss by not living among Chinese families? We'd like an apartment with a harbor view, but that might mean less space and higher rent. Do we want to live close to markets? How long would it take to get to the office? What about schools in the area? Recreational facilities for the kids?

Housing Costs

Residential rental costs have fluctuated enormously in recent years. From 1978 to 1981 they increased at first steadily and then dramatically, culminating in the 1981 'boom', when rentals reached an all-time high. Inevitably, a market crash followed and Hong Kong experienced an almost three-year-long depression in the property market. Following the signing of the Sino-British Agreement in late 1984, however, the market noticeably firmed and rents rose steadily through to the end of 1985.

From 1985 up to 1991 the increases in rents have been steady rather than dramatic. There have been fairly predictable ups and downs but overall the market has moved up -- some speculators would say, against all odds.

There is much talk that, in the run up to 1997, the property market must take a dive but there is still little sign that this will happen. However, things move quickly in Hong Kong and when the right -- or wrong -- rumor strikes, anything could happen.

Below are some typical monthly rents for properties in Hong Kong in 1991.

Description of property	Monthly rent
Repulse Bay, 2,300 sq ft, pool, seaview	$30,000
Mid-Levels, 1,600 sq ft, pool/squash, view	$48,000
The Peak, 3,165 sq ft, townhouse, pool/squash	$83,000
Discovery Bay, 1,600 sq ft, duplex, garden	$24,000
Pokfulam, 2,600 sq ft, pool, seaview	$33,000
Jardine's Lookout, 2,300 sq ft, pool, club	$40,000

Without some financial assistance from their employers, most expatriates would find the cost of Hong Kong housing prohibitive. For those without such assistance, there are older buildings containing flats that are comparable to local middle-class standards: comfortable though smaller, set in a higher-density neighborhood, and perhaps offering less-spectacular views. Another very good alternative is to find a nicer but more remote apartment in the New Territories, Aberdeen, Stanley, or commute by ferry from one of Hong Kong's outlying islands, such as Cheung Chau, Lamma, or Lantau.

Hong Kong's unmarried expatriates have a number of options available. There are the cheaper flats away from Hong Kong Island, but also small studio apartments ('service flats') in town. Another appealing option might be to rent a room with a Chinese family. In addition, the YMCA and YWCA, Caritas, and Helena May Institute hostels also rent rooms at very moderate rates. Other persons may find it possible to share flats, and there are advertisements for these in the daily papers. Certainly accommodation is one of the biggest problems for anyone coming to Hong Kong, and you will find that rents are high. There have been recessional periods, however, and supply and demand can vary. The American Chamber of Commerce conducts semi-annual surveys of housing costs in Hong Kong, and results are published in *AmCham* magazine in April and September issues.

Standards

Hong Kong flats vary considerably in size, style and in the availability of amenities and fixtures. There can seem to be contradiction between what is considered 'luxurious' here and what the expatriate might have had in mind.

You may be quite surprised at the number of apartment fixtures you took for granted back home but may have to buy here. A brief list: doorstops, toilet seats, towel racks, blinds, basic light fixtures, closets, bathroom medicine cabinet. Some flats offer a sink in the kitchen but no cupboards or counter space. You probably will have to provide those, plus the refrigerator and stove. In some cases, you will need to provide the wall-mounted hot water heaters for kitchen and bathrooms. Few buildings have tank-type water heaters, most are gas or electric European-style 'flash heaters'.

It is also important to note how the size of a flat is measured. All measurements are in square feet. However, this includes the common areas such as the foyer and lift areas etc, so when asking about the size of a flat ask for the 'net' area. When renting a flat, the owner will require a two-month deposit — not including the first month's rent — and it is usual to pay the agent 50 percent of the first month's rent as commission. That equals 3.5 months' rent in advance to move into your flat. You will also need to pay a deposit to the phone and electricity companies. For the phone company this is a $600 line connection charge, the electricity connection is usually $800. It takes about 10 days for a phone connection, electricity can usually be connected within a couple of days.

In many buildings, the wiring is not ducted in the walls. Lighting, power wires and the telephone lines are stapled at intervals along woodwork, around door frames, and across ceilings. Buildings are maintained by caretakers and building attendants who polish brass, mop hallways, and dispose of trash.

Lobbies in Hong Kong tend to be sterile extensions of parking garages — large areas (sometimes marble) of unfurnished space.

Coping with the Climate

High humidity is a six- or seven-month problem in Hong Kong, particularly on the Peak, which can be above the cloud line for part of the year. You'll need to take certain precautions in your flat to prevent damage to clothing (particularly leather goods), walls, furniture, and books. The use of dehumidifiers, silica-gel bags, mothballs, and/or tubular heaters in closets is recommended. Fungicides are available at hardware shops to wash walls, ceilings, and any areas where mold may grow. The climate is also conducive to roaches and other pests. There are exterminators with monthly maintenance programs.

Air conditioners seldom come with the flat, but their purchase for at least some rooms will make the long, hot humid summer more tolerable. Portable fans and ceiling models are possible substitutes. The installation of air conditioners in the windows -- or special openings if provided -- is normally done by the supplier. Reverse-cycle air conditioners provide heat in the winter as well and some new models also include dehumidifiers. Although the short winter is not very cold and freezing conditions are not experienced, heating is necessary as concrete blocks of flats are not insulated.

During the May-to-September typhoon season, it is necessary to take certain precautions around the flat, whenever typhoon signals and warnings are given. 'Typhoon boards' are sometimes provided. These should be fitted to glass doors and large windows for protection. It's also recommended you place an 'X' across the window with masking tape to protect against flying glass should a window be blown in by wind. Consult the landlord, caretaker, or co-tenants regarding details of precautions to be taken. Some buildings are particularly exposed to winds. Typhoons ('hurricanes' in America) seldom hit Hong Kong directly and people at times don't take warnings seriously. This is a mistake. They are destructive and dangerous, so heed all warnings.

Electricity and Gas

Hong Kong has a 200V, 50-cycle electricity supply. Electric cooking stoves usually require a special fitting with heavy wiring and more power than other appliances. Town gas is available for cooking and water heating on Hong Kong Island and parts of Kowloon. Elsewhere LPG tanks are usual on a delivery-as-requested basis with local suppliers.

If your washing machine, dryer, or dishwasher is 110V, 60-cycle and is used through a transformer, it will slow down on 50-cycle current. However, this probably will not affect the machine or the wash. One laundry problem, though, might be the supply of hot water. There is rarely a hot water heater in the wash area, so unless the machine heats the water itself, a heater should be purchased. One alternative is to buy a cold-water-only machine, of which there are many brands available in Hong Kong. Hong Kong has few self-service laundromats, so you may find a washer/dryer to be a wise investment.

Most flats have two types of electric wall outlets, based on required amperes. The 'power plugs' are wired more heavily and fuse at 15 amps. Power plugs are needed for all appliances up to two horsepower, and a heavier circuit for more than two horsepower. All outlets require either a large or small three-pronged plug. Several adapters may be needed to accept the many different sizes of prongs and to fit various plugs. These are inexpensive, but confusing.

For instance, there are flat and square pronged plugs and outlets, besides the large and small sized round prong varieties. It is unwise to use poor-quality plugs or adapters, and outlets should never be overloaded. Loose and badly fitted connectors can cause fires.

There are two private power companies in Hong Kong: Hong Kong Electric Company (Hong Kong and Lamma Island) and China Light and Power (everywhere else).

Hong Kong & China Gas Company supply Towngas which is piped to all homes in the urban area. LPG, or bottled gas, is used in more remote areas such as the outlying islands and parts of the New Territories. Cooking by gas is by far the preferred method in Hong Kong.

A warning about gas water heaters: Older model flash heaters have caused several deaths by asphyxiation in recent years. These are no longer on sale but some older places still have them. Check that yours is a 'safe' heater -- meaning self-ventilated modern flash heater. When using gas heaters in the bathroom open a window to ensure ventilation. Your supplier and the gas company can further advise.

Finding a Flat

English-language newspapers carry advertisements for flats to rent, to share, and to buy outright. The *South China Morning Post* has the largest classified advertising section. Through the newspapers, it is possible to contact the many agencies and have them assist in finding suitable accommodations. Competition among agencies is fierce, and a flat hunter should have no qualms about using several at one time. It's also a good idea to know up front just exactly how much of a fee you will have to pay the agent and for how long. The usual agency fee is half the first month's rent, payable by the tenant.

Securing an agent via the local English-language classifieds may be the quickest, most convenient way to locate a satisfactory flat, but it is by no means the only method. One alternative is to visit a neighborhood that particularly appeals to you and stroll its streets. Visit the local supermarkets and check their bulletin boards for listings of vacant flats. Or go to a building in which you might like to live (or at least see), and then contact the management personnel. If you have Chinese-speaking friends, another alternative might be to ask them to watch the classifieds in the Chinese newspapers. Very often those listings offer more apartment value for the dollar than can be found in the English-language ads. Finding a flat in Hong Kong can be extremely rewarding, but it's not easy, and the process of finding out what is available and then making the selection can take a month or more.

The rental price of most flats is offered exclusive of rates, utilities, and management fees. Rental of a building parking space may be an additional charge, and a caretaker may also expect his own extra payment. It is wise to inquire into all such possible extra costs when considering a flat as they can add to the total and are not controlled by rent legislation. It is also normal to split attorney fees for drawing up the lease between landlord and tenant.

Residential Areas

Many expatriate families live on Hong Kong Island, although rents are very much lower from Kowloon Tong out through the New Territories, and travel on the Kowloon Canton Railway (KCR) and the MTR is fast, convenient, relatively comfortable, and very safe. The two systems are interlinked so that riders can cross from system to system as simply as changing platforms.

The New Territories lifestyle is most readily adopted by those who prefer the country life or are willing to sacrifice easier commuting for more spacious living facilities. If rent prices continue to escalate in Hong Kong, more expatriate families could look to the New Territories as a good alternative to Hong Kong Island. Nevertheless, if you do wish to live on the Island, the most popular residential areas are the south side (around Repulse Bay), the Mid-Levels, and the Peak.

Mid-Levels

The Mid-Levels cover a long strip of hillside area from Conduit and Robinson roads at the western end of the Island to Jardine's Lookout in the center of the island. Most of the flats throughout the Mid-Levels have harbor views - from partial to spectacular. Although many newcomers find the harbor view very attractive, it should be remembered that flats facing the harbor look north and so may get very little sun. Western Mid-Levels around Robinson, Kotewall, and Conduit roads are a conglomeration of high-rise flats. While they may lack some of the open space to be found in the Mid-Levels farther east, the nearby Western District has a certain Chinese neighborhood feel about it that one does not find elsewhere. Public transport might take a little longer in some of these areas, but they are adequately served.

The middle Mid-Levels are handily located behind Central District and close to the Botanical and Zoological Gardens and Brewin Path Playground. This area includes the popular Bowen and MacDonnell roads, where spacious older and newer luxury blocks of flats can be found.

The eastern end of the Mid-Levels includes Stubbs Road, Shiu Fai Terrace, and the eastern end of Kennedy Road. Transport in this area can be difficult at peak hours because buses and mini-buses coming from the south side of the Island are full. Some parts of this area are close by pleasant walks - paths along bush-clad hills of the middle part of the Island.

School buses are available for most schools in this area. Many American families seem to choose between the Mid-Levels and Repulse Bay by deciding whether Dad (or Mom) travels 25 minutes to work or the children commute to school. Living anywhere on the north side of the Island allows fairly quick access to the Star Ferry, the MTR, and the Cross Harbour Tunnel. But walking up from Central is a steep climb, and even a short hike in the summer humidity is very exhausting. One can reach Kennedy Road from Wanchai by elevator — through the Hopewell Centre building in Queen's Road East. In 1993 a pedestrian escalator will climb from Des Voeux Road, Central up to Conduit Road.

The Peak

The Peak offers a good minibus service, and many people commute to work on the Peak Tram. The environment is pleasant and the journey to Central takes 20-30 minutes. Views of the harbor or the outer islands in the South China Sea are exquisite, except during spring months, when the Peak is often above cloud level. Dehumidifiers are vital on the Peak. Supermarkets, banks, beauty salon, and post office are available. The German Swiss International School and Peak Junior School are close at hand as well.

For government employees, there are several large blocks of flats and numerous smaller buildings on the Peak, some of them older and more architecturally interesting than the new ones. Some flats boast fireplaces and lots of brass handles and well-polished mailboxes, and a general air of gentility pervades most of the buildings. Many are also extremely exposed to typhoons. School buses cover most areas on the Peak.

North Shore

Jardine's Lookout has private homes, some garden apartments, and a predominance of two- and three-story buildings. Located above Happy Valley, it is an excellent district for those whose who wish to be reasonably handy to Central but live in a more suburban type of environment.

Happy Valley, Causeway Bay, and Wanchai contain some high-rise blocks of flats which appeal to expatriates. Generally, the flats are smaller there. However, each of these areas is conveniently located for shopping, and transportation is readily available. Causeway Bay and Wanchai are heavily populated, with Victoria Park being the main recreation area.

South Shore

Repulse Bay, Shouson Hill and Deep Water Bay on the south side of Hong Kong Island are, at peak traffic hours, 20-30 minutes' travel time from Central. Shouson Hill's apartment buildings tend to be smaller, with two- and three-story units most prevalent. Residents of this area can shop in Aberdeen as well as in Stanley. Aberdeen, which has the floating restaurants and was once just a fishing village, has now been redeveloped and industrialized. Minibuses are available along Shouson Hill Road. Repulse Bay seems to be chosen by families whose children attend the Hong Kong International School. Most of the housing is high-rise, though there is a distinctly suburban atmosphere in Repulse Bay. Most of the buildings must be reached by long, steep, driveways. Although Repulse Bay Road is well served by buses and minibuses, some expatriate commuters form carpools or rent hire-cars by the month, sharing the ride to work with several neighbors. Despite the difficulties of parking in town and the traffic congestion, a car can be a great help in Repulse Bay.

A small shopping center - housing a supermarket, bank and post office - is located on South Bay Road, and another on Beach Road. New arrivals should be careful not to be taken in by the beaches, particularly those of Repulse Bay and Deep Water Bay, which seem so pleasant when viewed in winter or on a clear weekday. On a summer weekend, the crowds and traffic at the southern beaches are unbelievable, and best avoided. There is the other matter of the swimming waters: during and immediately following a heavy weekend, they can be badly polluted.

Stanley, once a small fishing village, houses the local prison, some British military families, the Stanley Club, some small beaches as well as an expanding residential population. Located a few miles past Repulse Bay, Stanley has a large open market very popular with expatriates for its fresh fish and vegetables, rattan furniture and accessories, clothing, and much more. There is a supermarket and bus service to the Hong Kong International School and to Quarry Bay Junior School as well as frequent buses to Central and Shaukiwan. The residents of Stanley tend to feel they live in a real community.

Small apartment units two- and three-story and the more leisurely pace of traffic permits bicycling and walking for both youngsters and adults. Some of the buildings have swimming pools and garden areas.

The journey from Stanley to Central can take around 40 minutes during peak traffic periods, particularly between 7:30 and 9 am.

Chung Hum Kok is located on a peninsula between Stanley and Repulse Bay. It is becoming very much an expatriate location as the low-rise flats, often with swimming pools and gardens, appeal to many who are not keen on high-rise living. A small beach is within walking distance from most flats. Bus services operate to Central and North Point. A supermarket is well located on Chung Hum Kok Road. The journey to Central from Chung Hum Kok - as from neighboring Stanley and Repulse Bay - is a long one.

Other relatively new developments on the South Shore are in South Bay, just along from Repulse Bay, Red Hill, and Tai Tam. The American Club's splendid new premises are located in Tai Tam which is also not too far from the International School in Repulse Bay.

West Shore

Pokfulam has become popular in recent years. Large apartment buildings there include Scenic Villas and Baguio Villas. Some low-rise flats with garden areas can be found in Pokfulam on Bisney, Mount Davis, and Sassoon roads.

The housing estate at Wah Fu provides shopping facilities and restaurants, but this and other large housing developments such as Chi Fu Fa Yuen have increased the congestion.

Transport can be difficult during rush hours as the buses and minibuses operate mainly along Pokfulam Road, and from some areas this is a long uphill climb. Baguio Villas has a minibus service. School buses cover most areas.

Kowloon

Waterloo Hill, Homantin Hill and Beacon Hill are areas of high-rise buildings, excellent for public transportation, near supermarkets, and close to the Urban Council's public library. Flats vary in size from relatively small (1,200 sq ft) to quite large (2,500 sq ft). Many have terraces and views. There is considerable noise from airplanes landing at Kai Tak, and one would be wise to apartment-hunt in the late afternoon, when air traffic is heavy, to see how this affects the prospective living environment.

Kowloon Tong and Yau Yat Chuen are more suburban in feel. Here one- and two-story buildings, surrounded by gardens and on quiet streets,are available in completely residential settings. There is some noise from aircraft.There are few houses for rent, but many buildings contain only two or four flats. Kowloon Tong is 20 minutes by bus to Tsim Sha Tsui, and close to Kowloon City. The MTR provides speedy access to the Island.

Mei Foo Sun Chuen is a self-contained high-rise community in Lai Chi Kok. It has its own bus service every 15 minutes to the Star Ferry. There are water taxis from Mei Foo to Central, which take around 25 minutes, and the tunnel bus service is also convenient. Nonetheless, the journey is fairly long if you work on Hong Kong Island, even though the MTR has provided some improvement. Flats for bachelors, couples, and families are small but allow for people of all ages, family composition and income. Mei Foo is really a large town in itself, built to local middle-class standards. It is noisy and crowded, but its advantages are beautiful harbor views, shops of all kinds on the ground floors of residential buildings, restaurants, and parks and play areas, all of which have been incorporated into this project, developed by Mobil Oil.

New Territories

In the New Territories there are some magnificent townhouse-type developments, particularly around Sai Kung and Clearwater Bay. These and other New Territories areas were previously largely overlooked by expatriates, who reasoned that the isolation and long journeys overshadowed the advantages of the environment. This is changing with the development of infrastructure. Some shift to these areas is likely as rents in the more-popular areas of Kowloon and the Island continue to escalate and as new housing estates of detached and semi-detached houses are built at Yuen Long and Taipo.

Discovery Bay on Lantau Island is a fairly new development. Phases I and II were completed in 1983 and consisted of several low-rise, spacious apartments, many of which were on the beach-front. It was considered a quiet, peaceful place to live. The development has grown rapidly since then and Disco Bay, as it is known, now consists of several high-rise buildings accommodating approximately 7,000 people. There are plans to accommodate another 14,000 people if all the existing plans come to fruition.

Discovery Bay has its own 24-hour ferry/hydrofoil service. The journey to Blake Pier, next to the Star Ferry on Hong Kong side, takes 20--30 minutes. Residents have their own club, shopping facilities and primary school. Private cars are not permitted. Rentals, once much cheaper than either Hong Kong or Kowloon, are slowly coming up to par.

Domestic Help

Most expatriate families here employ a live-in or part-time domestic helper, who may be a Chinese '*amah*' or, nowadays, most often a Filipina or Thai. The duties for a live-in helper over a six-day week include cleaning, washing, ironing, some cooking or help with cooking and help with children.

Part-time help is just that, coming in for a few hours each day, or for two or three days each week.

Most domestic helpers have a sense of dignity and pride in doing a job well and in their own way. These same attributes can also account for most of the pitfalls. Perhaps the most important axiom for the new expatriate to learn is: 'Don't fight the system'. There are just certain things that domestic help like to do their own way. However, if you feel it necessary to do things a little differently, your instructions should be as clear and precise as possible.

For many Westerners coming to Hong Kong, this will be the first experience of living with someone from an Eastern culture. There are naturally bound to be conflicts and misunderstandings, but there is also much in the relationship that can be both enlightening and enriching. Most problems, you'll find, will arise over use of the kitchen and control over the household.

Virtually all Hong Kong flats have small quarters for live-in domestic help, which must be furnished, These furnishings include a bed, a chest of drawers, a table, and either chairs or folding stools, which can be purchased from a local market or from a family leaving Hong Kong. Families that by choice or as an economy measure can manage without domestic help are more common now in Hong Kong, and for them the *amah*'s room can sometimes make a useful study, den, or extra workroom.

The 1991 wages for a Chinese amah were around $3,500 per month. Traditional practice, rather than any legal requirement, dictates that an extra month's wages be paid at Chinese New Year. The live-in amah works six days a week and receives ten days leave per year plus the statutory public holidays.

In recent years, Filipina, Thai and Sri Lankan maids have become very popular among both Chinese and expatriate families. They are employed in Hong Kong on two-year contracts and employers (known as sponsors) are expected to pay the round-trip air fare from the home country, passport and visa fees, uniforms (if necessary), food, housing, and medical expenses. The Immigration Department issues all necessary documents.

The legal minimum wage for foreign domestic helpers is currently $3,300 per month with basically the same employment terms as for Chinese amahs.

There are several agencies which can help you get a maid from abroad but this can prove expensive -- especially for the prospective maid who is charged a hefty fee to get on an agent's books. A far better way is word of mouth. Most Filipinas -- or indeed Thai and Sri Lankans -- have a friend or relative they can recommend. There are also many already *in situ* who are about to end or break a contract. This latter option saves a lot of time -- and you can interview the maids yourself rather than relying on an agency recommendation. Should you go this way, make absolutely sure the maid is here legally. Check that she has a 'release paper' from her previous employer, otherwise you and the maid could both be in trouble.

Broadly speaking, Chinese *amahs* know Hong Kong, get better bargains when shopping and can help you with your Cantonese. Filipinas are usually easier to communicate with and have a more Western approach to child rearing (they are generally excellent with children). They are hardworking and have a very pleasant attitude to life. Although English is not their strong-point, Thai and Sri Lankans shine in the kitchen and can turn their hands either to Western or their national cuisine.

When it comes down to it , choosing a maid or amah depends on your own set of circumstances and personal preferences. Generally speaking the outlines above are fair but of course there will be specific exceptions like the fluent English-speaking Thai or the bad-tempered, lazy Filipina. Find out as much as you can about any prospective employee before signing anything.

If you just want part-time help, look at supermarket notice-boards. Rates vary depending on the type of work from $20 an hour up to $40. $35 per hour is considered normal.

Other Domestic Services

It is recommended that the expatriate family develop a list of other domestic services needed. Pest Control, window cleaners, floor polishers, caterers, babysitters and general handymen are just a few of the services you will find necessary living in Hong Kong.

The best places to locate these people are through other expatriates, classified sections of the local newspapers and the *Yellow Pages*. Two other good sources are the *Dollarsaver* and the *Kowloon Advertiser* which list page upon page of classified ads for all kinds of goods and services -- particularly aimed at expatriates. Subscriptions for both magazines are free. For the *Dollarsaver* call 528 0825 and for the *Kowloon Advertiser* call 366 1961.

Who's Who in Hong Kong Communications

Hong Kong's only guide to creative services in advertising, broadcasting, print production, public relations, publishing and allied fields. The first edition ran 312 pages and will be updated, enlarged and re-issued in 1992. Over 115 companies providing 65 categories of products and services were carried in the 1990 edition, which also included a "Quick Contact File" telephone finders guide to about 4,000 companies in Hong Kong.

The book's editor and AmCham's publications manager, Fred Armentrout, claims, "This is our most ambitious book since the original creation of our well known titles, *Living in Hong Kong* and *Doing Business in Today's Hong Kong* in the 1970s -- and it is about the same number of pages.

"We made the effort for three reasons: Americans are prominent in the communications industries here, there has never been greater need for companies in Hong Kong to use creative services in communications, and the existing professional infrastructure is disjointed and weak here and needs support.

Copies of the book are available in most local bookstores and directly from The American Chamber of Commerce in Hong Kong at HK$215/US$40 for non-members and HK$175/US$35 for members. Postage inclusive.

Chapter 4
LIVING & HEALTH

PHOTO COURTESY OF HONG KONG TOURIST ASSOCIATION

I t is very hard to generalize about the overall quality of life in Hong Kong since there are so many variables and intangibles to take into account. The first thing that might strike the newcomer is the high density of people here as well as the volume of noise and air pollution on the city's streets, particularly in the heavily congested areas of Tsim Sha Tsui, Central, Wanchai, and Causeway Bay. Hong Kong's great strength - its vitality and growth - is also liability, for it is not easy to walk around town without feeling at least a little constricted by the crowds, or without being assaulted by the deafening sound of construction equipment or the noxious fumes of the street traffic. On the other hand, there are places in or near Hong Kong where one can easily find fresh air and quiet, open spaces.

Where diet is concerned, Hong Kong's people - and the virtual army of outstanding chefs here - have taken advantage of the abundance and variety of fresh fruits and vegetables from countries throughout Southeast Asia. Unfortunately, despite the availability of such excellent fresh foods, the diet here is slowly being affected by Western traditions - namely the consumption of foods high in cholesterol. Thus, Hong Kong is seeing a higher incidence of cholesterol-related illnesses, such as strokes and coronary disease. The incidence of cancer here seems to be comparable to that found in other 'advanced' industrialized societies, although there seems to be an inexplicably high rate of lung cancer among Chinese women in Hong Kong.

In general, Hong Kong's health standards are quite high, particularly compared with those of most other Asian cities. It has comparable life expectancies to the West, and it has a lower infant mortality rate than the United States. The government has made a concerted effort toward disease prevention and eradication, which has resulted in a decreased incidence of infectious disease.

There were five cases of cholera in 1990 of which only two were local. Communicable childhood diseases are all under control due to an extensive vaccination program in hospitals, clinics, and schools. Hepatitis B, declared endemic in 1988, is the latest virus under fire by government health workers. All newborn babies are now routinely vaccinated against this as well as tuberculosis, diphtheria, polio, tetanus, and whooping cough. As of 1990, all one-year-olds visiting government clinics are given the measles, mumps, rubella vaccine (MMR) so that, in effect, children are now protected against nine common childhood infectious diseases.

Twelve cases of AIDS were reported in 1990 and the Expert Committee on the disease has been upgraded to an Advisory Council. This technicality will bring more awareness, funds and facilities to bear on the problem.

If you take basic precautions, you will be at absolutely no risk of contracting anything more serious than a common cold or bout of flu.

Drinking Water

Although Hong Kong has, in the past, experienced shortages of water, the quantity and quality of the water supply today is very high and up to international standards. Any harmful bacteria that might be found in home tap water actually do not come from the water itself, but rather from older pipes, where corrosion enables the bacteria to collect and grow. If you let your water run for a minute or so before drinking it, you shouldn't need to boil it. Nevertheless, boiling your water for at least 10 minutes is a good safeguard. You also can buy distilled water in 10-gallon plastic containers - or in small bottles by the case - and have it delivered to your home by A S Watson & Co Ltd (660 6688). In addition, you can find individual small bottles of distilled water and various imported mineral waters in local supermarkets and family grocery stores.

Swimming Water

The quality of Hong Kong's swimming water and beaches has deteriorated over the past few years. This decline is caused by a combination of pollutants that include animal and human waste and chemical and industrial effluents. There is a move by the government to rectify the state of the beaches but many people feel this is too little too late. Most local beaches fall well below World Health Organization safe swimming standards, something to consider before entering; especially so at the most popular beaches. The newspapers give wide coverage to the water pollution issue, considered a major problem in Hong Kong. At the beginning of summer, they will list what beaches are closed and which have been upgraded/downgraded based on government tests every two weeks. A rule of thumb by long-time residents is not to swim in the sea or if so, do it from a junk/private boat moored well away from known black spots.

Food

Food sold in Hong Kong's many restaurants and markets is of generally high quality. The city's Urban Council - the statutory body charged with maintaining Hong Kong's public health - regularly inspects premises of all restaurants, and issues food business licenses.

Hong Kong abounds with cooked food stalls known as *dai bai dongs*. Most of these makeshift restaurants are licensed by the same division of the Urban Council that oversees markets. You'll see these food stalls set up in small alleys, along busy streets and sidewalks, and within food markets themselves.Several hundred licensed stalls are currently in operation. The Urban Council is attempting to move all of these businesses into designated market complexes and is therefore no longer issuing licenses for *dai bai dong* operations. Food vendors, or hawkers, who roll their cook carts and sell interesting varieties of cooked cuisines on street sidewalks, are not sanctioned by the Urban Council. They run their concessions without a cooked food license. Thus, you partake of those local delicacies at your own risk. In general, it must be said that *dai bai dongs* and cook-cart vendors maintain relatively good hygienic standards. If you're not sure, just watch how they prepare the food and clean the dishes. You can learn a lot about any restaurant by looking at its 'kitchen'.

Also under the jurisdiction of the Urban Council are the city's more than 50 retail fresh food markets, which must adhere to the Council's licensing regulations, including the maintenance of strict sanitation standards. An actual trip to one of these markets can be a great cultural adventure, not only in the bargaining with vendors over the price of a pound of bananas, but also in the array of produce you'll find available. Some examples (depending on the season): papaya, mango, star fruit, lychee, pear, melons, apple, banana, durian, orange, plum, grape, greens, tomato, onion, gingerroot, mushroom, carrot, potato, crab, prawn, oyster, finfish, beef, pork, chicken, Chinese sausage, and a variety of spices.

Health authorities recommend completely cooking anything grown in Hong Kong or nearby China. Human manure 'night soil', rather than chemicals, is used to fertilize crops there. Since chemicals are not used in the production process, it is important to wash produce thoroughly because more live bugs tend to be found. To ensure the hygiene of the vegetables you eat, soak them in cold water or with a drop or two of bleach.

Medical and Health Services

There is no free national health service in Hong Kong. Doctor's appointments, medications, X-rays, operations and hospital care all have to be fully paid for by the patient. However, government employees and those of some government-subsidized organizations are given free or reduced-rate treatment, and many companies have medical schemes and contracts with doctors' firms who act as company doctors. Government medical services and emergency treatment are available to everyone at nominal charges at public hospitals.

Along with checking in advance what medical benefits are available here to you and your family, check your general state of health, dental needs, and eyesight before arrival. Details of any special treatment medication or prescriptions should be brought with you so that a local physician or specialist can authorize fresh supplies (foreign prescriptions are not filled here).

Smallpox vaccination is required, except for children under the age of one year, if you will have visited an infected area within 14 days of your arrival in Hong Kong. Other preventive innoculations are available free for children in Hong Kong. These include protection against tuberculosis, diphtheria, whooping cough, polio, typhoid, and measles. Although Hong Kong is not an unhealthy place, the same precautions as are recommended in most countries should be taken, particularly for children.

There are no specific dreaded diseases in Hong Kong that are different from those of the US or Europe, but because of overcrowding and the damp, hot weather during the long summer months, infections do occur more frequently and seem to last longer. As in all tropical countries, care should be taken in the cleaning and preparation of fresh foods, as a precaution against intestinal diseases.

Medical Emergencies

Knowing what to do in an emergency and acting as quickly and calmly as possible is the best way of preventing permanent injury and even loss of life. Apart from the obvious precaution of having a clean and well-stocked first-aid kit at home, you should also be prepared to dial 999 for police, fire or ambulance services.

A doctor should also be called if one is known to be available quickly, but in some cases of acute illness, accident, bites, deep cuts, poisoning etc, the patient should be taken by the fastest means available to the nearest hospital emergency room for free emergency treatment. If you wish to go to a private hospital, you must tell the ambulance driver. All six regional public hospitals (formerly known as government hospitals) offer a 24-hour emergency service:

Queen Mary (Pokfulam)	819-2111
Queen Elizabeth (Kowloon)	710-2111
Prince of Wales (Sha Tin)	636-2211

Princess Margaret (Lai Chi Kok)   742-7111
Tang Sui Kin (Wanchai)   831-6800
Tuen Mun (Tuen Mun)   468-5111

If you have an accident which requires hospital treatment on one of the outlying islands, you will be taken to Queen Elizabeth hospital by helicopter.

Hospitals

In December 1991, all government and government subvented (partially subsidized) hospitals were taken over by the Hospital Authority, an independent body. The changeover did not signify any great changes in the system — the same services are still available at basically the same low cost. However, much of the reorganization is still under discussion so it is difficult to say what changes may take place in the near future.

There are 13 public hospitals, 20 subvented, and 11 private hospitals providing a total of approximately 25,000 beds — or 4.3 per 1,000 population. This figure compares well to the United States' 5.3 and Britain's 6.8 beds per thousand population.

Private hospitals are listed in the *Yellow Pages* but the four most popular with expatriates are: Hong Kong Adventist on Stubbs Road which has dental and other specialty clinics, emergency room, and extensive preventive health awareness classes. They also run free ante-natal classes. Matilda Hospital, best known for its maternity wing, sits on top of the Peak. Many of the rooms in the colonial-style building have large balconies offering spectacular views of Hong Kong. It is certainly a quiet and relaxing place to have a baby — though a difficult place for visitors to reach. Canossa Hospital, on the other hand, is five minutes from Central and is considered a good general hospital. For Kowloon, Baptist Hospital in Kowloon Tong has a good reputation.

You will often find that your doctor prefers to work in one particular hospital. If you therefore have a preference for a particular establishment — especially if you are having a baby — take this into account when selecting a doctor.

Adventist   574-6211
Canossa   522-2181
Matilda   849-6301
Baptist   337-4141

More on Maternity

All of the private hospitals mentioned above have good maternity services. **Adventist** is equipped for traditional delivery as well as providing two birthing rooms. **Canossa** only accepts maternity patients with doctors affiliated to their hospital. They have four labor rooms and do not offer ongoing ante-natal classes. **Matilda** offers an extensive program of ante-natal and post-natal care in addition to fitness and exercise classes during and after the pregnancy. **Nethersole Hospital**, a government subvented hospital, has a maternity wing which offers, in conjunction with its out-patient clinic, an excellent service from the beginning right through to delivery. The cost is a fraction of private hospital charges.

Breastfeeding is not actively encouraged in many hospitals — especially the large public hospitals where a set routine seems to take precedence. The few places where nursing is *actively* encouraged are Matilda, Nethersole and Adventist.

Private ante-natal classes/exercises are available in several places. Check *Dollarsaver* or ask at your doctor's clinic for details. *La Leche League* (605-3810) for advice on breastfeeding, is well-established in Hong Kong and is a good place to meet other mothers. *The Hong Kong Baby Book — your one-stop guide to having a baby in Hong Kong* is probably a worthwhile investment ($98) if you are pregnant and new to Hong Kong. Alternatively, *Hong Kong Mother & Baby*, a bi-monthly newsletter, is full of interesting articles and advice on parenting in Hong Kong. The newsletter is available free of charge by calling 512-0441.

Clinics and Special Treatment

The government has retained control of the 68 clinics where various out-patient services are available. Treatment at these clinics costs only a few dollars and includes tests, X-rays, medicine, etc. There are also specialty clinics for maternity and child health guidance which includes free ante-natal and post-natal care of the mother and a full immunization program for the child. There are also 29 clinics run by the Family Planning Association (FPA), 25 methadone treatment centers and several 'floating' clinics — specially equipped boats which visit remote areas.

Doctors, Dentists and Specialists

Hong Kong has many highly trained doctors practicing Western medicine in government service and in private practice. Both universities now run medical schools, and many doctors also have specialist qualifications from other countries. The University of Hong Kong has recently started a school of dentistry. A list of all registered medical practitioners is published twice yearly in the Government Gazette. Recommendations about a family doctor, dentist, or specialist can best be obtained from friends, from your national consulate, and from your employer.

The adventurous may also be intrigued by the numerous Chinese herbal medicine stores and the promises of ginseng or other exotic medicines. Care should be exercised if such things are not familiar and their properties not fully understood. Acupuncture, acupressure and moxibustion are also generally available, trusted by both local and some expatriate residents.

Fees charged by private practitioners in Hong Kong range widely, from a few dollars to $400 or more for a consultation. Separate charges are usually made for laboratory tests, X-ray examinations, special diagnosis, and the cost of medicines if supplied directly by the physician or his own dispenser. Home visits are generally more expensive, but many doctors keep their clinics open after ordinary office hours to suit those who cannot attend during the day.

Dentists will usually provide an estimate for expensive treatment such as capping, crowns, bridges, and gold fillings, which may require several visits.

Pharmacists and Prescriptions

There are a number of excellent dispensing pharmacies from which you may safely and accurately obtain your prescriptions. Drugs cost considerably less in Hong Kong than in the United States.

Family health can generally be maintained by using common sense. Summer heat and humidity may cause rashes, stomach upsets, and prickly heat. Mosquito bites, eye infection (conjunctivitus) from swimming, and athlete's foot are all possible Hong Kong conditions for which medicines are available. All drugs are paid for by the patient. Many doctors in Hong Kong dispense the drugs they prescribe. Since you cannot get a foreign prescription filled, have a Hong Kong doctor issue a new prescription for any regular medication.

It is inadvisable to purchase prescription medicines under the counter. Hong Kong's wonderful ability to imitate has led the occasional unscrupulous entrepreneur to produce apparently exact copies of various medications and their packages.

All the familiar Western remedies for headaches, cold symptoms, constipation, cough, and overeating -- in short, most non-prescription patent medicines -- are displayed among the bubble baths, deodorants, cosmetics, and other toiletries Americans and British are accustomed to using at home. Children's powdered formulas, standard baby equipment, humidifiers, bottles, vitamins, etc are stocked, but certain brands may be difficult to locate. Sometimes shops wait several months to receive new shipments of those items or brands which they do carry.

Hong Kong's many opticians can grind lenses, provide soft and regular contact lenses, and have all varieties of glass for lenses, as well as huge assortments of frames from all over the world. Prices are reasonable by US and UK standards. A number of qualified ophthalmologists will prescribe lenses.

Pedicurists (who remove callouses, massage feet, and clip and paint toenails) often bill themselves as 'chiropodists.' Ask where they were trained if you want more than a pedicure. Several of these practitioners will come to your home by appointment. There is a Dr Scholl's salon as well.

Counseling services

There are relatively few counselling services in Hong Kong for English-speaking individuals and families. Westerners constitute a very small portion of the population and their family and social orientation is sufficiently different from that of the Chinese to make the problem of finding guidance services more than merely one of language differences.

A Survey of Mental Health Resources in Hong Kong, published in 1990, outlines the way the system works, lists several English-speaking help groups and private practitioners and also describes counselling services available in schools. The booklet is available through Dr Carol Betson, The Department of Community Medicine, Hong Kong University, Li Shu Fan Bldg, Sassoon Road or at the reception desk of the American Chamber of Commerce in Swire House ($25).

Another source of information is the *TV & Entertainment Times* which lists several support groups and counselling services in its 'Outreach' column.

Below is a list of some services. For details on the kind of counseling, meeting arrangements and the address, call the number given. Phone numbers often change as do the people running the various support groups so if you have a problem getting through to a particular group, call the **Community Advice Bureau (524-5444)** for the most up-to-date number.

Against Child Abuse	755-9933
Alcoholics Anonymous (problem drinkers)	522-5665
Al-Anon (for families of problem drinkers)	522-5665
Al-Ateen (for children of problem drinkers)	522-5665
Bereaved Parents Support Group	813-2884
Cansurvive (cancer support group)	328-2202 / 566-4560
Christian Counselling Service	526-4747
Comfort, Care, Concern (AIDS Helpline)	525-3433
Drug Abuse Telephone Enquiry Hotline	366-8822
Hong Kong Samaritans	834-3333 (hotline)
Marriage and Personal Counselling Service	523-8979
Mother to Mother	817-3626
Multiple Sclerosis Group	545-0303 (office hours)
Narcotics Anonymous	522-5665
Overeaters Anonymous	987-9180
Parents Against Drug Abuse	873-3776
Pills Anonymous	721-0880
Rape Hotline	572-2733

Children

Life in Hong Kong for children and teenagers is not unlike that of any large metropolitan city. There are basketball courts, swimming pools, movie houses, summer work programs, sports, hobby clubs, and music lessons. The main problems that children and their parents seem to face in moving to Hong Kong are those created by the transition from what is usually a suburban environment to an urban one. Twelve- to 15-year-olds will, for instance, have limited opportunities for dating in the evening unless parents are willing to allow youngsters on buses or in taxis by themselves.

With so much of adult social life centered on business entertaining and dinner parties, parents can't always be home in the evening. In addition, because many expatriate businessmen who are based here with families must travel extensively throughout the region, they may be home a great deal less than they were before they came. Furthermore, many expatriates are sent to Hong Kong for only two or three years so that families may think of themselves as transient. Less effort is therefore made to put down roots, to accept the place as 'home'.

All these factors tend to accentuate any previous family problems and to make the transition more difficult for children. Many teenagers on arrival feel that they have removed from the mainstream, from what's happening at home. Companies often try to transfer families in the summer months; therefore, children may encounter problems in making friends until the school year starts in September. In addition, teenagers will find it difficult to locate part-time jobs or to obtain visas that will permit them to work.

Some community groups do sponsor summer job programs. The Community Advice Bureau can advise on these and on holiday activities. Volunteer work in hospitals can be done, and the Mothers' Club of the Hong Kong International School - in conjunction with the school - sponsors and arranges lessons, crafts courses, and various activities during the summer months.

To the extent that parents feel that living overseas is exciting, broadening, and meaningful for the whole family, the difficulties of living in Hong Kong can be overcome. Joining groups and learning about - and working for - the community contributes greatly to any family accepting, and being accepted by, the community.

Drug Abuse

Despite the wide range of wholesome family activities available in Hong Kong, there is nevertheless - as in every major industrial city - a drug abuse problem here. The primary difference, between Western cities and Hong Kong is that while 'softer' drugs like marijuana and hashish are difficult and expensive to obtain here, heroin is very cheap, readily available, and the drug of choice among addicts.

Most of it is 90 percent pure (rather than 4-5 percent as in America and Europe), so that one experiment may prove fatal. It is generally smoked here rather than injected due to its potency.

The exact number of addicts is not known, however, government figures suggest that at the end of 1990 there were about 39,000 'active' addicts — 90 percent male, 10 percent female.

The government has made a concerted effort to combat drug abuse here, undertaking a four-point program: preventive education and publicity, treatment and rehabilitation, law enforcement, and international cooperation. To that end, the government has involved many thousands of students in anti-drug campaigns; established two dozen methadone treatment centers; extensively researched the use of various detoxification formulas; made significant heroin seizures; and played an active role in international anti-narcotics operations through Interpol and the United Nations.

The chances are good that you and your family do not fit the profile of a typical Hong Kong drug abuser: over 21, in the lower income group, generally employed as a casual laborer or as an unskilled or semiskilled worker, and living in very crowded conditions. However, drug abuse here is to be taken very seriously. If you'd like more information, contact the Narcotics Division of the Government Secretariat (867 2756) or the Government Information Services (GIS) Department (842 8777).

Street Crime

It is very difficult to generalize about crime in Hong Kong - or in any other city - because to someone who's been victimized, crime can indeed seem all pervasive. It must be said, however, that while the incidence of crime may not differ much between Hong Kong and a given Western city, the fear of crime for Westerners is not as pervasive in Hong Kong. All forms of public transportation, for example, are widely used at night. Stores often remain open until 10 or 11 pm - restaurants even later. And pedestrian traffic can be quite heavy in certain districts until the early hours of the morning.

The overall crime rate increased in 1990 with a total of 88,300 reported crimes compared to 79,860 just two years earlier. There was an increase in all areas of crime, most significantly in armed robbery. Stolen vehicles were a major cause for concern when it became clear that highly organized gangs were delivering luxury cars to China where they underwent various identity changes before being shipped back and resold. The 48 percent increase in this particular crime eased a little after Chinese authorities eventually agreed to assist in investigations. Triad and gang warfare is, as always, also a cause for concern.

Insurance

There are some 275 insurance companies currently authorized to transact insurance business in Hong Kong. As one might expect, all types of insurance coverage are obtainable. Policies may be purchased in US as well as Hong

Kong currencies. Insurance companies also provide claim services enabling assessment and payment in Hong Kong of losses under their policies.

Automobile insurance

Compulsory insurance against liability for bodily injury to, or death of, persons including passengers caused by the use of an automobile is required by Hong Kong law, referred to as 'third party insurance'. This coverage, with unlimited liability, can be obtained separately from, or in conjunction with, coverage for loss of or damage to the insured vehicle and to property belonging to persons other than the insured. Generally the premium is at tariff rate and is subject to no-claim discounts on an annual graduated scale up to a maximum of 60 percent if no claim is made against the company over a period of five or more years. If you bring a statement from your previous insurer that you have made no claims in past years, you can obtain this discount when your policy is issued.

Normally, these policies do not cover loss or damage caused by typhoons. Coverage against such loss is obtainable on payment of an additional premium and is recommended if the automobile is parked or stored in the open. Such comprehensive insurance will also be required if the vehicle is being paid for on a hire-purchase agreement.

Employees compensation insurance

Chances are, your employer provides you with thorough workmen's compensation insurance. If not, there are a number of companies from whom you can purchase it independently. If you are an employer of an *amah*, gardener, or chauffeur, the Employees Compensation Ordinance renders you liable to compensate such employees for any injury sustained by accident arising out of and in the course of employment - and to compensate the employee's dependents if such accident results in death. Insurance to cover this liability is therefore compulsory. Compensation calculated under the provisions of the ordinance is based on the employee's salary. The premium is at tariff rate.

Fire, typhoon, and burglary insurance

Almost all houses and apartment buildings are made of reinforced concrete or brick construction. The risk of fire -- except in the industrial, commercial, and crowded, low-income residential areas -- is not therefore very great. Nevertheless, insurance coverage is a sensible precaution. Typhoons are regular occurrences in Hong Kong. Not infrequently, they are of sufficient intensity to blow in windows and air-conditioning units and can cause considerable water damage to household and personal effects. Insurance coverage against typhoon loss or damage must be purchased in conjunction with fire insurance, the premium for which is at tariff rate.

Although burglaries occur infrequently in high-rent neighborhoods in Hong Kong, 'householder comprehensive' policies are available that insure against the loss of or damage to one's personal and household effects contained in the insured's private dwelling. Under such a policy, it is necessary to itemize art objects, silverware, jewelry, and other articles of substantial value; otherwise, no article is deemed of greater value than five percent of the total insured sum.

Personal-effects insurance

In addition to the types of policies mentioned above, personal-effects policies provide further coverage against loss when articles are worn or used outside one's home. Valuables, such as jewelry, watches, and articles of personal adornment that may be lost or forcibly taken away, must be appraised and itemized.

Comprehensive personal liability

Liability for injuries to persons and damage to property is governed by common law unless modified by statutory law, and is almost identical to that in the United States. Insurance against this liability may be obtained under a comprehensive personal liability policy.

Personal and travel accident insurance

Indemnity against loss of life, limb, and sight as well as permanent total disability, including reimbursement of medical expenses caused by accident while at home or abroad, on land sea, or in the air, can be covered by a personal accident policy bought on an annual basis.

When traveling abroad, similar coverage can be obtained under a travel accident policy valid for varying periods of one to 180 days. These policies are also obtainable from insurance booths in the departure lounge at Kai Tak. In conjunction with travel accident insurance, some companies will insure travelers against skyjacking. This insurance, at a nominal premium, pays the insured a stated sum per day for a stipulated maximum number of days during which he or she, as a passenger, is prevented from reaching the scheduled destination of the aircraft as a result of hijacking.

War-risk insurance

If you travel on business, check whether or not your life or disability policies are in effect if you go to or over a war zone. If not, policies can be written for each trip you make.

Medical insurance

Long-term illnesses can be expensive in Hong Kong, as elsewhere, and the costs of operations and hospitalization have increased in recent years. Most families will have medical and/or hospital insurance through their employers. Should you need to purchase major medical insurance on your own, you will not find it easy to obtain in Hong Kong. Except for Blue Cross/Blue Shield, most insurance companies do not offer the sort of comprehensive coverage to which most Westerners are probably accustomed. If you do not need extensive coverage, there are numerous policies available locally and these should be seriously considered.

For More Information...

The newly arrived resident in Hong Kong may require help on a wide variety of personal matters in daily life here, and only some suggestions can be covered in this chapter. Knowing where to obtain such guidance or information is important. Following are some of the places in Hong Kong where a visit or even a telephone call should provide the solution to most problems.

The volunteer staff of the Community Advice Bureau (CAB), 8 Garden Road, St John's Cathedral, Old Hall, answer calls from 9.30 am to 4pm, Monday through Friday (524 5444/526 1672). Their purpose is to provide 'free, confidential, impartial help and advice on all subjects'. Their excellent card index has been built up over the years and is regularly revised and updated so that they can handle inquiries on almost any subject. Their 'Hong Kong Information Sheet', compiled in conjunction with the YWCA and Women's Corona Society, will answer many questions.

The Government Information Services in Beaconsfield House can handle some reference inquiries (842 8777) and has a library and photographic record. Other government departments also have general inquiry services or an information officer. The Central Government Offices (entrance on Ice House Street) also have an inquiry counter and supply most government forms. The City District Offices (see preliminary pages of the Business Telephone

Directory) are distributed throughout Hong Kong and Kowloon and are designed to attend to all community and personal problems. The Consumer Council at 6 Heard St has a consumer Advice/Complaints office. Finally, many reference questions can be answered by the staff of the Urban Council Public Libraries at the City Hall and other branches, by the American Library in United Centre (Admiralty MTR station), and by the Public Record Office of Hong Kong in the Murray Road Car Park Building.

There is an American Citizen Services office at the US Consulate, but be aware the position is mainly intended to assist families of the 450 or so Americans attached to the US Government who work there. This leaves little time for others, outside of those services normally provided by the consulate. *Know your Consulate* is a free guide to its services available from the American Women's Association or directly from USCONGEN (US Consul General).

Chapter 5
COMMUNICATIONS

H ong Kong's communications sector is one of the most sophisticated and reasonably priced in the world. Characteristic of Hong Kong's innovative nature is the fact that the telephone was introduced here in 1882, just six years after its invention by Alexander Graham Bell! One can find advanced telecommunications, a broad range of periodicals, good English-language TV and radio stations (especially given the small English-speaking population here), and a variety of libraries.

Telephones

Every imaginable kind of phone can be found in Hong Kong, from a simple, standard-issue instrument to high-speed data links. Most important, any one of them can usually be installed in less than a week. All telephone lines are owned and controlled by the Hong Kong Telephone Company (Telco). Customer services for residential and business lines are described in detail in Telco's booklet, 'Tariffs for Customer Service' available at CSL outlets (more later) or by phoning 888-2888.

Basic residential telephone connection is provided for a flat rate of $168 per quarter plus $21 for a standard push-button telephone. There is a one-time installation fee of $600. Local calls are free. (It is quite acceptable to ask to use a phone in a shop or restaurant without expecting to pay anything.) International Direct Dialing (IDD) is installed free of charge on request, or you can ask for a PIN number which allows you to make international calls from any telephone. IDD calls can be made from public phones advertising that service or from any public telephone accepting credit cards or phonecards. Phonecards can be purchased from many shops.

Other services which are available on request include call forwarding, call waiting, abbreviated dialing, alarm clock, conference calling etc, all for a nominal monthly charge. 'Homefax 2' allows for a residential phone and fax machine to share a single line. A separate fax line can also be installed if necessary.

Phones can be purchased from one of several outlets — some more reputable than others. In the past, there has been a problem with suppliers dumping incompatible equipment on the market, so beware. It is best to go to a reputable dealer where the equipment is certified 'permission to connect' (to a Telco line).

Telco operate around 12 CSL shops which provide almost everything you need in one store. You can walk into a CSL shop and order a line (or two), a telephone of your choice, a fax machine, IDD and any other services you want, buy a phonecard, pay your bill and walk out again.

Telegrams and cables can be sent through Hong Kong Telecom International (HKTI), formerly Cable & Wireless. HKTI also handle telex installation, leased circuits, maritime communications and international television services. For more details look at 'Telecommunications Services and Tariffs from Hong Kong'. As most of these services would be used in a business and not in the average home,they are covered in detail in other AmCham publications such as *Establishing an Office in Hong Kong* or *Doing Business in Today's Hong Kong*.

After your telephone is installed, you will be given a directory collection card (directories are not delivered here). Directories are published in English and Chinese and are broken down into residential (white pages), business by name (white pages), business by category (yellow pages) and shoppers' guides. Many find the directory a valuable source of information regarding emergency services and procedures, severe weather warning system and typhoon warning signals. If you cannot find the number you need, call 1081 for English language directory enquiries (free).

Pager systems, and cellular phones are widely used in Hong Kong and there are hundreds of different ones to choose from. Pager systems can be extremely sophisticated and you can get cellular phones small enough to fit in your pocket. Shop around.

Postal Services

It has been known to happen: a firm in Central received a reply in the afternoon mail to a letter it had mailed at 10 am the same day! The Post Office makes frequent random checks of deliveries and prides itself on the fact that 95 percent of all letters mailed by 6 pm are delivered the following day. Hong Kong's postal service is unusually fast, efficient, reliable, and one of the least expensive in the world.

A letter sent to any Hong Kong destination costs 80 cents for the first 30 grams. Airmail prices begin at $1.80 for the first 10 grams. Airgrams cost $1.80. Letters, postcards, and paper are handled in the same manner as elsewhere. Literature for the blind, when it's clearly marked, does not require postage. You will find little difficulty in mailing small packets, or heavy or bulky parcels. The Post Office has an Air Parcel Post service (for packages under 20 kg), a Speedpost service (for fast movement of small items), and an Intel Post service (direct transmission from facsimile equipment).

Sea mail is very slow. Parcels to the US or UK take 6-10 weeks. Mail very early for Christmas. Although final posting dates for each country are published for Christmas cards and parcels, it is advisable to post things even earlier, especially if you have an aversion to queueing. This may mean doing your Christmas shopping in August (which requires considerable willpower). Sales are on then anyway, so you may as well buy, ship, and be done with it.

A leaflet, 'Postage Rates and Services', free at Post Offices, gives the mailing times for every day of the week for each country, as well as information on supplementary services available. *The Hong Kong Post Office Guide*, available for $166 at Post Offices and from the Government Publications Centre, is also very useful.

The Media

Newspapers

Hong Kong boasts some 69 daily newspapers and 610 periodicals. Of the Chinese-language dailies, 39 cover mainly news, while the others focus on television and cinema news, horse racing, or sex. There are five English-language dailies printed here: the *South China Morning Post*, the *Hongkong Standard, The Asian Wall Street Journal,* the *International Herald Tribune,* and *USA Today.*

The *Post* and the *Standard*, general-interest newspapers, have local and international coverage, and regularly feature syndicated news and feature stories as well as the columns of leading foreign journalists. The business sections of both carry listings of shipping in port and due, schedules of freight lines, and stock-market quotations. In the 'letters to the editor' columns, one can read ongoing dialogues among residents or between residents and government. Subjects cover a broad range, including censorship, public transport, cigarette smoking, taxation, pending legislation, book prices, the best method of punishment for criminals, the taste of the paper's cinema or art critic. Letters, by the way, are read by government and some changes are actually effected because of them.

There are also daily listings of City Hall Events and community service club luncheons, weather reports, sports, etc. Christmas posting dates appear at the appropriate time. Classified ads are abundant. Friday and Saturday are the days to post 'help wanted' ads in the *Standard* and *Post* respectively. Both papers are published seven days a week and can be delivered to your door.

The Asian Wall Street Journal is regional in scope and *Herald Tribune* international with a European emphasis, both are American newspapers which have achieved a strong readership in Hong Kong. Along with 'hard news' on local markets, the *Journal* offers lively features on trends and prominent business people. The *Herald Tribune* has what is probably the most comprehensive daily global overview in town. It is based in Paris, and over half of its readership is European.

Overseas editions of many foreign papers and magazines are flown in daily. Unfortunately, they are quite expensive. AmCham members enjoy free shopping passes to the China Fleet Club stores, where such American magazines are current and at the same prices as sold at home. Even without such a pass, you can probably find a bargain in periodicals as well. One vendor is said to have a contact with the plane cleaners at Kai Tak Airport. After receiving the already-read foreign papers from the planes, she gives them a fast iron and a fresh fold and they're set for resale in short order, all for your reading benefit!

Magazines

Hong Kong is one of Asia's major printing and publishing centers, so you will find literally hundreds of magazines here. Among the more popular local publications are *Asiaweek*, the *Far Eastern Economic Review*, *Asian Business*, and the *TV & Entertainment Times*. In addition, American, English, Australian and European magazines are sold at newsstands, bookstores and in MTR kiosks. There can be as much as six or seven weeks' delay as most are sent by surface mail. All 'time sensitive' magazines, on the other hand, are shipped via air or are printed here. *Time*, *Newsweek*, *The Economist*, etc, are all current and are sold at newsstands or by subscription. The Asian editions of these magazines are printed here in Hong Kong.

Radio

Hong Kong has 15 radio channels: seven operated by Radio Television Hong Kong (RTHK), three by Commercial Radio, two by British Forces Broadcasting Service (BFBS) and three by newcomer, Metro Broadcast. Eight of these stations broadcast in English and all run 24-hours-a-day. Radio 3 (RTHK) focuses on local and international news, discussions, and easy-listening music. Radio 4 (RTHK) is chiefly classical music and Radio 6 (RTHK) is the BBC World Service. Commercial Radio concentrates on popular music but also has regular news and weather broadcasts as well as some business features. BFBS, once widely transmitted, can now only be received in certain areas. Some programs are locally produced while others come from UK. The second BFBS channel broadcasts to the Gurkha soldiers in Nepalese. Metro Broadcast's three channels supply a variety of programs — with Metro News dedicated solely to local, international, sports, business and Asian news as well as regular weather reports.

Television

There are two English TV channels and two Chinese TV channels in Hong Kong which broadcast to the 94 percent of all households who have at least one set. Given the poor choice of programming, the relatively short broadcasting time (nine hours a day) and the hours the average person spends at work, it seems remarkable that anyone watches TV at all! Having said that, many households do own VCR's and with most films arriving on the video market within weeks, this seems to be a popular option. And then there's cable TV...

After much controversy and discussion cable TV has finally made it to Hong Kong — albeit just half a dozen channels up to the end of 1991. Gaining permission to own a satellite dish is extremely complicated — many feel unnecessarily so. Since the legislation passed through the government, a few satellite dishes have appeared on the tops of apartment buildings, but cable TV is not yet widespread, by any means.

Libraries

If you've been accustomed to having excellent library facilities close at hand, Hong Kong may well come as a disappointment, particularly where English-language materials are concerned. However, there are a few libraries that, despite their small size, make a good effort to provide their users with relevant, up-to-date materials.

Alliance Francaise has a main office and several branches which offer film and record libraries as well as French books. They are open to members and the general public.

A quiet, well-lighted oasis in Queensway, the American Library in United Center is basically a reference library on subjects pertaining to the United States, including extensive information on American colleges and universities. A user's card is issued free to anyone over 16 years old. In addition to reference material, there are a large number of books on America and by American authors, a good range of up-to-date American periodicals, and many videocassettes for viewing at the library.

The best source for American college catalogs, is the Institute for International Education. This is the oldest and largest college counselling organization in the United States and shares space with the American Library.

The Government Information Services Library is a reference library that deals with a variety of subjects such as the laws of Hong Kong, departmental reports, and official documents. A film library is stocked with 400 films from the United Nations, the GIS and the Central Office of Information in London. A photographic library and microfilm facilities are also available for public use.

The Urban Council runs a public library system with facilities in some 30 locations while the Regional Council operate a further 20 District Libraries as well as two mobile libraries. All the libraries are well used and all have an excellent choice of books, newspapers, periodicals, records, audio cassettes, video cassettes, slides and microfilm suitable for various age groups. The Urban Council also has educational, cultural and recreational programs in the form of book exhibitions, competitions, lectures, interest clubs, film and video screenings, hi-fi and compact disc concerts, screenings, story hours and organized library visits. The newest library, opened in 1990 at the Cultural Centre, specializes in books on the arts.

The British Council Library accepts membership applications at 255 Hennessy Road. This library contains books on English-language teaching, English literature, fiction, and reference subjects.

The Goethe Institute has a lending library of German books, records and films - as do most foreign government language centers.

Visiting scholars and others with legitimate interests may arrange to use the excellent libraries at the universities and polytechnics, for reference. The American Club library has a good selection of children's books and gets new books very quickly. There are fairly broad sections on Asia and China and a good selection of mystery novels and fiction. The Helena May Institute and Hong Kong Club and most private clubs have libraries for their members; again, modern novels and books on China and Hong Kong predominate. AmCham operates a small Business Information Center library of reference material and magazines. Access is free to members and $20 per visit to the general public.

Doing Business in Today's Hong Kong

A fourth updated and revised edition of *Doing Business in Today's Hong Kong* has been released by the American Chamber of Commerce in Hong Kong. This edition comprises 21 chapters divided into three large themes: Business Environment, Business Support Services and Sales and Manufacturing Industries, written by 25 authors. It is a book written by business people, for business people, many of the authors, of which, are members of the American Chamber of Commerce in Hong Kong.

"Our members are people on the ground and doing business here, and from here in China and Southeast Asia. They have been eyewitnesses to contemporary business history and are the makers of Hong Kong's business future — anyone wanting to do business in Asia who reads this book will be deeply grateful to these authors for having shared so much of what they know for the good of all," said Fred Armentrout, publications manager for AmCham.

The book's authors are attorneys from multinational firms, accountants, members of executive search firms, consultants with Hong Kong Government subvented business support organizations, bankers, textiles and apparel manufacturers, China trade consultants, and independent entrepreneurs based in the territory but with global investments.

The book is available from leading Hong Kong booksellers and directly from the American Chamber of Commerce. Member price HK$195/US$38. Non-member price HK$245/US$44. Postage inclusive.

Chapter 6
LEGAL
INFORMATION

The following is only an introduction to certain legal obligations and rights. All residents should take care to observe Hong Kong's legal requirements - which may be new to them - and a lawyer should be consulted whenever there is doubt about legal interpretation.

Immigration and Visa Information

If you are a foreign national considering a move to Hong Kong, the first thing to understand is that in order to enter Hong Kong for purposes of employment, or to establish or join a business, you must obtain an employment visa issued by the Hong Kong Immigration Department. In addition, your accompanying family members must obtain dependent visas. The employment and dependent visas must be obtained prior to arrival in Hong Kong. An application for a visa may be made at any British Embassy or British Consulate or diplomatic office in the world, although it is customary for applicants to lodge the application at any British Embassy or office closest to their home. The normal processing period is from 8 to 12 weeks.

Americans who come here on visitors' visas to investigate or to lay the foundation for new offices may introduce themselves to the American Chamber of Commerce in Hong Kong if they need advice and assistance. It will generally be necessary, however, to leave Hong Kong, apply for a visa, and then return after it has been obtained.

The only people for whom no resident visa is required are holders of:

(1) British (Hong Kong) passports,
(2) United Kingdom passports endorsed, 'issued on behalf of the
    Government of Hong Kong',
(3) United Kingdom Passports isued in the United Kingdom, the
    Channel Islands, or the Isle of Man.

An employment visa is normally granted to US passport holders for six months. The dependent visas are normally valid for the same period. Upon arrival in Hong Kong, you and your family should apply for multiple re-entry visas. This allows you to leave Hong Kong for business or holiday purposes and be readmitted as long as the visa remains valid. One month prior to expiration of the employment and dependent visas you and your family should apply for extensions of your visas.

Normally, multiple re-entry visas are given to students to match their parents' immigration status-that is, to expire when their parents' visas expire. Therefore, in cases where children go 'home' to school and visit their parents in Hong

Kong on vacation, some inconvenience may arise when the visa expires and the child is away from Hong Kong. Some parents have found it expedient for their children to apply to a British representative overseas (British Embassy, British Consulate, etc.) for a Multiple Visit Visa. Alternatively, the children can enter Hong Kong as visitors and request an extension of their visitor status before their 30-day visitor stay expires. Australians can stay in Hong Kong for three months without a visa, and UK citizens do not require visas. Therefore, their student children would be able to share vacations with their parents without visa formalities.

Employers of expatriates in Hong Kong are required to guarantee the repatriation expenses of their employees and dependents upon termination of employment, at which time the Immigration department will require a statement from the foreign resident's new employer to the effect that the repatriation expenses will be paid.

Persons who enter Hong Kong as visitors are not permitted to enter into employment (paid or unpaid), to establish or join any business, or to enter school as students. Except in the most unusual circumstances, visitors are not allowed to change their status. Tourists who overstay the period for which they are temporarily admitted are subject to fines and other penalties.

Application Procedures

At the time your application is made, you must list two 'referees', or sponsors, in Hong Kong. One of the referees is generally the local employer in Hong Kong. If the Hong Kong employer is the branch subsidiary of an overseas company, the legal framework of the branch or subsidiary should be finalized prior to application.

After the application has been forwarded to the Hong Kong Immigration Department, the Hong Kong sponsor will be contacted and asked to provide supporting documentation and to complete the sponsorship form. The sponsor must do this within two weeks of receipt of the sponsorship form from the Hong Kong Immigration Department. After the sponsor has completed the form and returned it to the Hong Kong Immigration Department, along with the necessary supporting documentation, the application is assessed and the results telexed to the British Embassy where the application was lodged.

The difficulty or ease of any application for a Hong Kong employment visa varies from case to case. Each application will be assessed on its own merits. The Hong Kong Immigration Department is advocating a localization policy.

Consequently, applications for Hong Kong employment visas are now more carefully scrutinized to determine whether a local resident could not fulfill the requirements of the job concerned.

As a general rule, a foreigner whose livelihood in Hong Kong is dependent solely on his or her ability to earn commissions will not be granted a Hong Kong employment visa because there is no assurance that the foreigner will be self-supporting here.

Dependent Visas

The spouse and children of a visa applicant can apply for Hong Kong dependent visas. Dependent status allows a spouse — whether male or female — to pursue employment opportunities in Hong Kong.

Right to Land / Unconditional Stay

UK passport holders and their families can apply for a 'Right to Land' endorsement which allows them to remain in Hong Kong free of any conditions. In order to qualify, the applicant must have lived in Hong Kong for a continuous period of not less than seven years. Those who have been deported, contravened a limited period of stay, stayed in Hong Kong as a refugee or otherwise lived in the territory unlawfully, are disqualified.

It is up to the applicant to supply evidence proving he or she has lived in Hong Kong for seven years. Letters from previous employers, tax returns, old passports are all considered valid documentation.

Other foreign passport holders who have lived in Hong Kong for more than nine years may qualify for 'Unconditional Stay' status. The terms are similar to those seeking 'Right to Land' status although final acceptance is at the discretion of the Immigration Department. It would be wise to check carefully with the Immigration Department (who are generally very helpful) or seek the advice of a solicitor.

Identity Cards

Under the Registration of Persons Ordinance, virtually anyone over the age of 11 who enters and intends to stay in Hong Kong for more than 180 days must apply for a Hong Kong Identity Card within 30 days of arrival, except for the following:

(1) The aged, the blind, and the infirm who have been approved by

the Commissioner of Registration for exemption.
(2) Children of consuls and consular staff who are under 18 years of age.
(3) Children under 11 years of age.

As part of an effort to restrict the entry of illegal immigrants, it is now necessary to carry this card at all times. Young people between ages 11 and 18 must have a Juvenile Identity Card, and adults over 18 an Adult Identity Card. It is a punishable offense not to carry this card. Police stop and check over two million people a year, including Westerners on occasion. Among the few persons exempted from the Identity Card requirements are the families of persons employed by the British government.

Identity Cards can be obtained by applying at one of the four Registration of Persons offices in the Territory. The locations: North Point, Aberdeen, Kowloon, and Tsuen Wan. You should go to a Registration of Persons office only if you are applying for a Hong Kong Identity Card for the first time. You must apply in person, and you will be required to provide documentation authorizing you to remain in Hong Kong for six months or more. You must submit your passport, one passport-size photograph, and such particulars as residential address, nationality, place and date of birth, occupation, etc. An application for a Juvenile Identity Card must be made for a young person by a parent or guardian, who will be required to furnish particulars on behalf of the applicant. The young person, however, must also go to the Issuing Office.

If you already have a valid Hong Kong Identity Card and are simply applying for a replacement, you can go to any one of the eight New Identity Card Issue Offices, listed in the blue 'government' pages (under 'Immigration Department') in the Hong Kong business telephone directory.

An adult should apply for an Adult Identity Card within 30 days of becoming a Hong Kong resident or reaching 18, and an application for a Juvenile Identity Card should be made on behalf of a young person within 30 days of his or her becoming a resident or reaching age 11. There is no charge for the issuing of an Identity Card.

When a person moves from Hong Kong or dies, his or her Identity Card should be returned to a Registration Office for cancellation.
American citizens residing in Hong Kong should also consider registering with the American Consulate. Registration can be effected by submitting a completed prescribed form to the Consulate. Among other things, registration enables consular officers to locate the citizen in the event of an inquiry from the United States.

Marriage

If a couple wishes to marry in Hong Kong, they must complete a Notice of Marriage on a prescribed form and submit it to a marriage registry at least 15 days before the ceremony. There are 13 marriage registries in Hong Kong, including that in the High Block of the City Hall, the most popular in town. In special circumstances, a marriage registrar may shorten the 15-day notice and waiting period.

The marriage ceremony itself may take place at any time within the three-month period following the end of the 15-day notice and waiting period. The ceremony may be performed either at a marriage registry or in a licensed place of public worship. Advance arrangements must be made for a ceremony at a marriage registry, and two witnesses are required to validate the ceremony.

A person under age 21 must secure the written consent of his or her father (or mother, if the father is deceased) or legal guardian before submitting a Notice of Marriage. A divorced person must present to the marriage registry proof of the dissolution of his or her former marriage, and a widow or widower must offer proof of the death of their spouse. There are no residency requirements for a marriage in Hong Kong and no restrictions relating to the nationalities of the couple.

Births

The birth of a child in Hong Kong should be registered within six weeks at one of the nine birth registries. Upon request and the payment of a nominal fee, a birth certificate will be issued following the registration; duplicate birth certificate can also be obtained later. When registering a child's birth, one of the parents must appear in person at the birth registry and show the identity cards and passports of both parents and (if available) a marriage certificate. If the parents are not married, the father's name will be included in the registry and on the birth certificate only at the mutual request of the mother and the father.

If one or both parents of a newborn child are United States citizens, the parents may wish to obtain a consular Report of Birth to prove the child's United States citizenship. The child's Hong Kong birth certificate and the parents' United States passports, marriage certificate, and divorce decree (if applicable) must be presented to the American Consulate before a Report of Birth will be issued. The fee is US$13. Parents from other countries outside Hong Kong should consult their consulate or commission regarding the procedure for registering a newborn child.

Divorce

A couple in Hong Kong desiring a divorce, judicial separation, or marriage annulment should consult a Hong Kong solicitor or foreign lawyer, depending on where the couple believes proceedings should be commenced. When considering possible jurisdictions, attention might given to the citizenship, domiciliary, and residency of the parties; and the different rules regarding financial support and child custody. It is possible for citizens of other countries to obtain a divorce, judicial separation, or annulment in Hong Kong, regardless of where the marriage took place, provided that reasonable residency or domiciliary tests are met.

The sole grounds in Hong Kong for divorce are that the marriage has broken down irretrievably. Those grounds, however, must be established by proving at least one of certain prescribed facts, such as the commission of adultery or that the couple has lived apart for more than two years even in an uncontested, requested divorce. Ordinarily, a divorce will not be granted in Hong Kong to a couple married for less than three years. Once granted, a Hong Kong divorce decree becomes effective six weeks later. A judicial separation can be obtained more easily and quickly; annulment, on the other hand, usually requires a time-consuming and difficult procedure.

In connection with granting a divorce, judicial separation, or annulment, a Hong Kong court can order property settlement, a lump-sum payment, or periodic maintenance payments for the benefit of either party or of the children. A court order will be based on the financial resources, earning capacities, and ages of the respective parties, as well as on their living standards and on the health and expectations of any children involved. The court may set a maximum term for any periodic maintenance payments and may later adjust those payments in the event of new circumstances. A Hong Kong court is also able under certain conditions to adjust the terms of a maintenance agreement entered into in another jurisdiction.

Finally, when granting a divorce, judicial separation, or annulment, a Hong Kong court can also provide for the custody and education of each minor child. So long as the child continues to be a minor, the court may, from time to time, order adjustments in the custody arrangements.

Death

In the unfortunate event of the death of a loved one here in Hong Kong, you can contact the Hong Kong Samaritans (389 2221), who have a 24-hour service to assist you not only with comfort and moral support but also with advice on the procedures and formalities necessary. There is also a free booklet available,

'What To Do When Someone Dies,' published by the Urban Council.

There are several important points to remember in the event of the death in Hong Kong of a friend or family member who is a citizen of a country other than Hong Kong. Remembering these points can prevent frustrating delays and legal problems.

First, the deceased person's body should not, in the period immediately following death, be moved without the cooperation of a physician or the police. Call the deceased's private physician, if possible, as he or she will know the medical history. If death occurred somewhere other than in hospital and a physician is not immediately available, the police should be called (dial 999) to remove the body to a nearby public hospital for examination and pronouncement of death by a physician.

A second point to keep in mind is that the consulate or commission of the country of which the deceased was a citizen can be of great help. In the case of a United States citizen, the American Consulate is prepared to assist in a number of ways, including (when the deceased's family is not in Hong Kong) making any necessary arrangements for the embalming and shipping to the United States of the body. If the burial or cremation is to be in Hong Kong, a funeral parlor and an appropriate priest, minister, or other spiritual advisor should be consulted.

Another point is that a travel agent, in addition to a funeral parlor, may need to be consulted if the body is to be shipped overseas.

Finally, the settlement of the deceased's financial affairs may prove more complicated than a settlement would have been, had he or she died in their country of citizenship. Thus, a Hong Kong solicitor or foreign lawyer, as may seem appropriate, should be promptly contacted. The family or a friend should also remember to return the deceased's passport to the commission or consulate of the country of issue, and his or her Identity Card to one of Hong Kong's Registration Offices.

Estate Planning

For a United States citizen, a move to Hong Kong generally does not require any major changes in estate planning. This is true because Hong Kong recognizes and enforces wills validly entered into elsewhere, and the rules in Hong Kong for the distribution of the assets of a person who dies without a will reflect the same concerns that comparable rules do in the United States. Furthermore, the Hong Kong tax on estates assets located in Hong Kong generally is creditable against any United States estate tax payable on those assets. For an expatriate from another country, however, a move to Hong Kong may be a reason to reexamine and adjust current estate plans, if only to take some advantage of Hong Kong's favorable tax rules.

Hong Kong not only enforces wills validly entered into in other jurisdictions, but it also affords the same respect to non-testamentary dispositions, such as gifts in contemplation of death, the designation of life insurance beneficiaries, and the creation of joint ownership in bank accounts and property, as is given by most states in America. With regard to the distribution of the residuary assets of a person who dies without a will, or with only a partial will, Hong Kong law provides first for the decedent's spouse and children, then (in the absence of children) for his or her parents, then (in the absence of all the foregoing) for grandparents and more distant relatives.

As a general rule, the estate of an expatriate who lived in Hong Kong at the time of death but who maintained close connections with his or her home country is principally settled in the home country. Hong Kong proceedings may, however, be necessary if there are noteworthy assets in Hong Kong, making the appointment of a local executor potentially valuable. If the expatriate did not maintain close ties to the home country, the estate is usually settled in Hong Kong. The estate of a United States citizen, regardless of the citizen's residence or domicile or the location of his or her assets, is subject to US federal estate taxation as well. The speed of estate proceedings in Hong Kong, therefore, is not of much benefit to the families of American citizens.

The Hong Kong government imposes estate duties on Hong Kong assets. The duty varies from a minimum of six percent on estates valued between $4,000,000 and $4,500,000 to 18 percent on estates valued in excess of $5,000,000.

Jury Duty

With only a few exceptions, most foreign residents of Hong Kong between the ages of 21 and 65, and conversant in English, are qualified and liable to serve as Hong Kong jurors. Among those few exceptions are commission or consulate officials and their spouses as well as members of the clergy, dentists, and doctors. Service on a Hong Kong jury does not jeopardize an American's citizenship.

Becoming a juror is a two-step process. First, a person's name is drawn from a public list - usually the list of Identity Card holders - and he or she is given notice of the drawing and an opportunity to claim a statutory exemption from service. Then, but not always right away, the person is summoned to appear for jury service. Once summoned, the person may be excused or given a postponement if good reason is offered, upon written application to the Registrar of the Supreme Court. Special hardship to the person's employer and family vacation plans have each been accepted as a good reason for an excuse or postponement.

A jury in Hong Kong may have either seven or 17 members, depending upon whether it is a 'common' or 'special' jury. Except in capital cases, a verdict does not require unanimous assent. Jurors in Hong Kong receive some compensation for their service.

Voting

Practically anyone over 21 years of age and who is a Hong Kong permanent resident, or has been resident in Hong Kong for the past seven years, is eligible to register to vote in Urban or Regional Council elections and District Board elections. There are currently around 1.85 million registered voters — 50.2 percent of the potential electorate of 3.7 million.

Fifteen of the 40 Urban Council members are elected as are one third of Regional Council members. In 1991 history was made when, after much discussion and deliberation, 18 members of the Legislative Council were directly elected.

Some US citizens residing in Hong Kong remain eligible to vote in state and local elections in their former home states, and all such citizens over 18 may vote in national elections. US citizens should contact the American Consulate or their former boards of elections for guidance and absentee ballots. A state can no longer use absentee voting in national elections as grounds for claiming resident income taxes from former residents living abroad, and many states do not even consider absentee voting in state or local elections in determining liability for income taxes. A United States citizen does not put his or her citizenship at risk by voting in a Hong Kong election.

Citizens of other countries should always consult their own consulates or commissions in Hong Kong if they are in any doubt about their legal position while living here.

Chapter 7
BANKING
INFORMATION

PHOTO BY JOHN LANGFORD

I t is said that Hong Kong has more banks per square mile than any other city in the world. You may therefore find you can transfer money to and open an account with the same bank you used in your home country. Banking facilities for both business and personal affairs are available at the approximately 166 licensed banks of more than 23 nations. A large number of major American and British banks have branches or affiliates here and there are numerous Hong Kong-based banks as well as branches of other foreign banking institutions. Many offer a full range of banking facilities in Hong Kong dollars, fixed-term deposits, loans, remittances, and other services. One service, Autopay, has been available for some years and authorizes your bank to automatically pay regular accounts for electricity, gas, telephone, subscriptions, and some stores. This avoids your having to write many individual checks, while also keeping you informed of the transactions involved.

Another service, Easy Pay System (EPS), has been adopted by many banks with retail services. With this system, you may pay for purchases at a participating restaurant or store by using either a bank credit card or automatic teller machine card. Your account is instantly debited, and funds are transferred to the merchant's bank account.

If the convenience of using multiple branches is a consideration, you should choose a well-established bank with several branches. But if having access to several automatic teller machines (ATM's) will suffice, join either the Hong kongBank/Hang Seng Bank whose ATM cards are interchangeable and who operate a huge ATM network, or join one of the dozen or so banks who are linked with JETCO. A JETCO card allows you to use the ATM's at any of the member branches — giving access to an even bigger network than HongkongBank.

There is some variation in the services provided by banks in Hong Kong. Some require applicants to provide references to open an account. Not all banks return canceled checks with the monthly statements, although American ones normally do. Service hours also vary from bank to bank but most institutions are open between 10 am and 4 pm weekdays, 9 am and noon Saturdays.

Although American banks in Hong Kong cannot open US dollar checking accounts locally, many can accommodate their customers by offering services through their US based branches. These banks may have supplies of the necessary signature cards and other documents and will forward them on your behalf to their domestic branches. Some can also handle subsequent check cashing and deposits relative to the accounts in the US, but a charge may be made for these services.

An alternative to a US dollar checking account in the US, if few US dollar remittances are made, is to open a local US dollar savings account and to obtain drafts for mailing overseas, or to make telegraphic transfers directly to a US bank. Remittances can be made in most currencies, but the use of these services may require you to go to the bank to request them, and so are less convenient than checks. There is normally an extra clearing charge. Inquire into the best way if you need to transfer US dollars locally.

Interest rates paid on bank savings accounts and fixed-term deposits are set by the Hong Kong Association of Banks, which meets regularly (usually once a week). This group also sets the Hong Kong prime lending rate at the same meeting. The Hong Kong government has not specified any practical rate limits, and the interest rates fluctuate more than in the US. The interest paid on savings accounts is not subject to Hong Kong tax, whereas interest earned on other local investments might be.

Most international banks will also take fixed-term deposits in major currencies. Ask your bank for the minimum amounts they will accept for these deposits.

Checks

Hong Kong regulations covering the issuing and cashing of checks are similar to the negotiable instrument laws of Great Britain. All checks issued in Hong Kong are considered 'bearer' checks unless the words 'or bearer' are deleted. Thus, if you write a check without crossing it, it can be cashed without endorsement by anyone, although banks usually require some identification. To protect yourself against loss of a check and to ensure that checks can be used as valid receipts, ask your bank to issue you blank checks that are already crossed. Or you can simply draw two parallel diagonal lines in the upper left-hand corner of the check and insert the words 'A/C payee only' between the lines. Always delete the words 'or bearer' as you fill in the payee's name. A check drawn in this manner may only be deposited to the account of the payee. If you cross your check but do not add 'A/C payee only', it must be deposited in an account, but not necessarily that of the payee.

Don't cross a check if you are cashing it yourself, as banks cannot pay cash against a crossed check. If you are using preprinted crossed checks, you can cancel the crossed portion by signing your full bank signature across the double lines. Allow time for deposits to be cleared before taking the money out.

Other hints on check writing: when writing dates, use the British sequence of day, month and year, or else give the month in writing rather than figures. Alterations on a check require your full bank signature, not just your initials. If the amount is in even dollars, end the amount written with the word 'only' instead of 'and no/100'. Information such as the invoice or account number of the bill you are paying should be written on the back, not the front, of the check. 'Check' is spelled in the English form — 'cheque' — in Hong Kong.

Loans

Financing for all purposes is available in Hong Kong, but terms, rates and collateral requirements vary considerably from time to time and from company to company. It is particularly important to shop around in Hong Kong at the time you need funds.

Because terms change rapidly, it is hard to say what is 'normal', but some general comments can be made. First, the bank or finance company is not required to disclose much information, so unless you ask specific questions, you might not get specific answers. Length of borrowing term may be considerably shorter than in the US: mortgages may be 15 to 20 years, unsecured loans three months to 32 years. The amount of financing available may be from 50 percent to 90 percent of the value of the collateral.

Mortgages are often written with a floating interest rate. In Hong Kong, this generally means that the interest rate moves up and down with changes in the prime rate. There is no legislated limit on the degree of timing from the government, and it can change on extremely short notice. As in the US, there may be other charges such as prepayment penalties, late charges, commission, appraisal fees, legal fees, or insurance. Occasionally some of these amounts may also change during the period of the loan, so be careful before making any agreement. The change in legal status in Hong Kong in 1997 has not as yet had an impact on mortgage financing.

Stockbrokers

There are a number of American, British, and Canadian brokerage firms represented in Hong Kong, with fully staffed offices providing the complete range of brokerage services. You can consult your broker at home as to whether to transfer your account to Hong Kong or maintain it there and open an additional account locally for securities and commodities trading in the US or UK. Commission rates vary between brokerage firms registered in Hong Kong and those registered elsewhere, so you might want to check what the relevant commission would be before choosing a broker. In addition, there are broker-age firms in Hong Kong for trading on one large local stock exchange known as the Unified Stock Exchange (established in early 1986), the Hong Kong Gold and Silver Exchange, the local commodity exchange, and other foreign security exchanges.

Currency

Hong Kong is part of the Overseas Sterling Area but is no longer a Scheduled Territory. Payments may be made between Hong Kong residents and others in Hong Kong dollars or any other currency. There are no restrictions on how much currency (domestic or foreign) may be brought into or taken out.

You can buy and sell all major currencies. Most currencies (Japanese yen, British pounds, US dollars, Swiss francs, etc) are available at banks and local licensed money changers at free market rates.

Since 1983, the rate of exchange of the Hong Kong dollar has been linked to the US dollar at the rate of HK$7.8 per US$1, but the actual amount received may vary slightly because of money market conditions and which bank or licensed money changer handles the transaction. Notes are issued in denomi-nations of $10, $20, $50, $100, $500, and $1,000 by two banks: the Standard Chartered Bank and the Hongkong and Shanghai Banking Corporation. (Also available, but not commonly used, is the one-cent note, one of the world's smallest pieces of currency). Coins are 10 cents, 20 cents, 50 cents, $1, $2, and $5. $10 bills are green; $20 purple; $50 blue; $100 red; $500 light brown; and $1,000 yellow.

Gold

There is a free market for gold, and dealings by residents and non-residents are unrestricted. No licenses are required for the freely permitted import and export of gold. There is also a gold futures market in Hong Kong. The strong local tradition in Hong Kong is to buy gold by the Chinese weight in taels (one tael being equal to 37.8 grams), and the price is still quoted daily for the tael as well as the ounce and kilo.

Miscellaneous

Don't assume all banks have the same basic policies with slight variations.

They don't. Some banks (mostly American) charge a fee if your current account gets below a certain amount — when it is in credit — and some banks have a service charge if you withdraw cash from an ATM with your credit card. There are lots of things to look for so don't assume that the biggest bank has the best deal, it doesn't.

There are several other points the newcomer should be aware of when dealing with banking issues in Hong Kong: You cannot open an account in a minor's name unless it has a joint, adult co-signatory.

Check carefully before utilizing banking services. There are often service charges added for things free or less expensive at home.

Money Changers

Licensed money changers abound in Hong Kong. They can be of use for after-hours banking needs (ie currency exchange) and most will cash a personal foreign currency check if they know you well enough (something most banks will not do).

Money changers will always add a service charge to any transaction, so if you use them be prepared to get a lower rate than at the banks.

Most banks in Hong Kong are more geared towards business clients than to retail clients. However, if pushed, your banker should be able to offer you the same quality of service he usually reserves for his business clients.

Chapter 8
BUSINESS MATTERS

PHOTO BY JOHN LANGFORD

W hile this book focuses on living in Hong Kong, rather than the business aspects, it's virtually impossible in a city as commercially minded as Hong Kong, to talk about one without including the other. Thus, in this chapter we address a number of business matters that most likely touch on one's personal life as well. For more details, we refer you to AmCham's companion volumes, *Doing Business in Today's Hong Kong* and *Establishing An Office In Hong Kong*.

Taxation

American expatriates working in Hong Kong for private enterprise are subject to taxation on their earnings by both the Hong Kong and the United States governments.

Hong Kong taxes

The Inland Revenue Department of Hong Kong imposes separate taxes on different classes of income arising in or derived from Hong Kong sources. This section is limited to the Hong Kong Salaries Tax, which is levied on income from employment in Hong Kong, including wages, salary, leave pay (unless paid by the employer for the purchase of transportation and expended for that purpose), and any fee, commission, bonus, gratuity, perquisite, stock option, or cost-of-living allowance. The place of payment is immaterial.

Benefits in kind that are not convertible into cash are not subject to tax, except for rent-free quarters provided by employers. If you are provided with free accommodation in Hong Kong by your employer, you will be deemed to have received rental income equal to 10 percent of the total income, other than rental, paid to you. This deemed rental income can be offset in whole or in part by rent actually paid by you either to your employer or to the landlord directly. If you are paid a lump sum by your employer, with no provision that a part of it is paid as a rental subsidy, the entire amount is subject to taxation. Therefore, care should be exercised in the manner in which both you and your employer report salary and other compensation.

Hong Kong has no system of withholding for Salaries Tax. The Hong Kong tax year is from April 1 through March 31. In April of each year your employer files an 'Employer's Return of Remuneration and Pensions' with the Inland Revenue Department and provides a copy to you. This form serves the same purpose as a W-2 form in the United States. The Inland Revenue Department will then send you a Salaries Tax Return, which must be completed and filed within one month.

Later in the year, you will receive an assessment notice from the Inland Revenue Department. This assessment demands payment of any outstanding balance of the prior year's tax liability, plus a provisional payment of the next year's liability. The assessment calls for payment in two installments. The first installment comprises the balance of the prior year's liability, plus 75 percent of the provisional tax for the next year. This payment is usually required early in the next calendar year. The remaining 25 percent of the provisional tax is paid about three months later. Payment of the provisional tax is similar to the requirement for the payment of estimated tax in the United States.

In summary, the amount usually subject to Hong Kong Salaries Tax is determined by adding all cash compensation (such as salary, cost-of-living allowance, tax reimbursement, and tuition reimbursement) plus (where quarters are provided or subsidized by the employer) 10 percent of such cash compensation as taxable housing income.

There are two ways the tax on your income can be assessed. It can be calculated on a graduated scale (see below), with whatever deductions and allowances you are entitled to, or you can be taxed at a flat rate of 15 percent - with no allowances other than charitable contributions — whichever is the lesser amount. In other words, the maximum you can be taxed is 15 percent of your total income.

The new tax assessment rates effective for the tax year beginning 1991/92 are as follows:

Net chargeable income (HK$)	Rate of salaries tax (%)
First 20,000	2 percent
Second 20,000	9 percent
Third 20,000	17 percent
Remainder	25 percent

Allowances and deductions

Single person's allowance	$41,000
Married person's allowance	$82,000
Child allowance-- 1st child	$14,000
2nd child	$10,000
3rd child	$3,000
4th to 6th	$2,000
7th to 9th	$1,000
Dependent parent	$12,000

Pre-1989/90, a married couple's income was taxed jointly, which meant a bigger tax bill than if the couple were not married. Public pressure, particularly from women's groups, has finally resulted in legislation allowing couples to elect to be taxed jointly or separately. Broadly speaking, it is better for a couple who both work full-time, to be taxed separately. Spouses working part-time or earning a small salary should consult an accountant or visit the Inland Revenue department in Windsor House for advice.

Some expatriates based in Hong Kong but having regional or area responsibilities are allowed to have their salaries tax assessed on a 'time' basis. On this basis, they are permitted to exclude from Hong Kong taxable income that portion of their income derived outside of Hong Kong. To qualify for the allocation of income between Hong Kong and offshore, according to time spent offshore, the following criteria must be met:

(1) You must be employed by a non-Hong Kong entity.
(2) A bona fide regional assignment is required; responsibility outside Hong Kong is necessary.
(3) Payment must not be in Hong Kong dollars; preferably, payment should be made into a foreign bank account.
(4) The non-Hong Kong duties must be substantial and not merely incidental to Hong Kong duties.
(5) The salary expense must be allocable to a non-Hong Kong unit and not wholly chargeable against the corporate profits of the Hong Kong unit.
(6) The appointment to a directorship of a Hong Kong company reduces substantially the potential of being allowed a time-basis allocation. An honorary or unpaid directorship should be alleged, but such arguments are not always successful.

Individuals wishing to qualify for time basis assessment should consult competent tax counsel.

United States income taxes

As mentioned earlier, US citizens and resident aliens living and working in Hong Kong are liable for US income taxes as well as Hong Kong salaries tax. Fortunately, there is a provision in the Internal Revenue Code that permits most American taxpayers working overseas to exclude all or a part of their foreign earned income. Even with this exclusion, however, American taxpayers are still required to file a tax return in which the income is reported and the exclusion is claimed. Failure to file a tax return can result in the loss of the exclusion.

US citizen taxpayers may qualify for the exclusion if they are bona fide foreign residents for a period including an entire taxable year or if they are physically present in a foreign country or countries for 333 days during a 112-month period. Once qualified under the bona fide residence test, taxpayers may claim the exclusion from the date of the initial establishment of their bona fide foreign residence. Resident aliens of the United States can only qualify under the physical presence test since they cannot be residents of the United States and bona fide foreign residents at the same time.

For 1991 the exclusion was US$70,000 but there is currently a bill in Congress proposing to increase this amount. It is therefore important that you keep up-to-date with what is happening back home.

The exclusion is elective for taxpayers who qualify under either the bona fide residence or physical presence test. It is computed on a daily basis at the annual rate shown above. For married couples, the exclusion is computed separately for the separate earnings of each. The exclusion may not be claimed by US government employees or military personnel for amounts paid them by the government.

In addition to the earned income exclusion described above, qualifying taxpayers may also elect to exclude housing expenses (including utilities and insurance) above an amount based on 16 percent of the salary of a US government employee at step 1 of grade GS-14 on the civil service pay scale. Both the foreign earned income exclusion and the excess housing cost exclusion are calculated on a daily basis for the number of qualifying days in the tax year.

Once you make either or both of the foregoing elections (foreign earned income and/or housing costs) the exemption(s) continue in effect until you revoke them. If revoked, you may not again elect the exclusion for a period of five years without the permission of the Secretary of the Treasury.

Even though all of your earned income may be exempt from taxation as a result of the exclusions discussed above, all investment income, whether from a foreign or US source, must be reported and is taxed in the same manner it would be if you continued to live in the United States. Preparation of income tax returns claiming the exclusions is complex, and you would be well advised to consult competent tax counsel before filing your first overseas return.

Taxpayers who sell their homes in the United States because of a transfer to an overseas assignment are given a four-year period within which to reinvest the resulting proceeds in a new home without paying capital gains tax. The new home may be in a foreign country.

American taxpayers traveling or residing abroad on April 15 (the normal date for filing US income tax returns) are given an automatic two-month extension for filing their returns and making payment of taxes due. Even though the time for filing and paying is extended, interest at the prescribed rate is charged on any tax due from the normal April 15 due date.

US citizens or resident aliens who have a non-US bank account or who have signature authority on a non-US bank account are required to file US Treasury Form 90-22.1 Report of Foreign Bank Account by June 30 of the year following the year in which they have the account or the signature authority.

There are several professional US tax advisers in Hong Kong who can provide counseling and prepare returns for US taxpayers living here. The American Consulate General in Hong Kong provides tax forms and IRS publications but does not have IRS personnel attached to it. There is a full-time IRS representative attached to the American Embassy in the Philippines, who makes periodic visits to Hong Kong and can be consulted by taxpayers requiring assistance.

Business Opportunities in Hong Kong

Among industrialized nations, Hong Kong is perhaps the last bastion of free trade and free enterprise. Hong Kong demonstrates the efficiency with which industrialists and traders respond to the laws of supply and demand, and its operations depend on profit incentives with minimum interference from government.

Hong Kong is a major manufacturing, banking, insurance, and shipping center ranking 11th among trading nations. Overall, the economy is good although 1990 saw the slowest growth in domestic exports for several years. In real terms, GDP was 2.4 percent in 1990 compared to 7.9 percent in 1988 and 2.3 percent in 1989. Inflation also rose rapidly during 1990/91, going from 8.5 percent in February 1990 to 14 percent in April 1991.

Hong Kong's largest imports continue to be raw materials, consumer goods, capital goods and food while the main exports are clothing, toys and dolls, electrical appliances, telecommunications equipment, photographic equipment, watches clocks and textiles.

Hong Kong continues to interest industrial investors, particularly those planning to establish some sort of fairly sophisticated manufacturing facility in Asia, because of its free enterprise philosophy and environment that provides maximum freedom for personal and corporate initiative. There are no government controls on imports and exports, other than those arising from international obligations or exercised for purposes of health, safety, and security. Capital equipment, raw materials, components, etc, may be imported freely from any source. There are very few customs tariffs in Hong Kong, and consequently there are few customs formalities to undergo for goods imported or exported.

In addition, there is an equally rare lack of restrictions on the foreign investor. For example, there is no objection whatsoever to any foreign company raising all or part of its capital through the local banking system. Alternatively, capital can be freely imported and, together with profits and dividends, freely repatriated. There are no regulations regarding permissible maximum percentage of foreign ownership or nationalities of company directors or employees. The government does not force the foreign investor to employ local people or to train them. All foreign-owned companies are treated legally and otherwise in the same way as are local companies.

Hong Kong also offers the advantage of low taxation. Tax is charged only on income or profits arising in or deriving from Hong Kong; no tax is levied on income or profits made abroad even if remitted to Hong Kong. Profits of unincorporated businesses are taxed at 15 percent, and profits of corporations are taxed at 16 percent.

Hong Kong is the gateway to the People's Republic of China. Manufacturers locating in Hong Kong achieve the advantage of proximity to the Chinese market. Another attraction is that Hong Kong is in the heart of the Asia-Pacific basin — an area that is growing faster than any other part of the world.

To manage a business in the Asia-Pacific area, many firms have found that maximum effectiveness and efficiency are achieved by being 'where the action is' — hence many regional headquarters are located in Hong Kong. If you are thinking of establishing a regional office in the Asia-Pacific area, Hong Kong should be your choice for several reasons; it is a free port, it has excellent banking and financial facilities, a sophisticated communications network, a stable government with a minimum of regulations and controls, low taxes, and a skilled labor force.

There are about 800 American companies with offices in Hong Kong. A previous survey by the American Chamber of Commerce in Hong Kong concluded that Hong Kong was still a preferred site for regional offices in spite of increasing costs. However, increased costs, particularly the very high rents of residential accommodations, have caused many companies to reassess their commitments and reduce the number of expatriate staff assigned here.

If you are interested in trade opportunities, investment opportunities, or in establishing a regional office in Hong Kong, the American Chamber of Commerce in Hong Kong can be of assistance. The functions of AmCham are described in the introduction to this book, and leaflets and references are available.

Employment for Expatriate Wives

To many readers it may seem odd in these enlightened times for this book to presume that if one spouse were unemployed in Hong Kong, it would be the wife. But reality dictates that, for a multitude of reasons, this is indeed the case. It is very common to find that a married woman has had to give up a good job and/or successful career to accompany her husband to Hong Kong. It rarely happens the other way around. The wife understandably might say to herself, 'My husband has a good job, with great perks and long vacations, but what about me? Can I get a job too?'

The answer is yes, but it will most likely be at a local salary (usually less than that at home), and it may take some persistence to find. Wives of expatriate businessmen have found a wide range of jobs — free-lance writing, antique store proprietorship, fund raising, bank managing, teaching, executive secretary, fabric manufacturing, social work, etc. Some work full-time; others, part-time.

The same skills that apply to job hunting back home probably apply here. Of course, you should directly approach all the organizations that interest you. You can also check the employment agencies and the classified advertisements in the newspapers. Many women think that the real answer to finding a job is through personal contacts — whether business or social. This is because many interesting jobs are never advertised, and an employer will simply put out feelers among his or her contacts in an effort to locate the right person. Don't hesitate to tell everyone you meet what you are seeking and what are your qualifications. If one potential employer says that he or she has no jobs available, ask to make an appointment with that person anyway in order to discuss the job market in your field and to gain further leads. Most people are happy to help a newcomer in this way. And you never know — a job may result.

It does not take long for a job hunter to discover the negative aspects of employment in Hong Kong. Salaries can be abysmal, as little as half the pay for similar work in the US. Some jobs have a 5.5 day work week, with only a two-week annual vacation, making it difficult for you to enjoy your husband's long annual home leave. Many jobs require fluency in Cantonese, and some government employers will not give full credit for American education, which may differ from the British system.

Despite these readily evident drawbacks, many women manage to find positions that utilize their particular skills and meet their personal and professional needs. Other women have decided that formal employment in Hong Kong is not for them and have become very actively involved in volunteer work with such organizations as the American Women's Association, the American Chamber of Commerce in Hong Kong, or the Hong Kong Arts Centre. There is no lack of interesting and useful things to become involved in while in Hong Kong — whether paid or volunteer.

You might find it helpful to take a look at educational and employment opportunities in 'Hong Kong for Expatriate Women', published by the League of Women Voters, Hong Kong Overseas Unit. *Employment for Expatriate Women in Hong Kong* compiled by members of the American Women's Association is on sale for $80 from AWA.

Hong Kong and China

The relationship between Hong Kong and the People's Republic of China is now going through some interesting dynamics. As Hong Kong goes through the process of adjusting to the idea of being absorbed by China in 1997, it seems to be meeting China going the other way. Despite occasional and expected spasms of self-doubt, the Chinese seem quite serious about opening up their country to Western investment, technology, culture, even economic theory.

This short section is not intended to offer a detailed study of the Hong Kong-China relationship, but merely to convey the tenor of that relationship and, it is hoped, to suggest some areas into which the inquiring mind might like to delve more deeply. Along with the companion volume to this book, *Hong Kong Connection - Doing Business in Guangdong Province*, AmCham also has a China Commercial Relations Committee, which is concerned with developing trade relationships and business transactions with China.

As agreed upon by China and Britain in the signing of the Sino-British Joint Declaration on December 19, 1984, Hong Kong's capitalist system will remain so for at least 50 years after China assumes control of the territory in 1997. Despite some skepticism voiced by Hong Kong Chinese over China's real intentions, the agreement nevertheless has brought a sense of renewed confidence to Hong Kong business people - albeit shaken by the massacre of civilian demonstrators in Tiananmen Square on June 4, 1989.

Since 1978, China has substantially increased its investments in Hong Kong. These cover a wide range of activities but concentrate on shipping, banking, real estate, insurance, retail outlets and manufacturing. Such investments not only contribute significantly to China's foreign exchange earnings, but are also making PRC-controlled companies important factors in the Hong Kong economy. See AmCham's book, *PRC Business Firms in Hong Kong and Macau* for more detailed information.

In addition, China has established several Special Economic Zones — similar in concept to free trade zones — just across the border from Hong Kong. They are intended to create an attractive environment for foreign investors, providing favorable treatment in such areas as taxation, labor, allocation of raw materials, and preferential supply of key infrastructure items such as electric power. So far, they have met with limited success, but the Beijing government appears intent on making them work. Meanwhile, foreign companies have adopted a relatively cautious approach to them because of the vagueness of many of the regulations governing investments in the zones. Nevertheless, the significance for Hong Kong is clear: the contrasting lifestyles and economic activities on either side of the Sino-Hong Kong border are gradually becoming less distinct. Many Hong Kong companies are taking advantage of cheaper labor and land and are moving their manufacturing activities — and the attitudes that go with them — across the border.

Simple transportation links are another factor that exemplify the improved China-Hong Kong relationship. Just a few years ago, the only way to travel to China was to take a train to the border and walk across the bridge over the Shenzhen River. Now there are direct flights from Hong Kong to Beijing, Guangzhou, and other cities; daily hovercraft services to Guangzhou; through train services; and even container truck routes. For more on this, see AmCham's book, *Doing Business in Guangdong Province*.

Chapter 9
SCHOOLS

PHOTO COURTESY OF HONG KONG INTERNATIONAL SCHOOL

There are about one million children in the Hong Kong schools system of whom fewer than 10,000 are English-speaking in English-language schools. During 1980, the government achieved its target of providing free education to every Chinese-speaking student for their first nine years of schooling — six years in primary and three years in secondary school. There is no free education for English-speaking students in Hong Kong but many companies pay for all or part of the tuition, textbooks and uniforms for the children of expatriate employees.

For students whose first language is not Chinese, there are a number of co-educational day schools available that accept children into the primary school at a somewhat earlier age than do American schools. It is advisable to apply to a school prior to arriving in Hong Kong as demand can be quite high, particularly in primary classes. Complete academic records should be provided on application.

Listed below are the main English-speaking international and ESF (English Schools Foundation) schools, with background on the schools, fees and other necessary information.

Private Schools — American System

Hong Kong International School
6-23 South Bay Close
Repulse Bay
Hong Kong
812-2305
Headmaster: David F Rittman

The Hong Kong International School was founded in 1967 and operates under the auspices of the Lutheran Church, Missouri Synod. Private and independent, it is fully accredited by the Western Association of Schools and Colleges (Burlingham, CA).

The school is housed in four buildings, spread over three campuses. An American curriculum and American-style educational program for students is offered. Instruction is in English, with French, Spanish and Mandarin taught as modern languages. Academic emphasis is on college preparation. Over 90 percent of students will go on to some form of higher education in the States. The high-school (grades 9-12) is located at **1 Redhill Road**. The building was completed in 1988 and is designed for 700 students. Facilities include: two school blocks, a center for arts and worship, a library of 50,000 books, 32 general classrooms, eight science and computer labs, a common area and a sports center containing a double-sized gym, indoor heated pool, squash courts, training and locker rooms. The building is designed around a large plaza and adjacent atrium intended to foster a sense of community.

Elementary (K-5) and Middle School (6-8) are located in the original school at **6-23 South Bay Close**. They are housed in two modern well-equipped buildings which contain two libraries, two gyms, three science labs, music rooms, a language lab, art rooms, chapel/auditorium, swimming pool, cafeteria and administrative offices. The elementary building is designed to accommodate open-style classrooms. Children are taught by the traditional, individualized method as well as by the modern team approach.

Pre-primary and kindergarten are based at newly-renovated premises at **26 Kennedy Road**. There is also a kindergarten in the South Bay school for those children living in the Repulse Bay area.

Total enrollment for 1990/91 was 1,560. Of this number approximately 60 percent were American, 10 percent 'host country' (Hong Kong and UK), and 30 percent from other nations.

Entrance requirements

1. The student must be able to participate in a class where English is the medium.
2. Applicants must have passed a physical examination within six months of entering.
3. Previous school records of the student must be submitted prior to acceptance.
4. For kindergarten, students must be age 5 by October 31 of the year of entrance.
5. For Grade 1, students must be age 6 by October 31 of the year of entrance.
6. Children of debenture holders who meet other entrance requirements are guaranteed admission at any time. Students from American/International schools have priority after debenture holders.

Annual fees

Pre-primary	$35,900
K-5	$71,800
6-8	$75,200
9-11	$82,100
12	$82,650

California International USA School
123-125 & 143 Waterloo Road
Kowloon Tong
Tel: 336-3812
Headmistress: Rose Ng

Established in 1986, the California School takes students from Grade 1 through to Grade 12. The student/teacher ratio is approximately 1:20.

Over 60 percent of the school is made up of English-speaking Chinese, with the remainder split between Japanese, Korean and Indian. The curriculum is based on the American system. The school has a pool, tennis court and library.

Teaching staff are American and English. Special tutoring is available for non-English speakers.

Annual fees

Grade		Regular	SAE (special assistance in English)
Grade	1-3	$44,400	$48,000
	4-6	$46,320	$50,400
	7-9	$50,160	$55,200
	10-12	$54,000	$60,000

Entrance exam in English and math required. No debentures.

Private Primary Schools — British System

Discovery Bay International School
Discovery Bay
Lantau
Tel: 987-7331
Headmistress: A M Naughton

Founded in 1983, DBIS has 120 nursery students and 350 primary students, up to primary 6. After graduating primary 6, students can go on to a secondary school of your choice or to West Island School, the ESF school zoned for Lantau.

Facilities are not impressive although the school has the use of a swimming pool in Discovery Bay. There is a football field, a small library and the usual singing, drama and ballet lessons. What it lacks in size, is made up for by an enthusiastic PTA who hold regular fund-raising events.

Annual fees

Nursery	$18,000
Reception	$21,000
Primary	$30,000
Debentures	$30,000

Hong Lok Yuen School
Hong Lok Yuen
Taipo, New Territories
Tel: 658-6935
Headmaster: Mr Wojciechowski

Hong Lok Yuen School goes from Primary 1 to 6 with two classes at each level. Apart from the regular teaching staff, specialist staff are employed for Chinese studies, music, PE and swimming. In 1990 the expansion program was completed, adding a library, gym, and rooms for art, music and Chinese studies.

On the same premises is **Orchard Kindergarten** which caters for children from three years of age up to five. They are taught by trained kindergarten teachers plus a qualified primary teacher for their last terms before entering primary school. Children from Orchard Kindergarten have first priority for places at Hong Lok Yuen School.

Kellett School
2 Wah Lok Path
Wah Fu
Pokfulam
Tel: 551-82334
Headmistress: V Steer

Kellett School was founded in 1978 and has approximately 380 children from ages four to 11. The purpose-built premises have 18 classrooms, two music rooms, art room, library, resources room, and an adventure playground.

The school is staffed by fully qualified teachers for each class plus specialist teachers for music, craft and remedial. The overall teacher/pupil ratio is 1:12. A school bus available in certain areas. Uniforms are required.

Annual fees

Reception	$30,800
Primary	$35,800

Corporate debentures are $100,000, private debentures, $25,000. Both are refundable and transferable (with certain conditions). Alternatively, parents can pay an annual, non-refundable $4,000 fee in lieu of debenture.

Private Secondary Schools — British system (and others)

Canadian Overseas Secondary School
166-166A Boundary St
Kowloon
Tel: 336-1116
Headmaster: Alvin Gillies

The Canadian School was established in 1983 and in 1990 had 580 students. The student/teacher ratio is approximately 1:25. Over 90 percent of the students are English-speaking with the remainder split between other Asian countries.

Almost all the teachers are Canadian and the curriculum is based on the Ontario system. Any credits gained at the school are transferrable to any school in Canada. Facilities include a science lab, audio-visual room, library, computer room, playground and volleyball court.

Uniforms are required. There is an entrance exam in English and math.

Annual fees
All grades (8-13) $38,000 per year.

Chinese International School
1 Hau Yuen Path
Braemer Hill
Hong Kong
Tel: 510-7288
Headmaster: Christopher Berrisford

CIS was established in 1983 and has rapidly developed into one of the top schools in Hong Kong. In 1990, there were over 800 students from Reception (nursery) through to Form 5 (11th grade). The school is bi-cultural with a strong emphasis on English, Mandarin and Cantonese. A large percentage of the student body comprises English-speaking Chinese although around 10 percent are either English or American.

The curriculum is based on the British system with students taking GCSE

'Dotting the eye of the dragon' before a good luck Dragon Dance performance

Space Museum in Tsimshatsui, Kowloon

A
performanc
Sunday after
Central, Hon

Causew
shoppir

孔道門

...onfucian
...mple

...affito in Tai O shows
...ditional 'junk'
...hing boats versus
...day's fishing
...ats at the
...ore.

Chinese buns
street s

Jardine's wa
tours b

Repulse Bay
Apartments

Annual Dragon Boat
Races

Bond Centre
one of the leading
commercial buildings
in central business
district, Hong Kong

Central district
harbour view 19

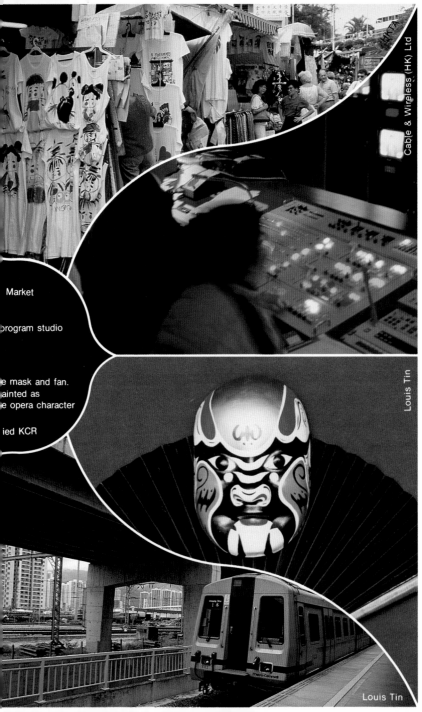

Market

program studio

mask and fan.
ainted as
opera character

ied KCR

Like Rolls Royces, portable phones are common in Hong Kong.

A new commercial area in Wanchai is still under construction

exams in the fifth form. In 1992, the school will begin teaching the International Baccalaureate Diploma (IB) for sixth form students. (See *L'Ecole Francaise Internationale* for details on the IB.)

Facilities include 59 well-equipped classrooms, science and computer labs, purpose-built art, music and language rooms, two gyms, a swimming pool, two extensive libraries, a dining room, complete catering facilities and a multi-purpose auditorium.

Annual fees
Reception to P2 $25,000
P3 to P6 $35,000
Secondary $45,000

Personal debenture is $75,000, corporate debenture $200,000.

Hong Kong Japanese School
157 Blue Pool Rd
Hong Kong
574-5479
Headmaster: Shiire Eiji

The Hong Kong Japanese School is the equivalent of primary and secondary schools in Japan. The same curriculum is followed so there are no restrictions in transferring to or from other Japanese schools. Teaching is up to Grade 9 so for university entrants, the final three years (10-12) must be completed in Japan.

There are approximately 1,700 students and a staff of around 110. No entrance exam is given for admission to the school but applicants must possess a certificate issued from their previous school. For non-Japanese applicants, there may be an exam to test language ability.

Annual fees
Primary 1 to Secondary 2 $9,108
Secondary 3 $11,028

German Swiss International School
11 Guildford Rd
The Peak
Tel: 849-6216
Headmaster: E Schierschke

N.B. *Cable & Wireless (HK) Ltd is now called Hongkong Telecom.*

Subsidized by the German government, GSIS is one of the more popular private international schools. There are two streams within the school : German and International (English speaking). The International stream has 600 students and follows the British school system while the German stream has 435 students and follows the German curriculum.

All German nationals are assured a place in the school but there is a two-year waiting list for the English stream. There is a bus service from the Star Ferry at additional cost.

Annual fees

Kindergarten	$25,000
Primary	$29,400
Lower Secondary	$36,400
Upper Secondary	$38,400

Private debenture is $30,000, corporate debenture is $60,000.

L'Ecole Francaise Internationale
(French International School)
34 Price Road
Jardine's Lookout
Hong Kong
Tel: 577-6217
Headmaster: G Gey

Another popular private school, FIS has relatively new premises in Jardine's Lookout. The school comprises 500 students in the French stream and almost 300 in the English stream.

The French stream takes children from age three (*petite maternelle*) up to graduation level (*Baccalaureate*) and follows the French curriculum. Classes are in French with English as the first compulsory foreign language. German, Spanish and Mandarin are also taught as modern languages.

The English stream takes English-speaking children from kindergarten (age four) to 18. The curriculum follows the British system up to GCSE exams (age 16) and then students follow a two-year International Baccalaureate course.

International Baccalaureate
The International Baccalaureate Diploma is recognized as a matriculation qualification for entries into universities throughout the world. Instead of

having to specialize by taking only three subjects at 'A' Level, students may take six subjects covering the humanities,science and languages — three at a higher level and three at a subsidiary level. As part of the course, students also undertake one afternoon a week of community service such as helping in the Vietnamese refugee camps. The course is demanding, but one that offers a broad all-round education; an ideal foundation for the university studies that a student will be able to follow anywhere in the world.

Annual fees

		French stream	English stream
Kindergarten	mornings	$14,580	$16,110
	full day	$20,910	$23,130
Primary		$23,490	$25,950
Secondary (1-5)		$27,480	$30,360
(6-7)		$33,930	$37,470*

*International Baccalaureate

Norwegian School in Hong Kong
Tai Po Bungalow
Kwung Fuk Rd
Tai Po
Tel: 658-0341
Headmaster: M Lillhein

This tiny non-profit school has only a dozen or so students and eight full time and part time staff. It is run by the Norwegian Missionary Society and the Norwegian Lutheran Mission. Instruction is in Norwegian — occasionally in Swedish or Danish if teachers are available. The syllabus follows Norway's system. The children are divided into four groups, depending on their age. Ages range from five to 15. There are no fees other than basic expenses.

Royden House School
110-118 Caine Rd
Hong Kong
Tel: 547-5479
Headmistress: Mrs Williamson
The Royden House School was founded in 1939 by Mr and Mrs EC Thomas and named after a missionary, Helen Royden.

The school offers kindergarten, primary and secondary education and caters to English and non-English speaking children of some 33 nations. English tuition is available for those whose English is not very good.

A specific age level is not required for a specific class. Rather, placement is determined by the student's knowledge and understanding. There are about 500 students in 13 classes and three kindergarten classes. Although grounds are limited for outdoor activities, students are bused to a playground once a week for sports.

Annual fees
Kindergarten $7,500
Primary $9,100-$9,600
Secondary $10,250-$17,500

Sear Rogers International School
109 Boundary St
Kowloon
Tel: 336-5358
Headmaster: C Kinbrough

The Sear Rogers International School was founded in 1982 by Helen Chu to meet the needs of English-speaking Chinese pupils. The curriculum is based on the UK system and English is the teaching medium.

The school offers education on primary and secondary levels — with the latter going up to GCSE level. There are no entrance exams for Primary 1 and 2, but admissions to all other classes are subject to interviews, written tests and academic records. As of 1991, there were 500 students enrolled at the school.

Annual fees
Primary $26,500
Secondary 1-3 $32,000
          4-5 $32,000
          6       $35,000

English Schools Foundation (ESF)

The English Schools Foundation grew out of the 1965 government education policy, the aim of which was to ensure that the cost to the Hong Kong public of a child attending an English-language school should not be more than that of a child attending a Chinese school. Any additional costs to the basic government subsidy, such as the provision and passages of teaching staff recruited from overseas, must be met by tuition fees.

ESF schools exist to provide education for a small minority of children whose language and non-local background make it impractical to attend the schools provided for the majority of pupils in Hong Kong and who need to be prepared for a future which almost certainly lies outside Hong Kong. Children of more than 40 nationalities fall into this group. The medium of instruction is English and the cultural background is European/International. The curriculum is based on the UK system of education.

There are currently 15 establishments under ESF management: five secondary, nine primary and a special education center for pupils with moderate to severe learning difficulties.

There is currently a zoning system operating and the choice of school is determined by the area of residence. Having said that, two of the three secondary schools on Hong Kong island are overcrowded and parents living in these 'catchment' areas should not assume that a place will be available for their child. It may be necessary to refer children to schools which have vacancies. *It is not possible to reserve places prior to arrival in Hong Kong.* For more information, contact the ESF directly. Tel: 574-2351. Fax: 838-0957.

Annual fees (to be revised in June 1992)
Primary $24,600
Secondary $40,700

Primary Schools --

Beacon Hill School
23 Ede Rd
Kowloon Tong
Kowloon
Tel: 336-5221
Headmaster: R P Lyden

Boundary Junior School
Rose St
Yau Yat Tsuen
Kowloon
Tel: 381-4362
Headmistress: J Davidson

Bradbury Junior School
43C Stubbs Rd
Hong Kong
Tel: 574-8240
Headmaster: R Brown

Glenealy Junior School
Hornsey Rd
Hong Kong
Tel: 522-1919
Headmaster: H Drummond

Kennedy School
19 Sha Wan Drive
Sandy Bay
Hong Kong
Tel: 522-4519
Headmistress: E A Gibb

Kowloon Junior School
20 Perth St
Kowloon
Tel: 714-5279
Headmaster: G T Davies

Peak School
20 Plunkett's Rd
The Peak
Hong Kong
Tel: 849-7211
Headmaster: K J Anglesey

Quarry Bay School
6 Hau Yuen Path
Braemar Hill
Hong Kong
Tel: 566-4242
Headmaster: D J Harrison

Shatin Junior School
3A Lai Wo Lane
Shatin
New Territories
Tel: 692-2721
Headmaster: B G Lewis

The Jockey Club Sarah Roe Centre
2A Tin Kwong Rd
Kowloon
Tel: 760-0441
Joint Heads of Centre:
M J Doherty / C T H Smith

Secondary Schools --

Island School
20 Borrett Rd
Hong Kong
Tel: 524-7135
Headmaster: D J James

King George V School
2 Tin Kwong Rd
Kowloon
Tel: 711-3028
Headmaster: M J Behennah

Sha Tin College
Lai Wo Lane
Fo Tan
Shatin, New Territories
Tel: 699-1811
Headmaster: D S Cottam

South Island School
50 Nam Fung Rd
Hong Kong
Tel: 555-9313
Headmaster: R E Brookin

West Island School (provisional name, temporary premises)
10 Borrett Rd
Hong Kong
Headmistress of primary school: P A Graham

West Island School is the latest addition to the ESF. New, purpose-built premises in Pokfulam are expected to be ready in 1994. The academic year 1991/92 consisted of just 120 first-year students.

Nursery Schools and Kindergartens

There are numerous private pre-schools and playgroups scattered throughout Hong Kong, Kowloon and the New Territories. Some are privately run and others come under the auspices of the Pre-School Playgroups Association (523-1611).

Large apartment developments such as Realty Gardens in Conduit Road, often have their own playgroups. And developments such as Discovery Bay have several private groups for all pre-school ages.

For further information: contact the Hong Kong Pre-School Playgroups Association, GPO Box 4049, Hong Kong, or look in *Dollarsaver* and on supermarket notice boards.

Universities

There are some post-secondary education opportunities in Hong Kong for expatriates. For those already attending a university and interested in Asian and Chinese studies, it is possible to enroll as an external student at the University of Hong Kong or at the Chinese University. It is not usually possible to gain admission as a regular student due to the competitive examination procedure. However, a few mature students may be accepted for full-time degree study.

For further information contact:

The Registrar, Chinese University of Hong Kong, Shatin, New Territories. (695-2111)

The Registrar, Hong Kong University, Pokfulam Rd, Hong Kong. (859-2111)

Hong Kong Polytechnic, Hunghom, Kowloon. (363-8344)

City Polytechnic, Argyle Centre, Tower 2, 700 Nathan Rd., Kowloon. (398-4321)

University of East Asia, Taipa, Macau. (Hong Kong contact: 859-9333) Apart from regular degree courses, the University of East Asia run several Open University courses with tutors and study areas both in Hong Kong and Macau.

Hong Kong Baptist College, 224 Waterloo Rd, Kowloon. (339-7333) Baptist College operates an external degree program with Ohio University in Athens, Ohio. Credits can be easily transferred to American universities.

Extramural studies

The universities in Hong Kong offer extramural courses which do not require previous university study. Offered during spring and fall semesters, courses are various and extensive. Asian studies courses in history, culture, arts and philosophy may be of particular interest to newcomers to the Orient. Contact extramural departments.

Chapter 10
TRANSPORTATION

PHOTO BY SUNNY CHAN

A lthough the land area of Hong Kong, Kowloon and the New Territories is limited, the variety and overall efficiency of the transport system will pleasantly surprise the new arrival. Buses, ferries, trams (streetcars), a funicular railway, a subway system, an electrified railway, taxis, hovercraft, minibuses — and of course private cars — are all used here. There's even a helicopter for hire.

With almost six million people on the move every day, it's not surprising that things get a little crowded at times. Rush hours are intolerable and if there is any way you can avoid them, do. The subway is jampacked, buses are a mass of sweaty bodies, taxis are impossible to find. However, off peak, the system works very well and all forms of transport are reasonably priced. The government keeps a watchful eye on all the various transport operators and does what it can to improve services whenever possible.

A useful publication for residents is *Public Transport in Hong Kong—A Guide to Services* published annually and available at the Government Publications Centre for $32. Also available is the Hong Kong Tourist Association's *Places of Interest by Public Transport*.

Road Transit

Private Cars

Private cars are an extravagance in Hong Kong. Limited parking space, high traffic density, costly fuel, and deliberate government efforts to curb ownership have all helped make private cars less and less appealing to many Hong Kong residents. Nevertheless, there are few cities where you will find such a high density of Rolls Royces, Mercedes and BMWs — not to mention the countless Japanese makes which are so popular.

The annual license fee for private cars in 1991/92 are as follows. The figures are revised (invariably upwards) at every annual budget.

Below 1500cc	$3,863
1501cc to 2500cc	$5,728
2501cc to 3500cc	$7,598
3501cc to 4500cc	$9,468
4501 and above	$11,263
motorcycles	$1,200

This includes a $48 Traffic Accident Victims Assistance Scheme (TAVAS).

New cars bought in Hong Kong are subject to a first-registration tax — a whopping 90-120 percent of the value of the car. Owners bringing their car from overseas are also subject to this tax which in this case is calculated as a percentage of the CIF (cost of car, insurance and freight). The age of the imported car is taken into account and a 25 percent per year depreciation is allowed. So if you really want to run a car in Hong Kong, look carefully at the excellent second hand market.

If you are from the United States and possess a valid driver's license from that country, or have an international driver's license, and are over 18, you may drive in Hong Kong for one year provided you are not a resident of Hong Kong. The same holds true for British citizens. However, eligibility varies from nationality to nationality so it is best to check with the Transport Department (829-5258) before taking to the road.

If you plan to stay in Hong Kong for more than one year, you must obtain a Hong Kong license at the outset. The registration and licensing of vehicles and drivers is carried out by the Transport Department at any of their four offices. All necessary forms are available at these offices. You will also need two passport-size photos, your passport, and overseas license (even if it has expired).

In Hong Kong you will have to forego the 'pleasures' of teaching your children to drive unless you get an instructor's license. A licensed instructor is the only person who may sit in a car with a learner. Learners must obtain a provisional license which costs $510 per year. Driving tests are quite rigorous and are taken in two parts. The first is a written test; the second a practical driving test, taken under normal conditions (much of the instruction is done in a simulator due to lack of road space). The total fee for the two tests is $1,036. There are long waiting lists so that as many as six to nine months may elapse between the two tests. A license costs $250 for one year, $798 for three years. Driving laws are very strict and there is not much flexibility for repeat offenders so once you have it, take care not to lose it. An international driver's license, valid for one year, costs $80.

Third party insurance is required in Hong Kong. Indeed, the penalty for not having it is a fine, three months in jail and the loss of your license for a year.

Should you be involved in a traffic accident in which personal injury results, you are required to report it to the police. On the other hand, if you have not been involved in any accidents, or made any claims on your insurance policy, you might be able to obtain a 20 to 60 percent discount on your insurance premium.

Parking can also be a major problem in Hong Kong, but there are private, multi-story carparks all over the territory. Charges for these carparks vary from $6 per hour in the New Territories to $14 per hour in Central. Monthly passes are available.

Driving is on the left so if you bring a car from the States or Europe (other than UK), it must be converted to right-hand drive immediately. Cars owned by consulates and their officials are exempt. Although conversion can be done, it is not recommended. Yet another reason to leave your car at home.

The vehicle license number belongs to you and can be transferred from car to car as you buy and sell. The retention fee is $560. The fee for a straight transfer of ownership is $1,000. The Chinese like to have 'lucky' numbers, which can be reserved — or bought at auctions held by the government from time to time. The money made goes to charity.

Some companies provide a car and driver for their executives. Drivers earn $4,000 to $6,000 a month (double wages at Chinese New Year) and are helpful in taking business clients around, meeting people at the airport and simply avoiding having to find a place to park.

Super grade gasoline in 1991 cost approximately $7 a liter. Many garages take credit cards. Servicing and repair is usually done best at garages operated by agents for particular makes. This can be expensive though. Less expensive are the many small garages around. It is advisable to go to one which has been recommended.

Membership of a motoring organisation such as the HKAA can ensure help not only in the event of a breakdown, but also in advising on insurance, vehicle inspections (mandatory for cars of a certain age) and the import or export of a vehicle.

Car Rental

With the presence of such self-drive car companies as Avis and Hertz, it is possible to rent a car for short or long term use. Requirements can vary from place to place but in general, you must be 25 or older and have had a valid driver's license for over two years. If you are American or British you may only have to show your current license. Other nationalities may have to present an international driver's license.

A Honda Accord costs about $500 a day and $2,710 a week to hire (including insurance). Not all places accept credit cards. You can find car rental companies listed in the *Yellow Pages* under 'Motorcar Renting & Leasing'.

Bicycles

Don't expect to do much cycling around Hong Kong. Bikes can be hired for pleasure at only a few shops in Hong Kong and Kowloon, but on the outlying islands there are quite a few places to hire — as well as space to cycle. Lantau, although somewhat hilly, is a great place to ride; as are areas of the New Territories.

Taxis

Although fares have increased, taxis remain inexpensive enough in Hong Kong for the private car to be increasingly superfluous. All taxis are metered and most taxi drivers have a basic knowledge of place names in English. If a driver doesn't understand where you want to go, try the name of a major landmark nearby, or try the phonetic pronunciations at the back of this book. If all else fails, the driver will ask you to repeat your destination on his radio-link and a despatcher at his headquarters will tell him where to go.

In Hong Kong, Kowloon and the 'new towns' in the New Territories, the taxis are red with silver roofs. The flagfall is $8 for the first two kilometers and 90 cents for every .25 kilometer thereafter.

In rural New Territories, taxis are green and the charges are $7 for the first two kilometers and 80 cents for every subsequent .25 kilometer. The same charges apply for Lantau's blue taxis.

Although taxi drivers should know all parts of Hong Kong and Kowloon, they don't. 'Hong Kong' taxis prefer to stay on the island and 'Kowloon taxis' prefer to stick to their patch. When one has to cross to 'the other side', they make every effort to get back to familiar territory as quickly as possible. Hence, there are areas in Kowloon where 'Hong Kong taxis' congregate where you can pick up an island-bound taxi who will accept a one-way cross-harbor tunnel fee (normally you have to pay the return tunnel fee). Such a place is near the Shangri-La hotel in Tsim Sha Tsui East. Similarly, 'Kowloon taxis' hang out in Paterson Street, not far from the Excelsior hotel. They normally park displaying their 'out of service' sign.

If a taxi's meter is covered with a cloth or displays the 'out of service' sign it usually means the driver is about to change shift and he has to go to a certain destination to meet the other driver. If you are going his way, he will take you. Shifts change at around 11am, 4pm and 11pm.

The taxi hotline for problems is 527-7177.

Buses

There are three franchised bus companies: China Motor Bus, Kowloon Motor Bus and New Lantau Bus company which only operates on Lantau.

The two main ones, KMB and CMB, provide the territory with an extensive, efficient service at reasonable cost. Both companies use double-decker buses which are generally clean and, off-peak, not too crowded. Air-conditioned buses are becoming more and more available and in a few more years, will probably be the norm.

Bus drivers can appear to be quite reckless but in fact there are few accidents. One of the biggest thrills is the bus ride to Repulse Bay or Stanley via Wongneichong Gap — sitting on the top deck. It's much more fun than a roller-coaster ride.

Most routes have a flat-fare system, with the fare being paid in exact change when you get on. The fare is usually indicated on the coin box near the driver.

Along with its regular services, KMB operates a number of deluxe coach services between major hotels and the airport. The four services go from the airport to Tsim Sha Tsui, China Ferry Terminal, Central and Causeway Bay, stopping at or near hotels enroute. Fares range from $10-12 (exact money required).

Finally, there is a non-franchised bus company, Citybus, which operates a deluxe bus service to Shenzhen, just across the Chinese border. They also operate a number of routes between Shatin and Kowloon as well as the open-top bus which goes to Ocean Park.

Minibuses (Public Light Buses, PLBs)

These air-conditioned, privately-owned 14- to 16-seater buses, were first used in the New Territories and made their first appearance on urban roads during the 1967 disturbances when strikes by bus drivers badly crippled the service.

These cream-colored vehicles with red stripes have no government-fixed routes although routes tend to be fixed by demand and familiarity. There are no set stops so you must flag them down if you want to get on. They are not allowed to stop at regular bus stops or on single or double yellow lines, so stand in an appropriate place if you want one to stop. Similarly, if you want to get off, just call to the driver to stop — or you can say *yau lok* which means you want to get off. The fare is posted on the windscreen. Pay when you get off. They will give small change but don't try asking the driver to break a $100 note unless you want a quick lesson in Cantonese swear words. Fares are generally between $3 and $6.

Cream-colored minibuses with green stripes do have fixed routes and fixed fares. They tend to go to off-the-beaten track places which are too difficult to get to by double-decker bus or where the demand for a big bus cannot be justified. Several routes go up the Peak. One particularly useful route goes to Matilda Hospital which is notoriously difficult to reach.

Rickshaws

The rickshaw, symbol of the colonial era in Hong Kong, is fast disappearing. The government no longer grants licenses so pullers either retire or die. There were only 13 licensed in 1991. Fares are negotiable — about $50 to $100 for a very short ride around the block. Picture-taking is about $50. For your own sake, agree on the price before you set off. Rickshaws are only for tourists and can only be found at the Star Ferry, Hong Kong side.

Rail Transit

Peak Tram

This is the famous funicular railway that goes from Central to the Peak, with four stops enroute. The fare is $8 ($13 return) for adults and $3 ($5 return) for children. On a clear, sunny day, the view from the observation platform is spectacular, so take a camera. There are two restaurants at the top: the Peak Cafe which has recently been renovated, and the Peak Tower where the tram actually terminates.

The lower Peak Tram station is opposite the American Consulate on Garden Road. There is a free open-top bus which shuttles between Star Ferry (near City Hall) and the Peak Tram station. (You will need to show your tram ticket on the bus going back to Star Ferry so don't throw it away.)

The tram is also used by many Peak residents. A monthly pass is available: $160 for adults, $65 for students (under 16).

Trams

Double-decker trams trundle along Hong Kong's original waterfront roads. Now, reclamation has put them further inland but they basically run from Western, along Des Voeux Road (Central), Hennessy Road (Wanchai and Causeway Bay) and King's Road (North Point) to Shaukiwan. If you have a couple of hours to spare, it is a terrific and relaxing way to see the 'real' Hong Kong. It costs $1 for the whole ride — or just a segment of it — 50 cents for children. There is also a special, open-top tram available for private hire. Call 891-8765 for details.

Mass Transit Railway (MTR)

Since its opening in 1980 the Mass Transit Railway (subway system), has been an enormously popular means of transportation among the people of Hong Kong. It carries over 2.1 million passengers every day, making it the heaviest trafficked carrier per kilometer in the world. Carriages are clean and functional — most of the space is for standing. There is minimal seating. It is efficient, reasonably priced and, above all, safe.

There are three lines which interconnect at several main stations: Island line, which runs from Sheung Wan to Chai Wan, connects with Tsuen Wan-bound trains at Admiralty. The Kwun Tong line starts at Yau Ma Tei and goes east to Lam Tin where a second harbor crossing joins the Island line at Quarry Bay. Passengers wishing to take the Kowloon/Canton Railway (KCR) should change at Kowloon Tong.

Prices range from $3 to $7.50 per ride though regular users generally buy a stored-value ticket. Each time you make a trip, the cost is deducted from your card. Stored-value tickets are available at $50, $100 and $200 and include bonus rides. These can also be used on the KCR, saving a lot of hassle at Kowloon Tong station. Tourist tickets are available for $25 — but you only get $20 worth of rides.

Most underground stations have banks, dry-cleaners, florists, instant photo machines, news stands, even bakeries. Six stations have Ticketmate stores where you can buy ferry tickets to Macau and parts of China.

Note: There are neither public toilets nor facilities for the disabled in the MTR.

Call 750-0170 for more information. Smoking, eating or drinking is not allowed, nor is large luggage.

Kowloon-Canton Railway (KCR)

With the dramatic growth over the past 10 years of places such as Shatin, Taipo and Fanling, the KCR has become an essential part of Hong Kong's public transport system. It was electrified in 1980 and over a ten-year period, the number of daily passengers has gone from from 20,000 to more than half a million. Although the train goes all the way to Lo Wu, you can only go as far as Sheung Shui unless you have a visa for China. If you are going to China, you get off at Lo Wu, walk across the border bridge and get on a Chinese train bound for Guangzhou (Canton). Alternatively, you can get an express train from Hong Kong to Guangzhou at Hung Hom station which goes straight through ($138).

Light Rail Transport (LRT)

These modern, electric trams are the newest mode of transport in Hong Kong. There are currently seven LRT routes running along a 23-kilometer stretch between Tuen Mun and Yuen Long. Initially criticized for their quietness, after causing several accidents by "creeping up" on cars and people, the system is finally gaining acceptance as motorists and pedestrians get used to their presence.

Water Transit

Star Ferry

Like the Peak Tram, Hong Kong ferries serve as both vital public transportation and as a first-rate tourist attraction.

The Star Ferry is most famous, and now has several routes. The most frequently used is the seven-minute Central to Tsim Sha Tsui ride which costs just $1.20 for adults and 60 cents for children. If you go downstairs, where you get to see the inner workings of the boat, it is only $1 for adults.

Other routes go between Wanchai Ferry Pier and Tsim Sha Tsui ($1.50 upper deck, $1.20 lower) and Central and Hung Hom ($1.20).

Call 366-2576 for more information.

Outlying Islands Ferries

Hong Kong & Yaumati Ferry Company (HYF) run triple-decker ferries between Hong Kong and Lantau and Cheung Chau, the two most popular and populous offshore islands. Lamma, just off the Aberdeen coast, also has a thriving community and is served by double-decker ferries.

At the weekends it seems as if everyone heads for the islands, and the ferries can get very, very crowded and noisy. If you can avoid the weekends, do. Apart from the unpleasant ferry ride, you do not see the islands at their best — mid-week and peaceful.

Weekday fares to Lantau (via Peng Chau) and Cheung Chau are $6.50 economy and $10 deluxe (air-conditioned inside, sun deck outside). On Saturday afternoons, Sundays and public holidays, the fares go up to $10 and $18 respectively. Return tickets are available at weekends for lower decks only. The journeys to Lantau and Cheung Chau both take an hour. There is also a limited, weekday hoverferry service to Cheung Chau and Silvermine Bay, (Mui Wo, Lantau) which only takes 25 minutes.

The Lamma ferry is $6 on weekdays, $7.20 weekends and takes about 40 minutes.

HYF also run a circular service between the islands, which is a delightful three-hour ride. Ferries go from Cheung Chau to Chi Ma Wan to Silvermine Bay to Peng Chau and back again. Fare $4.50 one way.

There are other interesting destinations with less frequent schedules. For example there is a twice-daily ferry to Tai O, the furthest point on Lantau. Or you can go to Po Toi near Stanley for a good seafood lunch. Check with the Hong Kong Tourist Association for schedules or call HYF (542-3081).

Discovery Bay Ferry Service

Discovery Bay on Lantau has no road link with the rest of the island and so all visitors and residents must approach by sea. There is a 24-hour ferry/ hoverferry service which takes 20-35 minutes depending on the boat. Fares are $20 per trip, $10 for children.

There is also a hoverferry service which links Discovery Bay with the rest of Lantau — at Silvermine Bay.

Transport to Macau and China

*Mac*au

There's a show of jetfoils, hydrofoils, jetcats, jumbocats, hi-speed ferries — and even a helicopter — zipping across to Macau every few minutes. With so much choice — and choices within choices — it is impossible to list all the fares. Basically they range from $48 for an economy seat on the hi-speed ferry to just over $100 for a first class seat on a jetfoil or jumbocat. The journey takes 50-90 minutes depending on which boat you take. The helicopter costs $852 per person ($952 at weekends), maximum eight people, and takes less than 20 minutes to traverse 40 miles to the Portuguese enclave.
Call 859-3359 for details.

The Macau Ferry Terminal is in the Shun Tak Centre, above the Sheung Wan MTR station in Western. The helicopter pad is also there.

China

There are many sailings/cruises to China and the various Special Economic Zones. Most leave from China Ferry Terminal on Canton Road in Kowloon. AmCham's books *Establishing an Office in Hong Kong* and *Hong Kong Connection — Doing Business in Guangdong Province* list all contact information.

Tickets for most boats and ferries to Macau and China can be bought either at their respective terminals or through Ticketmate outlets which are located in several MTR stations. Call 833-9300 for details. Ticketmate can also make hotel bookings for you.

There is a $17 departure tax for all vessels leaving Hong Kong waters.

*Water taxis / motorized sampans (**kai do**)*

It is illegal for water taxis to operate in Hong Kong harbor but they can and do operate from Aberdeen, Cheung Chau and other fishing villages where living on the water is a way of life.

A sampan can be hired to take you island-hopping, for example from Cheung Chau to the Frog & Toad pub on Lantau. Alternatively, you could go from Aberdeen to Sok Yu Wan on Lamma for a seafood dinner. Prices are negotiable, so bargain. Also remember to negotiate your return trip. The sampan may wait for you or may return for you later. If the latter, it may be wise to pay later — to make sure the sampan returns as promised.

Air Transit

Hong Kong International Airport

By any standard, Hong Kong International Airport, known as Kai Tak, is one of the safest and most efficient in the world, a result, ironically, of its being one of the most dangerous in which to land. As one pilot described arrivals from Australia: "So many hours of boredom followed by several minutes of sheer (blip) 'n terror!" The result is no pilot approaches Kai Tak with nonchalance and accidents are rare. You can often clear immigration, get your baggage and through customs within 30 minutes after you touch down.

With some 40 airlines operating from the airport, the traveler has direct access to over 70 cities worldwide. There is a departure tax of $150 for adults. No charge for children.

Access to Kai Tak is fairly straightforward: either by private car, air-conditioned deluxe coach or taxi. A taxi from Hong Kong side will cost upwards of $70 (including tunnel fee) and about $40 from Tsim Sha Tsui.

Chapter 11
SHOPPING

PHOTO COURTESY OF HONG KONG TOURIST ASSOCIATION

S hopping in a foreign city immediately involves some new thinking about currencies, exchange rates, and the cost of living, as well as some hunting around for special items that may not always be where you would expect to find them. Supermarkets have taken most of the hassle, and perhaps some of the fun, out of routine shopping. But Hong Kong still has variety, abundance, and not a few surprises and delights: custom-made shoes and handbags, alley and street markets, food stalls, and special sales at any time of the year. Although Hong Kong has almost no natural resources — except, of course, its enterprising people — it transforms its imports into every imaginable product as well as bringing in the world's luxuries for its boutiques and shopping arcades.

Living in Hong Kong for any length of time, however, is different from being a tourist on a quick shopping spree, and it is wise not to rush into the temptations of Hong Kong bargains until you can handle the currency with ease and make quick and reliable comparisons of cost and quality. Trying to 'think' in Hong Kong dollars as soon as possible is really the best approach, though it can also tend to dull the senses concerning the cost of living.

It isn't easy to generalize about the cost of living in Hong Kong because so much depends on one's lifestyle. It should be said, however, that in general Hong Kong is not a cheap place in which to live, mainly because of the high cost of housing. Imported goods can also be very expensive. You will, of course, want to make your own calculations, which will include such things as taxes, salaries, food, transportation, entertainment, perhaps school fees as well as some 'invisibles' like career prospects and travel opportunities. Probably no two people would agree on the results.

In recent years inflation has made everything much more expensive in Hong Kong, which cannot escape the influence of world trends. However, in comparison with recession and unemployment in some countries, Hong Kong has so far managed to maintain growth, balance its budget, keep taxes low, and provide virtually full employment.

Because of its free-port status, its history, its healthy tourism industry, and its overwhelming involvement in trade and commerce, Hong Kong has always been an excellent place for shopping. For some time after World War II, Hong Kong was a haven for shopping bargains and its cost of living remained low. However, the recent effects of world inflation, restrictive trade barriers against Hong Kong products, and a trend toward up-market exports have all had their influence. Hong Kong today is not quite the bargain basement it used to be, but it still offers the visitor and the resident very good value. The immediate effect on the new arrival, however, is that of confusion because of the huge variety of items available; the countless number of shops, arcades, alleys, boutiques, supermarkets and department stores; the large stocks on display in brightly lit windows, on counters, and in stalls; and the clusters of neon signboards hanging over the road.

Hong Kong has been described as one gigantic bazaar, and few tourists can resist the temptation to go on a shopping spree. Indeed, many come here just for this purpose. The new resident will find this wealth of shops and diversity of choice exciting, intriguing, and perhaps a little frightening. With the help of a map, however, most people quickly find that they can manage to buy essentials — whether they are staying in a hotel or apartment — and they will soon discover those areas in Hong Kong or Kowloon that sell particular goods. It is when specialty items are needed for the house, for the children, to give as presents, etc, that problems may arise.

To provide any sort of guide to shopping in Hong Kong is especially difficult, not only because of its very extent but also because Hong Kong changes so quickly. In addition to the opening and closing of shops with dazzling speed, there is the rapid development of whole new areas. Rebuilding and new building are the cause of most of this and mean that addresses and telephone numbers change often, new hotels and office buildings can add whole new shopping centers, the character of a district may change completely, or a new retail operation such as a fast-food store, a supermarket, or a department store can alter one's whole approach to shopping.

All of these things have in fact happened in Hong Kong in recent years. The overall effect has been to increase the number of shops, to broaden the range of goods available, and to bring more style and sophistication — albeit largely Western-influenced — into Hong Kong shopping.

Shopping Guides

There are several shopping guides on the market — some more useful than others. *Born to Shop* by Suzy Gershman and Judith Thomas is a comprehensive shopper's guide, as is *Hong Kong Yin and Yang* by Dana Goetz. Dana Goetz's real brainchild, however, is *Hong Kong Factory Bargains* which gives detailed information on which factories do what (from furniture to leather jackets to pots and pans) and which ones have in-house outlets, how to get there (most are in the back and beyond) and so on. The book also covers outlets in more accessible places. For jewelry shopping, there's *Hong Kong Gems and Jew-*

ellery by Joan Reid Ahrens and Ruth Lor Malloy and for home decorating, there's *Hong Kong Shopping Guide to Home Decorating* by Barbara Anderson-Tsang and Leopoldine Mikula. Home decorating is a very loose term, it seems, as the book covers everything from the obvious furniture fabric and curtain shops to the less obvious list of aquarium shops.

All of the above were either published or reprinted in 1990 or 1991, and some, like *Factory Bargains* is updated at least once a year, but for really up-to-date information, ask for a free subscription to *Dollarsaver* or the *Kowloon Advertiser*. These newsprint magazines are full of classified ads listing shop after shop, selling all kinds of things. They are particulary good for small, specialist shops like Nag Trade (horse equipment) and Eastern Fabric (Japanese home furnishings)

The Hong Kong Tourist Association publish a monthly *Official Handbook* which is free. Most of the shops listed, are aimed at the tourist market. The HKTA also publish several pamphlets on shopping, eating out and generally finding your way around. All are available from the HKTA Information Centre in the basement of Jardine's House or at the Government Publications Centre in the GPO building.

Shopping Centers & Malls

With the emergence of new towns in the New Territories and the vast expansion and redevelopment of housing estates in Hong Kong and Kowloon, purpose-built shopping facilities had to be built alongside. Thus, in the early 1980s, huge shopping centers began to emerge. One of the first was in **Tai Koo Shi**ng. Inside this vast complex is an ice-skating rink, several restaurants — including McDonalds and Pizza Hut — and hundreds of shops ranging from small specialist outfits to huge department stores such as Marks & Spencer and Wing On. This is one-stop shopping at its best. The Tai Koo Shing complex was quickly followed by others: **Shatin** has a huge one, as does **Tsuen Wan**.

Closer to the center of things, there is **Pacific Place** housing several movie theaters, restaurants, pubs, department stores and shops. **The Landmark** in Central is low on restaurants but has a basement supermarket and lots of high class fashion shops. High rents have squeezed the more interesting shops out to Central's perimeters. The first five levels of **Prince's Building**, also in Central, has an interesting variety of shops: Oliver's deli, a children's book-shop, Mothercare, Bed & Bath, KPS video rental, The Party Shop for party favors, plus lots of clothes shops, tailors and hi-fi/camera shops. Five minutes away from Prince's Building is **Worldwide House**, a maze of tiny bargain-basement shops. Factory outlets selling clothes of all descriptions, cosmetics at wholesale prices, and of course, restaurants and fast-food outlets.

Over in Kowloon, **Ocean Terminal, Ocean Centre** and **Harbour City** have combined to make one big shopping center, popular with tourists and residents alike. There isn't much you can't buy here — and prices are competitive. Across the road is **Silvercord**, famous for computer software though some of dubious origin. **Tsim Sha Tsui East** is a relatively new (early 1980s) complex of offices, hotels and shops. The shops are much the same as those in Worldwide House in Central, although catering slightly more to the tourist. There are also several travel agents in the area.

Department Stores

Until shopping malls became popular, department stores were the best way to do one-stop shopping, but now there is so much available all over Hong Kong that department store shopping is seemingly restrictive.

Although the major department stores all sell more or less the same things, they tend to specialize in different departments. For example, Seibu, in Pacific Place, has a terrific food hall, Wing On has an excellent hardware department and Daimaru has great household and kitchen equipment.

There are almost a dozen Japanese department stores here, mostly in Causeway Bay and they have also bought into older Hong Kong groups like Wing On and Dragon Seed. Other locals of note include Lane Crawford and Sincere.

China Products, China Merchandise and Yue Hwa all sell products from the Mainland. Embroidered tablecloths, bedding, towels and down jackets are all excellent value in these shops. They each also have an extensive herbal medicine department and supermarkets with foods from China.

Most of the Japanese department stores — Sogo, Daimaru, Mitsukoshi, Seibu and others — have wonderful bakeries which bake bread and cakes throughout the day. If you wander through the food department at baking time, you will find the smell of the freshly baked produce absolutely irresistible.

Markets

Apart from its modern shops and arcades, Hong Kong still retains many traditional, less formal areas.These include markets for fresh produce, side streets cluttered with stalls, and areas which specialize in a certain product.

'Wet' markets

The indoor, purpose-built fresh produce markets are run by the Urban Council. There are usually one or two in every district, catering to the local population. On Hong Kong side, there is Central Market, between Jubilee Street and Queen Victoria Street. In Wanchai there is one near Southorn Playground and one in Queen's Road East, and in Causeway Bay there is one in Bonnington Street and another in Jardine's Bazaar. There are others.

Central market is typical of all the others, selling fish and shellfish, meat of all descriptions, although mostly chicken and pork, and fresh fruit and vegetables imported daily from China, Thailand, Australia and many other places — offering a huge variety of fresh produce. The local Chinese abhor anything not absolutely fresh much preferring live fish to frozen, and very fresh vegetables. Droopy vegetables have no place on a Chinese table. As a result, you can be fairly sure the standards in these markets is kept high. For instant assimilation into the Hong Kong way of life, a visit to one of these markets is a must. The noise, the hustle and bustle and the local colour tells you more about life here than any amount of reading possibly can.

(At the time of writing, a section of Central Market was closed while construction on the Mid-Levels escalator was in progress. Although there are, temporarily, fewer market stalls, the variety is still there.)

You don't have to go to an Urban Council-run market to buy fish, meat and vegetables, there are countless street markets selling exactly the same goods. There is doubtless one not far from where you live.

Clothes Markets / Factory Outlets

Clothing is Hong Kong's biggest export item so it is not surprising that the home market is overflowing with overruns, samples, and seconds. Most of these goods — as well as clothes made specifically for the Hong Kong market — find their way to the many 'factory outlet' shops or to the markets specializing in clothes.

144

Factory Outlet shops, once literally a small room in the factory building, are now dotted all over Hong Kong and Kowloon and sell everything from silk lingerie to ski suits. Some sell only denim, others specialize in children's clothes. Others, have nothing but shirts and T-shirts. There are areas such as Mongkok in Kowloon and Wanchai in Hong Kong, where there are many such shops. They are easily recognizable by the jumble of clothes and people rummaging through them.

There are still quite a few factories who have on-site outlets for clothes and other products. For details see Dana Goetz's excellent book, *Hong Kong Factory Bargains* which is updated regularly.

Street markets selling mostly clothes, are scattered throughout the territory. **Stanley market** is perhaps the most up-market, selling washable silk, cotton sweaters and cardigans, leather jackets, denim for every shape and size and lots of children's clothes. Although it is not cheap by Hong Kong standards, and is aimed at the tourist, it nevertheless has its advantages: It is the only market where European sizes can easily be found. This is great news for those larger than size 10 who are sick of going into clothes shops in Central where nothing comes even close to fitting.

Sek Kong market, held only on Friday mornings, is a half-day outing and about as far away from Stanley as is possible to go. Sek Kong is almost on the Chinese border and is one of the bases for British troops stationed in Hong Kong. To get there, take a hoverferry or the MTR to Tsuen Wan and then get a bus to Sek Kong which goes over Route Twisk. The bus stops right outside the market — easily visible as crowds of people go every week to see the various wares spread out on the grass. The best things are sold in the first hour, so go early to avoid disappointment. It starts at 9am.

Some other markets specializing in clothes are in **Temple Street** in Kowloon, and **Jardine's Bazaar** in Causeway Bay.

Alleys and Lanes

Over the years, areas have developed where certain specialty goods can be found. A section of Pottinger Street, informally known as "ladder street", for example, does not sell ladders, but buttons and bows, ribbons, zippers, thread, elastic and all other sewing paraphernalia. Wing On street, or Cloth Alley, now relocated to Western Market (more later), sold nothing but fabric. Cotton, silk, curtain fabric, velvet, polyester. You name it, they had it.

The two best-known lanes are in Central and sell all kinds of things. Li Yuen Street East and Li Yuen Street West, run from Queen's Road Central down to Des Voeux Road. They both sell clothes, cheap watches, handbags, suitcases, clothing accessories such as belts and scarves, underwear and fabric. Walk down one and up the other (they are adjacent) and you will see everything on offer.

There is a street on Ap Lei Chau, Aberdeen, which sells nothing but boating equipment. All sorts of gadgets and widgets; fascinating to look at, even if you don't have a boat. And then there's Tung Choi street in Mongkok which sells all kinds of aquarium equipment and, in some places, the fish to go in them. There are streets which sell birds and bird cages, and others which sell fresh flowers. A section of Lyndhurst Terrace is just one picture framer after another. Similarly in Lockhart Road, there is a whole block of shops selling bathroom and kitchen tiles, and another selling wood, cut to order.

Supermarkets

There are two major chains of supermarkets in Hong Kong : Wellcome, run by The Dairy Farm, and Park 'n' Shop. Asia Provisions, the oldest supermarket in Hong Kong has just a few branches but hundreds of loyal customers who enjoy the more personal service.

There are branches of Wellcome and Park 'n' Shop in practically every district, housing estate, and major building. An on-going price war means that prices are very competitive and most goods are available. However, because of a dispute with tobacco companies in the late 1980s, both supermarket chains stopped stocking imported cigarettes.

Both chains tend to stock with a particular market in mind, and once the area is 'labelled', goods will be stocked accordingly. There seems to be little leeway in this policy which can sometimes be frustrating. Cheung Chau, for example, caters to the holiday crowd and is stocked with charcoal, barbecue forks and meat. There seems to be a total disregard for the residents who prefer a more normal diet. Supermarkets on the Peak and in Stanley cater to expatriates; you will find things there that you will find in no other supermarket in the territory. Likewise in downtown Mongkok, you will be lucky to find a supermarket selling good cheese.

Wellcome, Park 'n' Shop and Asia Provisions all offer credit accounts and a delivery service (Asia's is somewhat limited). Asia is particularly good for meats, especially lamb and offal. It is also good for more unusual items; if you can't find something at Wellcome or Park 'n' Shop, chances are you will find it at Asia. (For gourment goods see *Food Speciality Shops*)

Apart from the big supermarkets, there are hundreds of smaller ones around. Some offer a credit line and delivery, some don't.

Fast Food

While this Western type of snack bar has not displaced the traditional *dim sum* restaurant, or the street stalls (*dai pai dongs*), the fast-food chains have been welcomed into Hong Kong with open arms. McDonald's restaurants are to be found all over Hong Kong, Kowloon and the New Territories, so for Kentucky Fried Chicken, Pizza Hut. Maxim's, and Fairwood, both local chains, also have several outlets. For slightly more upscale fare, Oliver's Delicatessen have several sandwich bars offering a variety of foods as well as sandwiches.

However, when snacking is a way of life, there can never be enough fast-food outlets and the more traditional places have flourished despite the heavy competition. The ubiquitous, polystyrene lunch-box is still very much a part of life and, once you gain enough knowledge of the language and are willing to try one, you could be pleasantly surprised. An easy one to start with is *cha siu fan (*barbecued pork with steamed rice). Delicious!

A-Z Shopping Hints

"Here today, gone tomorrow". Never is this more true than when shopping in Hong Kong. New shops are constantly opening while old and not so old ones close down. Shopping guides can never keep up with the comings and goings and often, word of mouth is the only way to find a certain item or a particular place. This, therefore, cannot be a comprehensive list of places and products, simply a useful pointer in the right direction.

Antiques

Through its auctions, international fairs, and specialist dealers, Hong Kong has become one of the world's leading trading centers for several kinds of Chinese antiques. If you are an expert, you need not be told how to look for copies, fakes, or the 'instant antiques' — whether of bronze, porcelain, ivory, or jade. For the initiate, Hong Kong is an ideal place in which to learn about the finer points of connoisseurship because there is so much to see and handle. Art gallery exhibitions, specialist societies, and reputable dealers can all make Hong Kong a wonderful opportunity to enjoy and appreciate some of the fine points of antiques. However, do not pay a high price for anything without taking advice, and there will always be a room to bargain.

The traditional antique cum flea market area known as 'Cat Street', between Hollywood Road and Queen's Road West, is worth visiting, though many untidy shops and stalls have been upgraded into smart air-conditioned stores and, in the process, have lost something of their attraction for the browser. True blackwood and rosewood (and even teak) furniture is no longer made these days but can be found, for a price, in used furniture stores and antique shops, many of which can be found on Canton Road and Queen's Road East. You might consider whether this Oriental-style furniture will suit not only your home here in Hong Kong but also your next home where that may be — before investing too heavily. Ornaments, vases for lamps, and a variety of old and new Chinese items from snuff bottles to opium beds can also be found in Hong Kong. Macau has a similar and usually cheaper area of shops hidden away off the main street.

There are also reputable dealers in antiques located in the Ocean Terminal and some of the hotel shopping arcades. The auctioneers' announcements in the newspapers and the classified ads are other sources. Hollywood Road, which runs 2.5km above Central district, offers the highest concentration of small shops.

For the ancient, and not so ancient, as compared to genuine antiques, there are numerous shops elsewhere, from the Chinese department stores to tourist shops in Kowloon and the hotel arcades. Whether you are buying or collecting porcelain, jade, pearls, ivory, snuff bottles, or whatever, it is sensible to study the subject to whatever degree your interest goes. At the very least, you will want to learn some of the special vocabulary, how to test for authenticity, and to recognize antique from modern. To know the dates and some of the main reign periods of the Chinese emperors in the Ching and Ming dynasties will be a help, though the characters for reign marks on porcelain do not necessarily mean what they say!

Appliances

Electrical and gas appliances are mainly European, Japanese, or Hong Kong made. If you did not bring any with you and if you are faced with a bare kitchen and no air conditioners, dehumidifiers, or heaters, the outlay on appliances can be one of the first and most costly expenses. If you prefer second-hand machines, investigate newspaper and supermarket advertisements, check out used furniture stores and the Lammert Brothers. auction rooms in 9/F, Malahon Centre, 10-12 Stanley Street (522 3208), and ask among friends. Some items, such as air conditioners, may be already installed when you move in and can be taken over with the flat.

If you are looking for new equipment, Hong Kong's many appliance stores offer a wide range. It is best to decide on a particular brand and then locate the respective agent(s), some of whom will have retail outlets. The Hong Kong Electric Company runs the chain of Fortress stores, where you can find many different appliances. The Hong Kong and China Gas Company has show-rooms in Central and in Leighton Centre, Causeway Bay, among other locations. Some Japanese companies such as National (Matsushita) and Sanyo have showrooms in Central and in Kowloon, as does Philips. American appliances can be seen in Prince's Building showrooms. Weatherite is a Hong Kong brand, mainly for air conditioners. System One is a Japanese - owned chain of appliance stores.

It is wise to get full information and catalogs from the agents, but you may get a better price at one of the many electrical goods shops found in all areas and which carry stocks of all types of appliances, from toasters to TV sets. Be careful about the terms, installation, guarantee, servicing agreement, and new US demonstration models. Many shops, for instance, have a whole shelf of TV sets on display which seem to be switched on all day and night. Be certain you aren't given one of those. Most stores, however, will bring out new equipment still packed from the makers. It is useful to carry a tape measure when selecting your appliances — or any large items, for that matter — to be certain they will fit through doors or into odd-shaped kitchens.

Finally, you might consider renting a particular appliance, with an eye toward eventually purchasing it. Some stores, such as Gilman Home Appliances, will rent out appliances by the month with a hire/purchase option. If you later wish to buy an appliance you've been renting, the rent paid will be deducted from the purchase price.

Aquariums

Tropical and cold-water fish — and all related supplies and equipment — are available at the many specialist stores and stalls throughout Hong Kong. Tung Choi Street in Mongkok is a good place to start. The colors and graceful movements of exotic goldfish and the brilliant colors and strange shapes of saltwater fish make the purchase of such tanks very tempting. Some restaurants and stores use them as decorative items. Offices and shops may also have them for good fortune, based on advice from their 'fung shui' specialists. There is no shortage of equipment — pumps, lights, heaters, plants, etc — and a great choice of fish for a mixed-or single-type aquarium. The Hong Kong climate means that water-heating is expensive.

The disadvantage of investing in anything more than a small aerated tank for goldfish is that time, care, and cleanliness are essential for success. Feeding and cleaning are continuous chores, which can be problems during holidays. The loss of a whole tank of expensive saltwater fish from disease or neglect can break one's heart — and pocketbook.

Art

All types of art can be found in Hong Kong. If you are interested in Chinese art, visit the Hong Kong Museum of Art in the Cultural Centre or the two university museums before rushing in headlong. Knowing some of the history will make browsing much more rewarding.

Chinese scrolls and paintings can be found hidden away in Cat Street and Hollywood Road. A walk in this area will reveal several galleries and antique dealers with small and not so small collections.

At the other end of the spectrum are the gaudy oil paintings churned out for tourists — sometimes painted on velvet. Nathan Road and adjacent roads are a good source for this particular style.

Galleries along Wyndham Street often exhibit Western-style art and there are some fine collections of prints and old maps around. Check the *TV and Entertainment Times* for details on exhibitions.

Baby items

As mentioned in Chapter 2, baby clothes come in basically two types: cheap and very expensive. Clothes found in markets can be extremely useful — colorful towelling or 100 percent cotton trousers for newborns upwards for about $7 a pair; vests, underwear and t-shirts for $5 upwards — and they last very well. But they're not exactly *haute couture*, and for that reason, you may want to splash out at one of the many designer stores once in a while.

At the reasonable end of the designer market are *Tots Trading, Toys "R" Us* and *Mothercare*. At the top end are *Ba Ba, Lane Crawford, Benneton* and *Croco Kids*.

Apart from clothes, there is baby equipment to think about. For one-stop shopping, try **Wing On**. They have cribs, high chairs, car seats, strollers, walkers, baths, bedding, pottys, mosquito nets and most other things. Mothercare do too. **Chicco** in Daimaru and some other department stores, have a good collection of Italian equipment and Toys "R" Us stock everything 10 times over! If you have time, it is wise to shop around: baby baths, for example, are available in any local street market for a fraction of the cost of, say, one from Mothercare. Secondhand equipment is also available; check supermarket notice boards, *Dollarsaver* or the *Sunday Post* classified ads. By the way, locally made cribs are tiny. For American sizes, go to Toys "R" Us. Maclaren strollers are available at Tots Trading.

For day to day things such as disposable diapers, wipes, lotions, formula, bottles, baby foods, sterilizing tablets etc, go to Watson's, Mannings or any supermarket.

Bamboo and rattan

Here in Hong Kong bamboo and rattan offer a stylish and inexpensive alternative to traditional Western furniture. They can be found in many stores in Hong Kong, particularly along Queen's Road East. These stores all have books that feature photos of a broad range of furniture items. The customer simply picks the style and the color he or she likes, and the store will produce the furniture to those specifications. Stores also have a supply of upholstery fabrics, or customers can bring in their own from one of the many fabric shops in Hong Kong. It might also be worth looking at hardware stores that sell bamboo poles in different diameters and lengths. The imaginative do-it-yourselfer will find these and other manufactured bamboo items a delight to use in decorating the home. Try the small shops on Des Voeux Road and Jervois Street to see the range of material available.

For a variety of bamboo beach mats, Chinese bed mats, and floor mats, try the Chinese bedding stores. Bamboo Chinese pillows may not seem very comfortable, but they can be made into bed lamps with a little ingenuity!

151

Bedding

China Products, China Merchandise and **Yue Hw**a are definitely the best places to buy bedding. Cotton sheets, fitted or flat, pillowcases, bedcovers (limited choice), quilts with silk wadding, duvets — from polyester to goose down — and duvet covers are all available here. Prices are very reasonable. For more choice in bedcovers, try **Design Selection**, or any department store. Department stores also carry a wider choice in sheets if China Products' rather conservative line is not to your taste. Towels are also a good buy in the Chinese department stores.

Bicycles

Children's bicycles and tricycles can be found in toy stores and department stores — if you are lucky enough to have a safe area away from traffic where they can be ridden. Bicycles, however, are not used to the extent that they are in, say, Holland or Beijing. Hong Kong terrain and traffic do not permit this. You can find bicycles at competitive prices in shops along Wood Road in Wanchai. Some shops in remoter areas in the New Territories such as Tai Po and Sai Kung do rent out bicycles by the hour, mainly to youngsters, who ride them precariously. Bicycles can also be rented on Cheung Chau Island.

Birds and cages

Apartments are not the best places in which to keep birds, but balconies and verandahs have many a cage. Westerners prefer the usual canaries, budgerigars, parakeets, and cockatoos, but the Chinese custom is to have one of the exquisite though very small birds which sing delightfully. There is a wide selection of bird cages in Hong Kong, from imported and expensive types to locally made wire cages and charming wooden cages for smaller birds. Enthusiasts will enjoy the way owners take their birds 'for walks' to special Chinese teahouses, or hang the cages on trees, or carry them around with specially fitted cloth covers. Birdseed and all equipment for the cages is readily available, and there are special lanes or alleys in Wanchai, Western, and Kowloon where birds, cages and equipment are sold. Even the porcelain feeding pots and seed holders can be collectors' items in their own right and may be antique and expensive.

Books and magazines

Hong Kong has many stores for Chinese books and textbooks, and a smaller number for Western-language material. Six of the major bookstores are: **Hong Kong Book Centre, Kelly & Walsh, South China Morning Post Bookshops, Swindon & Co.,** the **Times Book Centre** and **Bookazine**. As its name suggests, Bookazine sells a wide variety of magazines as well as books. Specialist bookstores include **Wanderlust**, for travel books, **Rainbow Books** for children's titles and **The Professional Bookshop** for business and law books. Most stores have more than one outlet, check the telephone directory for details.

Limited titles — of books and magazines — are also available in Watson's, Mannings and most hotels.

Prices charged in Hong Kong bear little resemblance to the cover price. Most bookshops use an extremely inflated exchange rate making books and magazines very expensive. Wanderlust uses the daily exchange rate plus 15 percent so, depending on the currency and the economic climate, you can get some good deals there. **The China Fleet Club** has an amazing collection of American magazines and a fairly good selection of books, which they sell at the straight exchange rate of $7.80 (or thereabouts). This makes them the cheapest in town — but you need a pass to gain access to the club. (For this, you either need to be a member of the armed forces or of a private club which offers China Fleet Club passes to their members. Many clubs do. Chances are that you can get one — or that you know someone who will lend you one. It's worth finding out as the club, which operates like a PX, is an excellent shopping center. (Members of the American Chamber of Commerce receive passes.)

Cameras

It is difficult to stay in Hong Kong for any length of time and not be tempted to buy a new camera. There are numerous dealers and possibly the widest, most up-to-date range in the world. Think carefully about what you want before venturing into a shop, as you may be overwhelmed by the choice and end up being persuaded to buy something you really don't need or want.

For helpful, reliable service, go somewhere like **Photo Scientific** in Stanley Street or **Kinefoto** in Pottinger Street. You may pay a little bit more than in Nathan Road but at least you will receive accurate information from people willing to spend time with you. Nathan Road is notorious for its rude shopkeepers .

Again (see "*Books*"), the China Fleet Club is a good place to go. If you want a video camera, for example, they will be familiar with makes which can easily be used in the States as they deal with American servicemen all the time.

If you do go to Nathan Road, be on your guard for the standard rip-off attempts. Make sure your camera comes with a worldwide guarantee — and check the numbers correspond — (sometimes secondhand cameras are repackaged and sold as new). Also make sure you get all the parts you asked for — for the price you agreed. Sometimes, they will claim the price does not include the lens (the lens, by the way, should have its own worldwide guarantee). Of course not all Nathan Road shopkeepers are like this, and in a sense, it is unfair to put you off in order to avoid the unscrupulous few. But it is a fact of Hong Kong life, and you should be aware of it.

Carpentry and interior decorating

Before furniture stores became common, it was difficult — in fact, almost impossible 20 years ago — to buy ready-made furniture. Carpenters were then in even greater demand for making furniture ranging from blackwood and rosewood items to ordinary kitchen cupboards. Times have changed, but local carpenters are still in great demand for built-in bedroom or kitchen furniture, for instance, and for repairs of all sorts. Friends and neighbors can probably give you the name of a reliable carpenter.

If it's a home decorator you're looking for, one of the easiest places to find one is in your own building. It's very likely your building manager knows which apartments are or have been renovated, and who is doing the work. And, neighbors willing, you can easily inspect the man's work and decide for yourself. In addition, a few general handyman companies now advertise a wide range of services; but hiring a specialist is probably more effective. Have a look in *Dollarsaver* for some names. Explain (or, better, draw) very clearly what you want. Procedures can vary from a few measurements noted on a slip of paper to a full-scale quotation, and the standard of work can be very high if you are patient, supervise the work, and correct any misunderstandings. There is, however, such a demand for small contractors to fit out new shops that persuading someone to do a small job in your flat can be difficult.

Carpets and rugs

Many flats have wooden parquet floors made of beautiful teak blocks. These were a noisy, if cool, choice before air conditioning became common. The other problem with a beautiful polished wooden floor is to keep it polished and beautiful hard work, particularly in summer. Carpets and rugs are a good investment in Hong Kong. Wall-to-wall carpeting is widely available in all grades of quality and price, and you can have it fitted professionally by the store or do it yourself.

Hong Kong carpets are world - renowned and adorn many a palace, hotel, office, or home in countries far away. They are made of imported wool, and factories such as that of Tai Ping Carpets (which also has a showroom in Hutchison House) can make almost any style to order — in any size, wall to wall, with smooth or sculptured designs. These carpets, and the equally beautiful wool and silk carpets imported from China, can last a lifetime but are very expensive, so choose carefully. A gorgeous floral pattern or Oriental design may look just right in a Hong Kong setting, but a one-color carpet might be easier to live with in the long run. Chinese Arts and Crafts and Hong Kong Oriental Rug Company always have a good selection from which to choose.

'Persian' rugs are very popular in Hong Kong, and sellers will sometimes turn up unexpectedly at your door, laden with a tempting selection that can be hard to resist. The knowledgeable expert, however, would probably not buy in this way. There are several shops that specialize in these lovely carpets. In addition, there are frequent sales of such carpets in Lammert Brothers auctions that you might find useful, especially if you know how to distinguish quality.

For balconies, verandahs, roof areas, kitchens, and dens, indoor-outdoor carpets and carpet squares can be used to make effective transformations. Most shops selling curtain material and blinds also deal in carpets.

For cleaning your carpet, there are a number of firms in Hong Kong. Peking Carpet Expert Services has been around for a long time, but many others are now listed in the Yellow Pages.

Cars

As mentioned in the 'Transportation' chapter, it is an expensive matter to import, license, and run a car in Hong Kong today. Whether recent increases in all costs, from initial price and registration to car parking charges, will reduce the number of cars has yet to be determined. Legislation requiring government testing of old cars may also affect the prices of secondhand cars.

If you have the money and a car park, there is no shortage of dealers offering new cars from almost every country. Two and three year installment plans are offered, during which full comprehensive insurance is required. Air conditioning is now generally fitted on new cars and taxis.

Secondhand cars are usually advertised in newspapers. Ownership transfer forms must be filled out for the Licensing Office, and this is important if you are to avoid claims for parking fees and police summonses caused by the previous owner. Such claims should also be cleared at the Licensing Office.

If the mileage recorded on the odometer of a second-hand car seems suspicious, and if you cannot judge the car's condition, or if it is nearing the time for a test, you can pay for the agent of that make to give you a report. The flourishing Hong Kong Automobile Association will also do this for a reasonable fee.

Children's needs

For baby items, see *"Baby Need*s". For older children, basic clothes like jeans and t-shirts are everywhere. As are running shoes, jackets and underwear. Harder to find, are girls skirts and dresses — unless you like frills. There seems to be a tendency towards "cuteness" in Hong Kong which not every child either likes, or suits. American, British and European shoes are available but are very pricey. Local shoes don't last as long and are not as good as Western makes. Having said that, **Lily Shoes** in Causeway Bay make very good, leather school-type shoes.

Children's furniture is available at **Ikea** and **Toys "R" Us** as well as numerous custom-built furniture shops along Hennessy Road.

Sporting equipment such as skateboards, footballs, bicycles and roller skates are all at Toys "R" Us as well as other, specialist sports shops. Check with the Community Advice Bureau or ask at your child's school if there is something you cannot find.

Finally, if you prefer not to spend all your money on new equipment for your baby or toddler, there are a number of secondhand shops in the city where you can find good bargains. The Community Advice Bureau is a reliable source for names.

Chinese medicines

You probably will not want or need to try Chinese medicines, and it is not wise to experiment without some knowledge of what you (or they!) are doing. However, the Chinese medicine shops are widely patronized here by Chinese residents and are definitely worth seeing, even if you don't buy anything, Ginseng, usually Korean or American varieties, is available in various forms and rather expensive. Ginseng was the first item of trade imported to China from America and the state of Wisconsin has an active business with Hong Kong. Chinese department stores also sell various Chinese medicines from China. Tiger Balm is popular with some Westerners — rather like a very strong form of Vicks Vapo-rub.

Chinese tea

In a hot climate such as Hong Kong's, tea drinking really has much to recommend it. You may be familiar with some forms of Chinese tea, but Hong Kong truly has a remarkable selection, in tins, packets, cakes, pewter containers, and now even tea bags. Chinese department stores and some special shops on Queen's Road beyond Central Market and in many other areas sell not only teas but also tea bowls, small teacups, and, of course, tea caddies and teapots. There is a rich history and mystique behind it all. Try experimenting with various strengths of Chinese tea. If children like it, hot or cold, so much the better, because it is a much better thirst quencher than any of the canned and sweet drinks that even the youngest children drink nowadays.

Chinese tea may also be appropriate as a gift to friends abroad. Most Chinese restaurants will bring you Chinese tea immediately, often in glass tumblers. Others, such as Chinese vegetarian restaurants, will ask you what particular kind of Chinese tea you would like. Tea replaces water in these cases and is offered without charge.

Chan Chun Lan Tea Co Ltd is one of several stores that carry a wide range of teas and will pack and mail tea containers abroad.

Clothing

In recent years, Hong Kong has become more prosperous and, hence, more fashion - conscious. The number of new boutiques in Central Hong Kong and in the shopping arcades in Kowloon are one sign of this. As daring and colorful as the fashion can be, the business world nevertheless still tends to demand rather formal wear for male executives. Women can be more casual in sleeveless dresses and whatever is in fashion. There are some restaurants and clubs that still demand formal attire at lunch and dinner, even on hot summer days and evenings; though there has been a relaxation in recent years.

The Hong Kong winter is very mild, with no frost or snow, and it is also the dry season so it is easy to bring or buy suitable medium-weight clothing.

The summer, with its average daily temperature of 82 F and its warm evenings, can be very tiring during the five months of May through September, as the relative humidity is often in the 90's and makes the temperature simply unbearable. To be smart, cool and fashionable in such conditions is even more of a problem. However, the number of (air-conditioned!) department stores, boutiques, and shopping arcades filled with everything from handbags and *haute couture* to swimwear and Italian shoes means that everything is available — at a price. If you wear an unusual or especially large size, you may have difficulty with some items such as shoes or bras. Hong Kong still has its famous short-time tailors for men and women, and shoes, bags, jewelry are often made to order.

Although Hong Kong exports so much beautiful and fashionable clothing, not all of it is actually available here, as manufacturers concentrate on the export market and try to avoid local copying and competition. Locally made clothing that does come on the Hong Kong market, however, is attractive in price, quality and design.

Apart from the department stores, boutiques and brand-name shops like Giordano, Benneton and Crocodile, there are many stylish bargains to be had in the lanes and factory outlet shops. In the latter, you will often find clothes made for famous Western companies such as Banana Republic, The Gap and Britain's C&A. Stock is very erratic though — one day they will have nothing, and another day, you will be spoilt for choice so it's always a good idea to monitor your favorite stores closely.

Coffee

If you prefer something other than instant coffee, you can find beans and ground coffee in most supermarkets. Some supermarkets and delicatessens offer freshly ground coffee. **Tsit Wing Coffee Co** in Queen Victoria Street has all kinds of beans from Columbian to Blue Mountain at unbeatable prices. Tsit Wing also has small outlets in Admiralty and Central MTR stations.

Computers

Most brands of computers are available in Hong Kong, as is software. Though there are good buys possible with the hardware, the software is much more expensive than overseas.

You've no doubt heard of the days of the copycat computers. The Hong Kong government takes a dim view of infringement of trade mark or copyright and there are regular crackdowns. However, there is a lively market in so-called 'compatibles'. There are three major computer equipment centers — Silvercord on Canton Road in Kowloon, Golden Center on Nathan Road in Shamshuipo and the Hong Kong Computer Center on Lockhart Road in Wanchai.

Curtains and blinds

When air-conditioning was unknown and houses in 'colonial' style had open verandahs, the bamboo and rattan blind was ideal as a sunshield and for ventilation. Those traditional uses persist and some decorators use them indoors in place of venetian blinds or curtains. There is a selection of woven or tied types with thick or thin strips, and it is possible to have them made to fit the window or space available, with or without strings and pulleys to adjust them. Most rattan furniture shops will make them to order. There are specialist shops all along Queen's Road East.

On the other hand, the use of curtains is widespread throughout Hong Kong. There are many curtain stores in town. Take a look along Queen's Road East, or try one of the small curtain shops near the Lee Gardens Hotel, in Causeway Bay. You will probably want to line your curtains as the Hong Kong sun can be intense and thus fade colors quickly.

Dogs, cats, and other pets

Following a rabies scare about five years ago, the number of dogs has decreased, particularly strays and mangey, uncared - for animals in the New Territories. Most reputable pet shops keep their animals in well-constructed display pens, and even the 'worst' of a litter can look very appealing. However, these specimens are not always the best pedigrees, nor are they always in the best of physical health. For a good animal, it is better to consult the Hong Kong Kennel Club or a reliable veterinarian. Pet shops, however, do have a useful range of medicines, foods, shampoo, combs, etc, as do several supermarkets. A dog in Hong Kong ought to be protected by a flea collar.

Ads regularly appear in the newspaper for pets and the notice boards in the supermarkets usually have someone wanting to give away extra kittens or place a child's pet due to relocation. The Royal Society for the Prevention of Cruelty to Animals (RSPCA) is another place to ask and both inexpensive and important to join if you have a pet.

You should take note that your dog must have a license, which is issued at the time of the innoculation for rabies (required every three years). It is against the law *not* to license your dog.

Note: You cannot bring your pets into Hong Kong without them serving a quarantine of three to six months depending upon country of origin.

Electricians and plumbers

Unless you're a do-it-yourselfer, there can be various crises such as blocked drains and toilets, electrical wiring to alter or renew, burned-out sockets on toasters or kettles, leaking taps, and broken windows that demand the work of a professional. Locks and keys are another common problem. A few firms advertise 'complete' repair and maintenance. As in the case of a home decorator, your building manager might know somebody who could do a good job, and if you aren't sure, you can probably inspect their work right in your building.

Fabric

One of Hong Kong's best-known lanes was 'Cloth Alley' where any kind of fabric could be bought. The choice was enormous and the prices very reasonable — if you bargained. In 1989, the shopkeepers were all given notice to quit as the two buildings which formed the alleyway were due to be demolished. Happily, this coincided with the uproar surrounding plans to demolish Western Market, one of Hong Kong's oldest and, architecturally more interesting, buildings. Why not renovate Western Market, make it a 'craft market' and move 'Cloth Alley' inside?

So, billed as "Hong Kong's Covent Garden", the market opened in late 1991 and many, though not all, the 'Cloth Alley' shopkeepers moved in. The variety is still there, though prices have crept up a little.

Fans

Hand-held fans are readily available and are made of anything, from bamboo to camphorwood or ivory. While they were widely used before the appearance of air conditioning they are seldom used now, though they do make very good gifts. Another item that has made something of a come-back is the old-style ceiling fan with the long wooden blades. They are much more efficient than modern designs and can be a very practical alternative, or supplement, to expensive air conditioning if you have the room height for one. Watch the *Dollarsaver* and *Kowloon Advertiser* shopping guides and classified ads for these.

Fax machines

Over the past five years, fax machines have become an indispensable piece of office equipment the world over. In Hong Kong, things have moved on a step with personal fax machines becoming commonplace.

Like cameras, the fax market is overwhelming so it is best to do some research before plunging in. Some questions you need to answer are: do you want a phone, fax and answer machine in one unit? do you want to be able to transmit artwork of any kind? do you want two separate numbers for fax and phone or can they share a number? Do you need a repeat dial function? abbreviated dialing? and so on.

Hong Kong Telecom have a service called *Faxline* 2 where, for a small sum ($28 per month), they will install your phone and fax on the same line — but will give you two ringing tones and two numbers. This saves you the cost of installing a separate fax line ($600). Check with Telecom before buying a machine as some older models don't have the functions needed to share a line.

Flowers

If you have a garden in Hong Kong and also have the time (or someone else) to look after it, consider yourself extremely lucky. The most likely arrangement you will see here is a verandah, entrance, rooftop, or interior of a flat used for the display of plants. But what an abundance you'll find. The Chinese people have a great love of flowers, and even in the smallest flat or balcony there is likely to be a green potted shrub, flowering plant, or miniature tree garden arrangement, some of which are very valuable.

Festivals in Hong Kong also demand flowers, the main occasion being Chinese New Year, when the special markets abound with peach blossom branches, flowering plum, miniature potted orange trees (*gum gwat*), willow stems, and the delightful 'hanging-bell flowers' (*diu-jung fa*). The markets also have

161

poinsettias (which first appear around Christmas), chrysanthemums, tulips, gladioli, narcissus bulbs, and a massive display of many other flowers and plants. Prices are high, but no Chinese household's New Year celebration is complete without a vase of flowers and maybe some peach blossoms and an orange tree.

At all times of the year, however, there is a wide choice of beautiful flowers and plants, some grown in nurseries on the Island and in the New Territories, and other countries. Tulips, chrysanthemums, gladioli, orchids, roses, and other more exotic cut flowers are widely available at street stalls, markets, flower shops, and nurseries. Flower shops in the hotels and commercial building arcades will also arrange to have 'Interflora' orders delivered for you anywhere in the world for gifts and special occasions.

You will probably soon locate a flower stall or nursery near your home that you like. Some will supply plants on a regular basis and will tend or re-pot larger shrubs or potted plants when necessary. Many plants get very pot - bound if not looked after, and the soil needs renewing. It can be a tiring and messy job to re-pot them on a balcony or roof unless you are an enthusiast.

It is probably also worth visiting flower stalls and nurseries away from your home area, though you will be tempted to come away with a car full of plants. These nurseries vary somewhat in price, stock, and helpfulness. They are listed under 'Florists-Retail' in the Yellow Pages (about 500 entries); those include nurseries that deal mainly in plants and trees.

Flower stalls in Central District are located on D'Aguilar Street just above Wellington Street, Wyndham Street and on Garden Road near St John's Building. Others are at the corner of Repulse Bay Road on South Bay Close and in Stanley Market. There are nurseries on Shouson Hill Road, Pokfulam Road opposite Wah Fu Estate, and on Mount Davis Road. In December, these and many other shops and stalls have Christmas trees if you want the real thing rather than plastic. Beginning around the first of November, you can also find advertisements for Christmas trees in the local papers.

Most nurseries can supply heavy soil for pots, but you can probably find a good selection of potting mixtures, plant foods, seeds, and equipment from certain department stores and flower shops in the arcades. Both large and small gardening tools, locally made and imported, are also available. **The Anglo-Chinese Trading Company**, on D'Aguilar Street above Wellington, is a reliable source for seeds and flower bulbs.

The Agriculture and Fisheries Department also has government nurseries that grow large numbers of trees, shrubs and flowering plants for public gardens and tree planting. Seedlings and young trees can be purchased there, too, if you phone in advance to visit the nurseries and then carry away what you select.

Food specialty shops

It is often said that in Hong Kong everything is available — at a price. This is especially true when it comes to gourmet and specialty foods.

Several hotels have bakeries and delicatessens; two of the best are in the Holiday Inn hotels. The Mandarin also has a very good bakery as does the Furama Kempinski. The Park Lane in Causeway Bay discounts its daily breads and sweets by 5% from 5-6pm nightly . But when it comes to stocking more than two or three items, there are really only a couple of places: **Oliver's Delicatessen** (Prince's Building) and **Seibu's** food hall (Pacific Place Mall). Here you can get good selections of cold meats (especially salami and other sausage), cheeses, spices, fresh herbs, cookies and fresh bread. Not to mention a hundred other things.

Oliver's also stocks a wide variety of wines and 'handmade' chocolates. **See's Candies** (basement of Landmark Building) also specialize in chocolates. Seibu has a limited selection of frozen kosher dinners, while **Beverly Hills Deli** (primarily a restaurant) in Lan Kwai Fong also stocks kosher meals and foodstuffs.

USA & Co in Duddell Street, has an amazing collection of American junk food. Just the place to go if you're feeling homesick. They also have a fine collection of American wines.

Lorence & Company are wholesalers specializing in Italian foods and **Haagen Dazs** just has wonderful ice cream and ice cream cakes. Special birthday/anniversary cakes can be ordered. Indian spices, basmati rice and other foodstuffs are available in Canal Road in Causeway Bay or Chungking Mansions in Tsim Sha Tsui. Most of the Japanese department stores have a good variety of Japanese foods — including freshly made *sashimi*. **Daimaru** probably has the best selection.

Health food shops are few and far between. There's **Eden's** in Prince's Building and several branches of **Watson's** have a health food section. Some supermarkets sell a few odd things such as herb tea and 'healthy' cereals. Oliver's sell unsweetened soy milk.

Furniture and furnishings

All you ever want to know about furniture and furnishings is probably in the *Hong Kong Shopping Guide to Home Furnishings* which was published in 1991. The book contains information on all kinds of shops and services available in Hong Kong.

Basically, one of your first decisions is the level of involvement you want from others. Do you want an interior decorator to come in and do everything for you? What kind of budget do you have? Do you want to do it all yourself? Are you expected to use your home to entertain your or your spouse's clients? Once you have thought it through, you can begin to look around for what you want.

Almost any kind of look can be achieved as almost every style of furniture and furnishing are available. Shops along Lockhart Road sell marble by the meter, there are several Italian, Scandinavian, English and American furniture shops. If you're on a tight budget, have a look in Queen's Road East at all the bamboo and rattan furniture which can be made to measure in a matter of days. Then, of course, there's the traditional Chinese blackwood and rosewood.

For cushions, cushion covers, and curtains, shops along Queen's Road East or near Lee Gardens Hotel will make them up for you. They also sell fabric though, for a wider choice, go to the newly re-vamped Western Market. **Design Selection** in Wyndham Street have ready-made cushions and cushion covers, bedspreads and rugs made mostly with beautiful fabrics from India. Wellington Street between D'Aguilar and Lyndhurst Terrace has about a half dozen upscale fabric shops for curtains and upholstery.

For secondhand furniture, look in the newspaper or *Dollarsaver* for 'expat sales'. The Sunday 'Trading Post', in the classified section of the *Sunday Post*, is also a good place to look. Also on Sunday, Radio 3 have a buy and sell phone-in to which it is worth listening.

Gold

There are so many shops and jewelers selling gold in Hong Kong that some understanding of it is necessary to cut through the confusion. Anyone investing in gold ought to first have studied the matter carefully. It can be bought by weight: ounces, kilograms, or Chinese taels and leung. It can be of 24-karat purity or mixed with other metals, as in most jewelry. It can be bought in large or very small weights. It can be bought through some banks as a gold account, which is merely a paper record. It does not earn interest, and it may go down in value as well as up. Gold in jewelry is not pure and is decorative rather than for investment. Chinese gold is still mainly traded in taels and is 24 karats, fairly soft, and very yellow in color. It is still regarded as a traditional investment in Hong Kong, one of the world's biggest markets. Jewelers also carry a large stock of chains, rings, bracelets, gold bars, and other ornaments.

Hairdressers and barbers

There are many hairdressers and barbers throughout Hong Kong. Most expatriates seem to find a hairdresser quite near home where they can go whenever a quick cut, set, shampoo, or whatever is needed. The alternative is usually a recommendation from friends or a visit to one of the shops in the leading hotels or shopping arcades, where there is no language problem. Prices are usually shown in the window for all different services — haircut, shampoo, manicure, pedicure, waving, tinting, etc. At one time there was a predominance of Shanghainese barbers, many of whom came to Hong Kong in the 1940s and 1950s. Now there is the choice between expatriate hairdressers, young Hong Kong Chinese trained abroad, and the more traditional shops. You occasionally also see small open stores on the street, where the traditional barbers with simple equipment ply their trade and old Chinese women use twisted threads to remove facial hair (and give a snarl to any would-be spectators). The Yellow Pages list hairdressers under 'Barbers' and 'Beauty Salons', though many of the latter are actually for men.

Hardware

There are a lot of hardware shops that sell a surprisingly wide variety of items: tools, brass, screws, hinges, nails, drills, and much more. It's a do-it-yourselfer's paradise. They tend to be clustered in areas like Wellington Street in Central, Shanghai Street in Kowloon and Lockhart Road in Wanchai . The above areas also sell paints, brushes, varnishes, and lacquers. Department stores such as **Wing On** and **Sincere** also have an excellent selection of tools and hardware.

Housewares

The cheapest and probably most plentiful sources for kitchen items, pots and pans, plastic ware, and cleaning equipment are the many small Chinese provision stores, found everywhere. Supermarkets stock most essentials, and department stores such as Wing On, Lane Crawford, USA & Company, Sincere, Tyeb, Daimaru, Sogo, Mitsukoshi, and Matsuzakaya also have many items as well, such as kitchen knives, thermos flasks, and crockery — all at very competitive prices.

Jade

Hong Kong is one of the world's best places to buy jade, though it is all imported from Burma, China, Australia, and Taiwan. There is 'old' jade and 'new' jade, and it comes in many colors — white, red, lavender, brown, black — though jade is mostly thought of as being green. The exquisite imperial or kingfisher jade is jadeite from Burma, very expensive and very precious. The clarity of the emerald green color greatly affects the price. The nephrite, found in China, accounts for most of the other colors.

The color of some jade can be imitated or enhanced with dye, and so unless you are an expert or can obtain reliable advice, there are obvious dangers in buying jade. Experience comes from seeing and handling as much jade as possible, and in any case, an expensive item should never be purchased until you have learned something about this varied and beautiful stone. The jade merchant who buys jade at an auction in Burma has to take a chance and buy a whole rock before it is cut open to reveal how much jade it contains. But when you buy jade jewelry or ornaments, don't take any chances.

Jewelry and antique shops in every area provide the opportunity to see and appraise a beautiful variety of rings, necklaces, bangles, and pendants. The greatest concentration of jade shops is in the **Jade Market**. Some 400 stalls display their wares daily between 10 am and 3:30 pm under the Gascoigne Road Flyover, between Kansu and Battery Streets, in the Yaumatei section of Kowloon. The Hong Kong Tourist Association has an excellent Fact Sheet on this subject.

Jewelry

The number of jewelry shops in Hong Kong is one of the first things that any new arrival notices in almost any shopping area, though many of the shops are located in the hotels, in Tsimshatsui, and in shopping arcades so that they are highly visible and convenient for tourists. The absence of customs duties makes jewelry cheaper here than in other parts of the world. Prices for fine craftsmanship, though increased in recent years, are still reasonable. Any precious stone can be bought and set in any design, and there are many fine local designers. Repairs and new settings can be done. Hong Kong is also one of the world's centers for diamond jewelry and investment in quality stones.

Keys

Its relatively low crime rate to the contrary, Hong Kong seems to have an obsession with locks, keys, safes, and security in general. Everything is available, from Chubb safes to a simple kitchen door lock. When you lock yourself out or when spare keys are needed, there are many keymakers and locksmiths with street stalls. Some new stores have also installed key-cutting facilities. Pedder Lane and neighboring alleys in Central all have a choice of several.

Lighting and lampshades

There are all kinds of lighting shops in Hong Kong from the traditional table lamp with custom-made silk shade to the ultra modern spotlights and chrome ceiling lights to old, cut-glass chandeliers. Imported fixtures tend to be expensive but locally made lamps and lampshades are a bargain — and they are very well made. Shops such as **Henry Lampshades** and **Hong Kong & Shanghai Lampshades** sell porcelain and bronze lamps and will make the shades for you. **Hop Shing Loong** in Morrison Hill Road probably has the best selection of imported ceiling, wall and outdoor lights. Places like **Paul Tsui Enterprises** and **Soong Arts & Lamps** will make your favorite vase or porcelain pot into a lamp, complete with shade. They also have a wide variety of antique vases, which they will make into lamps.

Linens

Department stores keep all the usual items such as sheets, towels, tablecloths, tea towels, and handkerchiefs. Check sizes carefully; if necessary, sheets can be made to order. The embroidered table-cloths, placemats, and handkerchiefs with initials come in sets or separately and are mostly handworked in China on Irish linen, Swiss cotton, or polyester fabrics. They are beautifully made and make excellent presents for friends abroad, and are cheaper than in most other parts of the world. Some places to try are **Chinese Arts & Crafts** and other mainland Chinese owned department stores, **Oriental Handiwork Company Ltd**, and the **Swatow Drawn Work Co Ltd**. You can also buy imported canvas for all types of needlepoint and petit - point.

Luggage

If you have just arrived in Hong Kong, luggage may not be your first priority, but as a travel and tourist center this city does offer a wide range. Leather, fabric, fiberglass, canvas, plastic — you name it. All the famous brands are here from Samsonite to Mandarina Duck. Many brands are copied and like "compatible" computers, sold in Central's lanes (Li Yuen Streets East & West) under their own brand names for a fraction of the price. Some original designs are also available in the lanes and are very good value indeed. Shops selling suitcases usually also sell a wide variety of handbags, purses and wallets.

Mattresses

Mattresses of all kinds can be bought here. Hong Kong makes one popular brand, Airland, and those at the top of the range are very good. In fact, in a recent survey conducted by the Consumer Council, Airland mattresses were considered the best value for money.

Slumberland and Spring Air from the States are available, as are top brands from Germany, Malaysia, Japan and Singapore. Most department stores sell them and will allow you to test them in the shop. This is essential. If you are going to spend a third of your life lying on it, it may as well be comfortable.

For alternative bedding, try **Eastern Fabric** in Wyndham Street, for Japanese futons. They also sell the wooden bed-bases to go with them.

Musical instruments

Pianos (European, American, Japanese, and Chinese), guitars, drums, accordions, recorders, and other Western musical instruments are all available at several shops in Hong Kong and Kowloon. So are piano tuners, who are in great demand because of the changes in humidity. Chinese musical instruments such as the *sheng, pi-pa,* and *er-lu* are also for sale. **Tsang Fook Piano Company** and **Tom Lee Piano Company** are two leading dealers, but other dealers and agents are listed in the Yellow Pages. For Chinese musical instruments, try the **Yue Hwa Chinese Products Emporium Ltd** on Nathan Road. A good place to find excellent bargains is in the classified section of the the local newspaper.

If owning a musical instrument like a piano seems like an inconvenience, but you'd still like to play in Hong Kong, it's easy enough to rent one here. Many of the music stores rent pianos and organs at a fairly reasonable rate, delivery included.

Opticians

There are numerous optical shops in Hong Kong, particularly in the Central District. the choice of frames, styles, and lenses is extensive,and both soft and hard contact lenses are easily available. All optical shops will test your eyes first, but there has been some criticism of their qualifications to do so. If you have an existing prescription, remember to bring it, if only for comparison. Prices are reasonable and many visitors take advantage of the selection and facilities. Glasses are not included in most health-care schemes. The Optical Shop, with almost 50 branches is probably the most popular shop. They offer a fast professional, courteous service.

Pearls

These are available as beautiful strands, brooches, and rings, but prices have gone up and quantity declined as Japanese coastal waters have become more polluted. Stick to well-known names such as Mikimoto, and beware of cheap imitations. Also widely available are freshwater pearls and Australian pearls. The best shop is **The Pearl Gallery.**

Picture framers

Many people bring or collect in Hong Kong pictures, maps, scrolls, or embroidery. Most framers are located on Lyndhurst Terrace, Wellington Street, and Hollywood Road. Prices are reasonable and the choice of frames, styles, and glass (plain or nonreflective) is good. The quality of material and workmanship can be chosen to match the value of the item being framed. Humidity and sunlight do most to damage framed items. Some framers, such as Galerie du Monde Ltd, can do high-quality work to museum standards. Put felt pads behind your pictures to help avoid moisture damage.

School uniforms

When you enroll your child in any of the schools in Hong Kong or Kowloon, you will be advised what uniform is required and directed to one of several tailors.

Sewing patterns

These are hard to find sewing machines shops. USA & Company stock them.

Shoes

Hong Kong makes and exports shoes and handbags, and all the famous makes are imported in a good range of sizes. Everything from rubber sandals to high fashion can be found. Many new boutiques in shopping arcades on both sides of the harbor now add to the large number of specialty shops and department stores, which all sell shoes. Buying a pair of shoes in Hong Kong isn't necessarily without its problems, though. It is sometimes very difficult to find the larger sizes in American shoes, selection is limited and the buyer just might have to have his or her shoes made. Street stall shoe repairers now have to compete with 'shoe-bars', which provide excellent while-you-wait service in many department stores and commercial buildings like Worldwide House in Central.

Sporting goods

In recent years there has been a great improvement in the availability of athletic equipment. The boom in health-consciousness is truly universal. Shoes for sports and jogging, tents and packs for hikers and campers, sport clothes, tennis racquets, golf clubs, water skis, even softball equipment all reflect the growing interest in Hong Kong in recreation and leisure activities. Nevertheless, be warned that while nearly all types of athletic equipment are found here, you might have problems finding, for example, a good softball glove or racquetball racquet. On a grander scale, however, you can buy your own Hong Kong - built junk or cruiser at a surprisingly reasonable cost.

Stationery and printing

Writing paper, stamps, pens, envelopes, and aerograms may all be needed soon after arrival. Printed visiting cards are also widely used in business and social introductions. These are often handled by your employer if a company style is followed. Small side-street printers in Central specialize in cards, and rubber stamps (here called 'chops'). Man Wa Lane off Bonham Strand in Western has many of these stalls. Che San on Pottinger Street off Queen's Road Central is a large general stationery shop, but there are many others.

Stamps and airmail letters with stamps already on them are obtainable at post offices. Airmail letters without stamps and envelopes are found at stationers and street stalls. Boxed stationery, files, office supplies, Christmas cards, diaries, art supplies, etc, can all be bought at stationers or department stores and supermarkets.

Stereo equipment and accessories

While stereo equipment is not quite the bargain it might have been 10 years ago, it is cheaper here than most any other place in the world. What is perhaps most impressive about buying equipment in Hong Kong is the spectacular range and sophistication one finds. To even list a few dealers would do injustice to the many, many others found here. However, the Nathan Road area of Kowloon and the Causeway Bay district are two places where shoppers might start to look. As with buying camera equipment, however, it does pay to know exactly what you want, what is being sold to you, and, if you anticipate moving, whether that equipment is adaptable to other situations. It is also wise to check with the main distributor or agent first for models, price guides, and availability. Whether it is a stereo set for the car or a large system for the home, you should have no difficulty finding it. These are now even very upscale boutiques for serious audiophiles such as in Prince's Building inf Central. *The Yellow Pages* have extensive lists.

As for 'software' to run on your stereo system, have no fear. Anything that's readily available back home can probably be found in Hong Kong in the format of your choice: record, cassette tape, laser disc, and compact disc. While it is true that Hong Kong offers a good range of recordings in all these formats, you will probably find it hard to locate older or more obscure recordings.

Tailors

Probably less tailoring is done in Hong Kong these days because ready-made garments of good quality are more easily available. A recommendation from friends and neighbors is usually a good start, as choosing a tailor from among some 2,500 available can be somewhat risky. You can buy your fabric separately and ask for a particular style, or the tailor will show sample books of both fabrics and styles, and go from there. Shirts, dresses, slacks, and suits can all be made quickly, although it is best to have more than one fitting and not to hurry the work. Some tailors will visit offices or homes for fittings. Styles, buttons, linings, and zippers can all be chosen.

Tobacco

With the "tobacco war" raging between tobacco companies and the two supermarket chains (making cigarettes unavailable in these outlets), government legislation banning TV commercials for tobacco products and limiting of smoking in public places -- not to mention a 100 percent tax on each packet of cigarettes -- it is surprising that anyone still smokes. But they do. American and British cigarettes are sold on the streets at magazine and newspaper stalls. Small shops selling soft drinks and candy also stock them. For pipes, pipe tobacco, cigars, rolling tobacco and cigarette papers go to **Tabaqueria Filipina** who have half a dozen outlets around town. **Davidoff** cigars are available in the Landmark, Mandarin Oriental or Peninsula hotels.

Toys

Hong Kong is renowned for its toys, and doubtless has earned its good reputation. Unfortunately, the home market is not good. There are hundreds of toy shops in Hong Kong but on close inspection, the toys are cheap and badly made, ready to fall apart after five minutes. There is little legislation in this area so don't assume a toy is safe because it is allowed on the market. Use your common sense: a tiny plastic tea set may look cute but it can be lethal to a baby who may choke on a piece. Assume that, unless otherwise stated, all paint on wooden toys is toxic. Especially those made in China.

To be safe, it is best to stick to brands you know, where safety standards are printed on the box. **Toys "R" Us** is stocked with American and European toys and is probably the best value in town. But you will get nothing out of the ordinary here, they stock (in vast quantities) what they *know* will sell and don't take chances on more esoteric things. **Crystal & Co** sell Quadro climbing frames which can be designed and re-designed as often as you like. **Jack in the Box** carries all major wooden toy lines at its Western Market outlet. There are two shops in Prince's Building and Tots Trading has good values at its Repulse Bay and Happy Valley locations. Baby toys are available at most baby stores like **Mothercare, Tots Trading** and **Chicco.**

For older children, **Hobby Horse** in Prince's Building has some interesting things. Also look in the toy departments at **Wing On** and **Daimaru.** Look in the Yellow Pages for specialty shops selling sports equipment, remote control cars etc.

TVs, VCRs and laser disc players

TVs and videocassette recorders are readily available and very popular in Hong Kong. In the last couple of years, laser disc players have become very popular too. There is a vast choice of the most up-to-date equipment — mostly from Japan — so have a good look around before you buy. Hong Kong uses the PAL system which is incompatible with the States' NTSC. If you are planning to buy equipment to use here and take to America later, you must buy multi-system equipment. If you just plan to use it here, a single system PAL unit will be fine. Another advantage of a multi-system TV and VCR is that you can play tapes sent to you from the States.

The PAL system is also used in UK, Australia, New Zealand, and India. NTSC is in North America, Canada, Japan, Taiwan and Korea and SECAM is used in France, Germany and the former USSR. Other countries in Europe are divided between PAL and SECAM.

If you do not want to buy new equipment, there is quite a good secondhand market (if you're quick off the mark, as they sell fast) or you can rent. Check the Yellow Pages for information.

There are many, many video/laser disc rental places. The big chains like KPS have the widest range and also offer a delivery/pick up service. Smaller places may have a more interesting choice though.

Wallpaper

Twenty years ago, it would have been extremely unusual to see an apartment with wallpaper on its walls — probably because, without air conditioning, it would have peeled off in a matter of weeks. Now, however, it is quite normal and there are several shops which specialize in wall coverings. Have a look at **Tat Ming Wallpaper Co** in Vicwood Plaza or **Waly Decorative Products** in Prince's Building.

These shopping hints could extend indefinitely, from Abalone to Zucchini, but that would take all the fun out of your own explorations. If you really want something not mentioned here, and don't know where to start looking for it, call the Community Advice Bureau, you'd be amazed at what they know!

American Foods and Beverages in Hong Kong

In a unique cooperative publishing effort, the American Chamber of Commerce and the US Foreign Agricultural Service have produced this directory which includes over 200 agents, importers and representatives of US exporters. About 30 broad categories of foods and beverages are covered.

In keeping with its program of combining various industry-specific directories with text chapters that offer readers an introduction to the industries in the local Hong Kong context, AmCham has included sections surveying the Hong Kong market for US agricultural commodities and guides to exporters such as profiles of "Food Retailing in Hong Kong" and "Airline Caterers and Ship Suppliers." There is also a directory of executives of hotels, clubs and restaurants in the territory.

"In per capita terms, Hong Kong's citizens consume more American foodstuffs than any other country or territory in the Far East, and their taste for things American seems to grow every year," notes AmCham's 1990 president, John Kamm, in the book's preface. American Foods & Beverages in Hong Kong explains the American presence here and gives a guide to important people in the business.

The book is available directly from AmCham and at leading bookstores in Hong Kong. Member price HK$135.00/US$24.00. Non-member price HK$165.00/US$28.00. Postage inclusive.

Chapter 12
LEISURE
ACTIVITIES

PHOTO COURTESY OF HONG KONG TOURIST ASSOCIATION

I n this edition of *Living in Hong Kong*, clubs, societies, associations, arts and sports venues, have all been updated. In addition, there is a section on children's activities. The chapter has been broadly divided into sports clubs, arts and museums, miscellaneous clubs and children's activities. Although some listings may overlap, we hope it is arranged in a logical, easy-to-find way.

Information on club activities has been omitted since meeting places and times change regularly. If you are interested in learning more about a particular club, call or write to the address given. If the telephone number has changed, call Directory Inquiries (1081) or the Community Advice Bureau (524-3444) for the latest information.

Sports clubs and associations

Sports Associations
Listed below are associations that provide venues and sometimes training, for a number of sporting activities. Call first to see if your sport is available.

Hong Kong Sportworld Assn
109 Caroline Hill Rd
Causeway Bay
895-1023

South China Athletic Assn
Caroline Hill Rd
Causeway Bay
577-6932

Hong Kong Sports Institute
Shatin, New Territories
605-1212

YMCA
Salisbury Rd, Kowloon
369-2211

Island School Sports Club
Island School
Borrett Rd, Mid-Levels
524-7135

South Island School
Nam Fung Rd
Deepwater Bay
555-9313

Hong Kong International School
23 South Bay Close
Repulse Bay
812-2305

Sports Clubs

Archery
Hong Kong Archery Assn
GPO Box 7258
Hong Kong

Backgammon
Hong Kong Backgammon Club
1811 Wing On House
71 Des Voeux Rd, Central
523-4112

Badminton
Hong Kong Badminton Assn
1002 Queen Elizabeth Stadium
18 Oi Kwan Rd, Wanchai
838-4066

Ballooning
Hong Kong Balloon and
Airship Club
18B, Block E
Wylie Court
Wylie Rd, Kowloon
385-2669

A private pilot balloon license is
necessary. The Club will advise how
to go about getting one.

B*asketball*
'Open League'
Hong Kong International School
South Bay Close, Repulse Bay
812-2305

Bowling
No specific organization. Lanes at:
South China Athletic Assn
Caroline Hill Rd
Causeway Bay
890-8980

Boxing
Hong Kong Boxing Assn
GPO Box 3370
Hong Kong

Bridge
Hong Kong Contract Bridge Assn
906 Nathan Centre
580 Nathan Rd, Kowloon
332-3232

Canoeing
Hong Kong Canoe Union
1010 Queen Elizabeth Stadium
18 Oi Kwan Rd, Wanchai
572-7008

Chess
Hong Kong Chess Federation
202 Hoi Tang Bldg
31 Queen's Rd, Central
841-8527

Cricket
Hong Kong Cricket Assn
c/o Kowloon Cricket Club
67-4141

Cycling
Hong Kong Cycling Tour Assn
121C Wong Cheung Industrial Bldg
781 Lai Chi Kok Rd
Kowloon
387-0650

Cyclist Club
1/F
267 Lai Chi Kok Rd
Kowloon
720-7788

Hong Kong Cycling Assn
1013 Queen Elizabeth Stadium
18 Oi Kwan Rd, Wanchai
573-3861

Diving
Sea Dragon Skindiving Club
GPO Box 10014
Hong Kong
574-7951

Bunns Diving Club
188 Wanchai Rd
Wanchai
891-2113

Hong Kong Underwater Club
GPO Box 4232
Hong Kong

Fencing
1004 Queen Elizabeth Stadium
18 Oi Kwan Rd, Wanchai
891-4448

Field Hockey
Hong Kong Hockey Assn
GPO Box 4982
Hong Kong

Fishing
(for license)
Water Supplies Dept
11/F Leighton Centre
Causeway Bay
890-0333

Flying
Hong Kong Aviation Club
Sung Wong Toi Rd
Kowloon
713-5171

Football (American Gridiron)
Hong Kong American Football
League
G/F, 65 Hollywood Rd, Central
547-3821

Golf
Royal Hong Kong Golf Club
Fanling
New Territories
670-1211

Royal Hong Kong Golf Club
Deepwater Bay
812-0334

Clearwater Bay Golf & Country
Club
Clearwater Bay
New Territories
719-1595

Discovery Bay Golf Club
Discovery Bay, Lantau
987-7271

Chung Shan Hot Springs Golf Club
(Guangdong, China)
c/o Hong Kong Office
504 Pedder Bldg
12 Pedder St, Central
521-0377

Gymnastics
Hong Kong Amateur Gymnastics
Assn
905 Queen Elizabeth Stadium
18 Oi Kwan Rd, Wanchai
573-4159

Handball
Hong Kong Amateur Handball Assn
1010 Queen Elizabeth Stadium
18 Oi Kwan Rd, Wanchai
574-6934

Horseback Riding
Pokfulam Public Riding School
75 Pokfulam Reservoir Rd
550-1059

Lantau Tea Gardens
Ngong Ping, Lantau
985-5718

Hong Kong Services Saddle Club
Lo Wu Camp
New Territories
091-4355

Ice Hockey
Hong Kong Ice Hockey Federation
B8, 9/F Causeway Centre,
Harbour Rd
827-5033
or c/o Shan Weir
529-5390

Ice Skating
Lai Chi Kok Amusement Park
Lai Chi Kok, Kowloon
741-4281

City Plaza
Tai Koo Shing
567-5388

Lawn Bowls
Hong Kong Lawn Bowls Assn
GPO Box 1823
Hong Kong

Mountaineering
Hong Kong Mountaineering Union
PO Box 70873
Kowloon Central PO
Kowloon

Orienteering
Hong Kong Orienteering Club
PO Box 20142
Hennessy Road PO
Hong Kong

Orienteering Assn of Hong Kong
901 Queen Elizabeth Stadium
18 Oi Kwan Rd, Wanchai
Hong Kong
891-2691

Roller Skating
Amateur Roller Skating Assn
G/F, 109 Caroline Hill Rd
Causeway Bay
895-1023

Hong Kong Sports World Assn
c/o City Plaza, Tai Koo Shing
567-0391

or c/o Telford Gardens
Kowloon
757-2211

Rowing
Hong Kong Amateur Rowing Assn
Shatin Rowing Center
27 Yuen Wo Rd, Shatin
New Territories
699-7271

Rugby
Valley Rugby Football Club
GPO Box 10279
Hong Kong

Running
Hash House Harriers
PO Box 20289
Hennessy Rd PO
761-2252

Hong Kong Distance Runners Club
GPO Box 10368
Hong Kong

Sailing
Royal Hong Kong Yacht Club
Causeway Bay
832-2817/812-0365

Hong Kong Marina
Sai Kung, New Territories
792-1436

Aberdeen Marina
Aberdeen
553-3032

Aberdeen Boat Club
Aberdeen
553-3032

Hebe Haven Yacht Club
Hebe Haven, New Territories
719-9682

Softball
International Slow-Pitch Softball
Assn
c/o Scott Jordan
1B Vienna Court
41 Conduit Rd, Mid-Levels
540-6114

Hong Kong Softball Assn
(fast-pitch)
Tin Kwong Rd, Kowloon
711-1167

Squash
Hong Kong Squash Rackets Assn
Hong Kong Squash Centre
23 Cotton Tree Drive, Central
869-0611

Several private clubs have squash
courts, see the "Private Clubs" section in the Appendices.

Swimming
Hong Kong Amateur Swimming
Assn
1003 Queen Elizabeth Stadium
18 Oi Kwan Rd, Wanchai
573-8594

Or contact the Regional or Urban
Councils for information on public
swimming pools.

Tennis
Hong Kong Tennis Centre
(17 courts)
Wong Nei Chong Gap Rd
574-9122

King's Park (6 courts)
Kowloon
385-8985

Kowloon Tsai Park (8 courts)
Kowloon City
336-7878

Tin Kwong Road (4 courts)
Kowloon
711-1532

Victoria Park (14 courts)
Causeway Bay
706-1186

Hong Kong Sports Institute
Tennis Club (15 outdoor, 2 indoor courts)
Shatin, New Territories
605-1212

Hong Kong Tennis Assn
911 Queen Elizabeth Stadium
18 Oi Kwan Rd, Wanchai
890-1132

Several private clubs also have tennis courts, check the "Private Clubs" section in the Appendices.

Walking
Hong Kong Federation of Hikers & Outdoor Activities Groups
2/F Front Portion
61 Shantung St, Kowloon

Windsurfing
Windsurfing Assn of Hong Kong
GPO Box 10833
Hong Kong
521-8480

Main centers with qualified instructors are in Stanley, Cheung Chau and Sai Kung.

Arts and museums

This section is divided into four main groups: venues for drama/musical productions and other cultural activities, clubs and associations pertaining to the arts, and museums.

Venues

City Hall
Central (at Star Ferry)
522-9928

The City Hall opened in 1962 and comprises two buildings, known as the low block and the high block. The low block contains a concert hall, theater, exhibition hall and restaurants. The high block contains an exhibition gallery, recital hall, Hong Kong's busiest marriage registry, libraries and committee rooms.

Hong Kong Academy for Performing Arts
1 Gloucester Rd, Wanchai
584-1500

Opened in the 1980s, the Academy incorporates dance, drama, music and technical arts in preparing individuals for professional careers in the arts. Also on site are three theaters, an orchestral hall and a recital hall.

Hong Kong Arts Centre
2 Harbour Rd, Wanchai
582-0200

The Arts Centre aims to promote a balanced mixture of international and local performances and exhibitions. They also run several programs and courses aimed at children. The Centre consists of the Shouson Theater, a recital hall and the Studio Theater. It also houses the Pao Sui Loong Gallery for fine arts exhibitions.

Hong Kong Coliseum
9 Cheung Wan Rd
Hunghom, Kowloon
765-9211

A large-capacity, multi-purpose indoor stadium, it is ideal for pop concerts, ice shows, sporting events and other extravaganzas.

Hong Kong Cultural Centre
10 Salisbury Rd
Tsim Sha Tsui, Kowloon
734-9009

The Cultural Centre is the latest addition to Hong Kong's skyline, its controversial architecture is hard to miss. Inside is a concert hall, two theaters, an arts library, two restaurants and outside, there is a garden. Beside the old clocktower beside Kowloon Star Ferry Terminal.

Hong Kong Museum of Art	*Hong Kong Space Museum*
10 Salisbury Rd	10 Salisbury Rd
Tsim Sha Tsui, Kowloon	Tsim Sha Tsui, Kowloon
734-2167	*734-2722*

Situated next door to the Hong Kong Cultural Centre, the Space Museum is a distinctive dome-shaped building. Inside is an exhibition hall and a space theater. Shows at the theater go on throughout the day. Call for details as shows change periodically. Shows are in Cantonese with simultaneous translation into English, Mandarin and Japanese.

Ko Shan Theater
Ko Shan Rd
Hunghom, Kowloon
334-2331

Hong Kong's first open-air theater, perfectly suited for Chinese opera, variety shows and major film screenings. It is one of the venues for the International Film Week in the spring (March - April).

Queen Elizabeth Stadium
18 Oi Kwan Rd, Wanchai
891-1727

Located in Wanchai at the western border of Happy Valley, opposite the race track, the Queen Elizabeth Stadium is a 3,500-seat, air-conditioned area used for local and international sports events and cultural programs. The World Snooker Championships, international indoor tennis and badminton competitions and other major events are often held here. The complex also houses the headquarters of several sports associations.

Town Halls and Civic Centers

In recent years it has been government policy to provide venues for various social, sporting and cultural events in more remote areas — or where the population is large enough to warrant its own facilities. To this end, several town halls and civic centers have recently opened giving each area a focal point for meetings, drama productions and other events. To date, there are nine centers: **Lut Sau Hall** in Yuen Long, **Ngau Chi Wan Civic Centre** on Clearwater Bay Road, **North District Town Hall** near Sheung Shui, **Sai Wan Ho Civic Centre** in Sai Wan, **Sha Tin Town Hall, Sheung Wan Civic Centre** in Western district, **Tai Po Civic Centre, Tsuen Wan Town Hall** and **Tuen Mun Town Hall.**

Every month the Urban Services publishes a program of upcoming events in all the above-mentioned venues. Copies are available at all URBTIX (Urban

Services Computerized Ticketing System) outlets or you can become a registered patron of URBTIX by writing to:

URBTIX Central Booking Office
Level 9, Administration Bldg
Hong Kong Cultural Centre
Tsim Sha Tsui, Kowloon

As a member, you will receive a program in the mail and can book tickets by telephone. Non-members can get tickets at the theater where the show is scheduled to take place, or at URBTIX outlets which include many of the above venues and all six Tom Lee Music Company shops.

Clubs and associations pertaining to the arts

This section is divided into i) arts-related clubs whose members meet for lectures, discussions and appreciation, ii) theater, music, dance and film groups and iii) miscellaneous arts groups.

Arts-related clubs and associations

Hong Kong Anthropological Society
c/o Dept of Anthropology
New Asia College
Chinese University of HK
New Territories

Hong Kong Art Club
1/F, 21 Bisney Rd
Pokfulam
542-3223

Fine Arts Society
University of Hong Kong
Pokfulam

Friends of the Art Gallery of the Chinese University of Hong Kong
GPO Box 9861
Hong Kong

Friends of the Cultural Centre
c/o the Cultural Centre
Tsim Sha Tsui, Kowloon
734-2819

Indian Arts Circle
GPO Box 13005
Hong Kong

Oriental Ceramic Society of Hong Kong
GPO Box 6202
Hong Kong

Royal Asiatic Society
GPO Box 3864
Hong Kong

Society for the Advancement of Chinese Folklore
c/o the Hong Kong Tourist Assn
35/F Jardine House, Central

Theater, music, dance and film clubs

Theater groups

American Community Theater
(ACT)
GPO Box 110097
Hong Kong

Chung Ying Theater Co
G/F, 10 Borrett Rd
521-6628

Fringe Club
2 Ice House St, Central
Hong Kong
521 7251

Hong Kong Players
GPO Box 8218
Hong Kong

SKADS
(Sek Kong Amateur Dramatic Society)
c/o Borneo Lines
BFPO 1

Music

Apart from the groups listed below, there are several places where music can be heard regularly. The Hong Kong Philharmonic play year-round — with a two-month summer break. Subscriptions are available, offering discounted tickets. Call 721-2030 for information. The Hong Kong Chinese Orchestra also have regular performances.

Sunday Jazz at the Excelsior Hotel's Dickens Bar has been a popular feature for many years. Combined with the excellent curry buffet, it is the ideal way to spend a rainy — or even sunny — Sunday afternoon. Jazz can also be heard in bars and restaurants in the Lan Kwai Fong area, especially at the Jazz Club (call 845 8477).

There are free lunchtime concerts at St John's Cathedral on Wednesdays throughout the year and the Fringe Club sometimes offers lunchtime recitals. The acoustics at Pacific Place make it an excellent place for ensembles and choral groups — especially over the Christmas period when choirs perform Christmas carols.

Hong Kong Folk Society
GPO Box 4370
Hong Kong
336-1795

Hong Kong Singers
GPO Box 5260
Hong Kong

Hong Kong Jazz Record Society
GPO Box 10536
Hong Kong

Hong Kong Piping Society
(bagpipes)
10/F West Bond Centre
Queensway
810-1100

Dance

Hong Kong Morris
895-4550

Union Church Reel Club
Union Church
Kennedy Rd, Mid-Levels

Jean M Wong School of Ballet
1139 Wongneichong Rd
Mid-Levels
577-2112

Discovery Bay International School
(ballet)
Discovery Bay, Lantau
987-7331 / 987-6517

Hong Kong Arts Centre (ballet)
Harbour Rd, Wanchai
582-0230

Hong Kong Academy for Perform-
ing Arts (ballet)
1 Gloucester Rd, Wanchai
584-1500

Film Clubs

Apart from the many cinemas in Hong Kong, there are a few film clubs which
show foreign-language films and films which would otherwise not make it to
Hong Kong screens.

Alliance Francaise
123 Hennessy Rd, Wanchai
527-7825

The British Council
Easey Commercial Bldg
255 Hennessy Rd, Wanchai
831-5138

The Goethe Institute
(German Cultural Center)
14/F Arts Centre
2 Harbour Rd, Wanchai
802-0088

Miscellaneous Arts Groups

Hong Kong Craft Guild
GPO Box 12837
Hong Kong

Hong Kong Flower Club
GPO Box 119991
Hong Kong
358-2365

Ikebana International
GPO Box 3029
Hong Kong

Pottery Workshop
c/o The Fringe Club

Hong Kong Artistic Orchid Assn
GPO Box 9038
Hong Kong

The Hong Kong Craft Guild publishes a monthly newsletter detailing up-coming craft workshops, seminars and other information. New members - with or without craft skills -- are always welcome.

Museums

There are several small museums in Hong Kong — each specializing in a particular collection. As well as this, there are some permanent exhibitions which are worth a look. The Hong Kong Tourist Association publish "Museums and Arts & Crafts" which gives up-to date-information and information on how to get to the various museums.

Art Gallery, Chinese University.
This gallery displays a unique carved seal collection (name stamps, not animals, called 'chops' in Hong Kong), fine Chinese paintings of Guangdong province's Lingnan School and calligraphy from the Ming period to modern times. Free admission. 695-2218

Museum of Tea Ware, Hong Kong Park
Housed in one of Hong Kong's oldest colonial-style buildings, Flagstaff House, the museum has about 500 pieces of tea ware, mainly of Chinese origin. The museum is situated in Hong Kong Park, formerly Victoria Barracks. Closed Wednesdays. Admission free. 869-0690

Fung Pin Shan Museum, University of Hong Kong.
This museum contains Chinese art objects, mostly ceramics and bronzes. Closed Sundays, free admission. 859-2114

Hong Kong Museum of Art, Hong Kong Cultural Centre.
This splendid new museum was opened in late 1991 and houses the art collection which was once in the City Hall. The museum aims to raise the standard of art education and appreciation through the collection and display of historical and contemporary works. As well as the galleries, the museums offers guided tours, lectures and films. Closed Thursdays. Admission: Adults $10, children $5. 734-2167

Hong Kong Museum of History, Kowloon Park.
This museum has archaeological finds, ethnographic collections (eg local folk songs), historical photographs and other artefacts relating to Hong Kong's history. The museum also hosts special-interest exhibitions from overseas. Closed Fridays, free admission. 367-1124

Hong Kong Railway Museum, the old Tai Po station, Tai Po.
Interesting, small museum not only for railway buffs. Closed Tuesdays, admission free. 653-3339

Hong Kong Science Museum, Tsim Sha Tsui East, Kowloon.
Hong Kong's first 'hands-on' museum was a great success as soon as it opened in 1990. Unfortunately, enthusiastic crowds and inexperienced staff meant that many of the exhibits were broken in the first few days. Most have since been repaired or replaced. The museum is a great place for kids — if you can avoid school trips when it is very crowded. Best seen in the early evening Closed Mondays. Admission: Adults $25, children $15. 732-3232

Hong Kong Space Museum, Tsim Sha Tsui .
This dome-shaped museum is one of the largest planetaria in the world, but has no telescope. There is a Space Theater, and two exhibition halls offer various exhibitions throughout the year. Closed Tuesdays. Admission: Adults $10, children $5. 734-2722

Miscellaneous Clubs

This section lists i) special interest clubs, ii) clubs and associations with national affiliations, and iii) women's organizations.

Special interest clubs

The Hong Kong Amateur
Astronomical Society
GPO Box 2872
Hong Kong

Sky Observer's Assn
4/F, 23 Kim Shin Lane
Cheung Sha Wan, Kowloon
386-1658

The Hong Kong Archaeological Society
c/o The Hong Kong Museum of History
Block 58, Kowloon Park
Kowloon
367-1127

The Classic Car Club of Hong Kong
1208 Tai Yau Bldg
181 Johnston Rd, Wanchai
891-1886

Gemmological Assn of Hong Kong
PO Box 97711
Tsim Sha Tsui, Kowloon

Hong Kong Wine Society
c/o Hong Kong Polytechnic Library
Kowloon

Hong Kong Kennel Club
23B Stanley St, Central
523-3944

Hong Kong Cat Fanciers Society
D11 Repulse Bay Towers
119A Repulse Bay Rd
812-7140

Hong Kong Amateur Radio Transmitting Society (HARTS)
GPO Box 541
Hong Kong

Radio Assn of Hong Kong
2/F Wyndham Mansion
30 Wyndham St, Central
522-5783

Cathay Camera Club
2/F Beaconsfield House
Central
812-1657

Clubs/societies with national affiliations

Alliance Francaise
123 Hennessy Rd, Wanchai
527-7825

American Women's Assn
C7 Monticello
Kennedy Rd, mid-Levels
527-2961

American University Club
GPO Box 6452
Hong Kong
541-3372

Australian Assn
PO Box 89461
Kowloon City Post Office

British Council
3/F Easey Commercial Bldg
255 Hennessy Rd, Wanchai
831-5138

Canadian Club of Hong Kong
PO Box 1587
Hong Kong
Fax: 812-7635

Filipino Club
10 Wylie Rd
King's Park, Kowloon
388-8193

Goethe Institute
14/F Arts Centre
2 Harbour Rd, Wanchai
802-0088

Indian Assn of Hong Kong
20/F Sino Centre
582-592 Nathan Rd
Kowloon
332-0461

India Club
24 Gascoigne Rd
King's Park, Kowloon
388-8184/311-2392

Italian Cultural Society of HK
801 Hutchison House
Central
522-0033

Hong Kong Japanese Club
38/F Hennessy Centre
500 Hennessy Rd, Wanchai
577-3669

Japanese Society of HK
c/o Japanese Consulate
25/F Bank of America Tower
Central
522-1184

Jewish Recreation Club
(temporary premises)
4/F Melbourne Plaza
33 Queen's Rd, Central
801-5440

Korean Residents Assn HK
503 Korea Centre Bldg,Central
543-9387

Netherlands Assn
3A Babington House
Babington Path, mid-Levels
549-0656

Northumberland and Durham Assn
GPO Box 8503
Hong Kong

New Zealand Society of HK
GPO Box 8817
Hong Kong

Royal Society of St George
GPO Box 5506
Hong Kong

St Andrew's Society
c/o Lowe, Bingham & Matthews
22/F Prince's Bldg, Central

St David's Society
PO Box 20393
Hennessy Rd, Wanchai

St Patrick's Society of HK
GPO Box 615
Hong Kong

Spanish Society
(La Sociedad Hispanica de
Hong Kong)
GPO Box 11751
Hong Kong

Swiss Assn of HK
GPO Box 9873
Hong Kong

Women's Organizations

American Women's Assn
C7 Monticello
48 Kennedy Rd, Mid-Levels
527-2961

Financial Women's Assn
G P O Box 8474
Hong Kong
868-0262

Helena May
35 Garden Rd, Central
522-6766

*Hong Kong Assn of University
Women*
GPO Box 11708
Hong Kong

Hong Kong Council of Women
GPO Box 819
Hong Kong

*Hong Kong Assn of Business and
Professional Women*
GPO Box 1526
Hong Kong

Soroptimist Club of HK
GPO Box 6690
Hong Kong

US League of Women Voters
GPO Box 1683
Hong Kong

Women in Publishing
2C Chancery Lane, Central

Women's Corona Society
GPO Box 8151
Hong Kong

YWCA
McDonnell Rd, Mid-Levels
Hong Kong

Zonta Club of Hong Kong
GPO Box 428
Hong Kong

Volunteer Work

Employment opportunities for spouses certainly exist here. Full-time usually means a five-and-a-half day-week which leaves little time for the family. It also means you will only get between two and four weeks vacation — while your spouse can probably get away for a couple of months. Part-time work is often very badly paid, and again, terms and conditions not that favorable. For more rewarding work, you might try volunteering your services to one of the many organizations seeking help. The telephone numbers are elsewhere in this book — or can be got by calling the Community Advice Bureau (who themselves need volunteers) 524-5444.

Adventure Ship
American Chamber of Commerce
Cheshire Homes
China Coast Community Advice Bureau
Duchess of Kent Children's Hospital, Sandy Bay
Ebenezer School for the Blind
Hans Anderson Club
Helping Hand
Hong Kong Arts Center
Hong Kong Society for the Blind

Matilda Child Development Center
OXFAM
Red Cross
REHAB
Riding for the disabled
RSPCA
Samaritans
Spare a New Toy Appeal (SANTA)
St James Settlement
TREATS

Children's Activities

If you had a traditional Western upbringing, running around in the country, picking apples in the fall, driving your first car at 16, meeting friends in a coffee bar or drugstore after school and so on, your first reaction to life in Hong Kong for *your* children might be one of horror.

But don't despair, it really isn't that bad. There are plenty of things to do which your kids will love, and once settled into their new school, they will fall quickly into place.

Hong Kong is fundamentally a safe city for children. Yes, there is a drugs problem in some schools but it is confined to a minority of schoolchildren and is nowhere near as bad as in UK, Europe or the States. Your children will have to learn how to mix with several nationalities and will soon discover that it is indeed a big and interesting world outside their home country.

Facilities for children have greatly improved over the past 15 years. This is partly due to the population increase and partly a realization that children growing up in high-rise buildings with little or no access to the great outdoors, had to have purpose-built facilities. Swimming pool and sports complexes have been relentlessly expanded by the Urban Council of Hong Kong in all major built-up areas, adventure playgrounds with good, safe equipment were created, and schools and youth organizations offer all kinds of sporting and non-sporting activities. The Jockey Club — a non-profit organization which by law must plow millions of dollars of its enormous profits back into the community every year — also got in on the act and built what is the most popular leisure park for adults and children alike — Ocean Park and Water World.

What follows are three sections: i) purely leisure (non-organized activities), ii) sporting activities and iii) non-sporting activities.

Purely Leisure

Ocean Park, Middle Kingdom and Water World

On the south side of Hong Kong, near Aberdeen, is the best amusement park/ marineland/aquatic fun land in Hong Kong.

Ocean Park and Middle Kingdom

Open year-round, the Ocean Park complex consists of a marineland, amusement park and the Middle Kingdom, a walk-through museum tracing China's history through all 13 dynasties. The marineland, reached by cable car, consists of a wave cove where you can watch seals and sea lions from above or below the waterline, the Atoll Reef, filled with over 5,000 fish (including small sharks) with viewing on four underwater levels, a walk-through shark aquarium and Ocean Theater where a killer whale and several dolphins perform, as does the American Eagles professional diving team. There is also a huge walk-through aviary with beautiful parrots, flamingos and hundreds of other species in well-landscaped surrounds.

The amusement rides are included in the price of admission and include the hair-raising "Dragon", one of the world's longest and most exciting roller coaster rides with two 360 degree curls. The roller coaster is perched on the cliff edge and if you have your eyes open long enough, you will see quite a spectacular view. Other rides include `white water rafting' up and down man-made rapids and various giant swings.

Most of the activities take place on the headland — with access via cable cars. This in itself is a spectacular ride — and not for sufferers of vertigo. Alternative access is by the 'world's longest escalator'. The aviary and some of the rides are halfway down the escalator and it is tempting, after visiting these areas to carry on down to the exit. Be warned, this exit is miles from the main entrance/ exit and nowhere near Water World — if that is your next destination. If you have arranged to meet others at the main gate, or if you want to pick up the Citybus back to town, go back the way you came, on the cable car.

Prices (1991)
Adults $140
Children $70
Over 60 free

Prices include access to Middle Kingdom and unlimited rides in the amusement park. Every adult can bring two children between the ages of 6 and 11, free of charge.

There is a Citybus operating between Admiralty bus station and Ocean Park (quite difficult to get to by regular bus). You buy the Ocean Park ticket plus roundtrip bus ticket on board. Prices, adult $156, children $78.

Water World

Adjacent to Ocean Park, but with a separate entrance (and entrance fee), Water World is aquatic fun at its best. Open from April to October, the park is a popular meeting place for kids after school and during school holidays. There are things here for every level of swimming competency from super water slides, to toddler pools with swings and slides in the water. There is also a wave pool which, when in action, creates quite big waves. Kick boards and huge, inflatable rings are available inside.

Prices (1991)
Adults $60
Children $40
Season pass $250

Roundtrip Citybus ride available from Admiralty. Prices including entrance to Water World, $76 adults, $48 children

Other amusement parks are in Lai Chi Kok (see below) and Happy Dragon Recreation Park near Tai Wai KCR station in Shatin (699-7399). There is also a bike park next door to Happy Dragon and a small water park — with just two water slides and rapids — called Big Splash, at DD464 Clearwater Bay Road. Call 719-5233 for details.

Zoos, parks and country parks

At first glance, Hong Kong looks like the archetypical concrete jungle with every available square inch covered. In fact, only about 26 percent of the land is built on, the rest is open space — much of it designated as Country Park land.

Zoological and Botanical Gardens

Five minutes from the heart of Central, and just opposite the governor's house, is the Zoological and Botanical Gardens, a quiet haven away from the hustle and bustle of town. While the gardens are pleasant for a quiet walk or sandwich lunch, it is the zoo which is of most interest to children.

There are jaguars, lynx, tree kangaroos, anteaters,and porcupines but the undisputed stars of the collections are the primates: monkeys, gibbons, and tamarins. There are also over 500 species of birds — some extremely rare and which are being bred as part of an international breeding program. In fact the zoo is well-known internationally as a breeding center for various birds and animals. The rare Palawan peacock, for example, has been sent to zoos in 21 countries throughout the world.

There is also a playground for youngsters but it is in dire need of renovation and is not recommended. The best time to visit is in the morning or at dusk. In the heat of the midday sun, most of the animals retreat inside their cool, concrete houses. Admission is free.

Lai Chi Kok Zoo and Amusement Park

Located in Kowloon, this zoo does not share the good reputation of the Zoological Gardens. The amusement park, however, can be fun. There is also an ice-skating and a roller skating rink. Entrance: adults $10, children $5.

Parks

There are two kinds of park in Hong Kong: vest-pocket parks which are basically a pleasant sitting-out area with perhaps a small playground, and large, multi-purpose grounds, such as Victoria Park and Kowloon Park and Hong Kong Park.

Victoria Park, which divides Causeway Bay and North Point, has tennis and squash courts, swimming pools, basketball courts, a jogging track — and a pleasant sitting out area with a small playground. It is also the site of the Hong Kong Tennis Classic, the annual go-karting championships and the Chinese New Year flower market.

Kowloon Park is smaller and is situated on the corner of Nathan Road and Haiphong Road, just by the mosque. The Hong Kong Museum of History is on the park's grounds which also has a swimming pool, and indoor games hall for squash, badminton, basketball, table tennis, and dancing. There is a 'sculpture path' which includes works by both / local and international artists. At Chinese New Year, the park transforms into a huge flower market.

Country Parks

There are three main areas where country parks are located: the New Territories, Hong Kong and Lantau. There are several parks within each area. For those interested in walking, camping and other outdoor pursuits, the best thing to do is to purchase three maps from the Government Publications Centre: the Hong Kong Trail, the Lantau Trail and the Maclehose Trail, back them up with detailed maps of the area (the trail maps are very basic, but show where the trail goes), read up about the area in one of the many nature-style books on sale, then go off and explore.

Don't forget that even though you are never far from civilization, it is still easy to get lost. Take a torch, plenty of water, warm clothing and *tell someone where you are going*. The dry, cool season is the best time to go walking (November to January) but it is also the most dangerous as it is the season for hill fires.

The Maclehose Trail is probably the most famous as there is an annual race to complete the 100 kilometer path. Gurkha soldiers have won the race every year since it began, taking approximately 13 hours while even the fittest civilians take around 20 hours.

Sporting activities

Most schools run extra-curricular activities, summer schools and camps. For the latest details call the school and ask. (Summer schools are generally open to all children, not just those who are already enrolled.)

The YMCA and YWCA both have extensive youth programs with courses in art, computers, judo, swimming, Cantonese and lots more. One such course, run by the YMCA, is called "Cooking for Mom and Dad" and teaches children how to prepare food. Could prove very useful one day! Call for details.

Many of the sports clubs and associations listed on earlier pages also have youth teams, training sessions and such like. If you are interested in a particular sport, contact that organization and ask. A few which definitely run youth programs are: Hong Kong Fencing Assn (891-4448), Hong Kong Amateur Swimming Assn (572-8594), Hong Kong Amateur Gymnastic Assn (573-4159), HK Squash Rackets Assn (529-8558), Hong Kong Hockey Assn,

Hong Kong Rugby Football Union (HKRFU) (566-0719), Hong Kong International School Youth Sports Program (American football, basketball, cross-country, floor hockey, gymnastics, rugby, soccer, swimming, track, volleyball, badminton, bowling, squash, tennis and water polo).

The Hong Kong Sports Institute (formerly the Jubilee Centre) also runs several sports programs. The Institute is the base for most of Hong Kong's professional athletes. All the coaches are professional and the training programs are geared to competition. Summer sports programs include: trampoline, gymnastics, fencing, and tennis.

In conjunction with the Recreation and Sports Service, a territory-wide tennis coaching scheme is run during the summer months. Any player showing potential may be invited to join the Nursery Squad following the results of the 'Mini-Masters' competition. Contact the HK Tennis Assn for details.

The Outward Bound School runs 'character building' courses for adults throughout the year and during the Christmas, Easter and Summer vacations, there are courses for students. The courses teach leadership and survival skills as well as physical skills such as rock climbing, sailing and swimming. For details, call the school at 792-4333.

There is a very active Little League program in Hong Kong with approximately 400 children involved. The season goes from September through May with an occasional clinic during the summer vacation. There are currently four divisions with practice once a week. Parent involvement is welcomed as there is always a demand for umpires, coaches, managers and general helpers.

Little League can be contacted at GPO Box 11372 or through the Hong Kong International School.

Non-sporting clubs

Hong Kong Children Arts Society
GPO Box 1112
Hong Kong

The Hong Kong Arts Centre offers children's art classes and organizes an annual Children's Festival in December.

Ballroom dancing. Courses at the American Club go from October through March. Members' children are given first priority. The course consists of 12 classes and two dinner dances. Courses at the China Fleet Club are for adults only.

Chess. The Hong Kong Chess Federation, in conjunction with the Urban Council and the *South China Morning Post* holds annual Students' Championships in August.

Scouts, Girl Guides, Boys' and Girls' Brigades.

Hong Kong Council of the Boys'
Brigade
G/F Block A
Lok Man Sun Chuen
Tokwawan, Kowloon
714-9253

Girls' Brigade (Hong Kong)
address as above
715-8839

Hong Kong Girl Guides Assn
8 Gascoigne Rd, Kowloon
332-5523

Scouts Assn of HK
Morse House
9 Cox's Rd, Kowloon

For details on US Scouts and Guides, contact the registrar at the HK International School.

Hong Kong Youth Hostels Assn
1408A Watson's Estate, North Point
570-0985

Chapter 13
EXCURSIONS & TRAVEL

New Territories

Located about 15 miles (25 km) north of urban Kowloon, the 376 sq mile (974 sq km) of the New Territories was leased from the Chinese in 1898 to provide the fledgling colony with a hinterland. (It was that lease and its approaching deadline of midnight, June 30, 1997, that provided the catalyst for the Sino-British Agreement of 1984 which returns all of the colony, not just the NT, to the PRC).

According to the original lease, the New Territories begins at the aptly named Boundary Street located in urban Kowloon near the airport. In practice, the New Territories starts once you are on the other side of the mountains, through Lion Rock or Tate's Cairn tunnels.

There are several ways to see the New Territories, but be warned. No matter where you've come from, what state in the US, what country in the world, it is a fair guess you have not come this far to sit in a holiday traffic jam in blistering heat with your car boiling over. Therefore choose your time well, because traffic through the Lion Rock tunnel, along Clearwater Bay Road and Castle Peak Road can be horrendous.

New Towns housing half a million people or more have replaced some of the small villages (Shatin, Taipo, Tsuen Wan, Tuen Mun) and great swathes have been cut through rural areas to make way for highways, but it is still possible to see some of the rural life and lands that gives the NT its reputation.

Beaches Thirteen 'gazetted' beaches (which means they have facilities, lifeguards and changing rooms and are maintained by the Urban or Regional councils)are concentrated along the old Tai Po Road along the south shore of the Tuen Mun/Tsuen Wan Districts. They are Castle Peak, Kadoorie, Butterfly, Old and New Cafeteria, Anglers', Gemini, Hoi Mei Wan, Casam, Lido, Ting Kau, Approach and Tung Wan on Ma Wan Island. On the east coast in the Saikung district are eight more: Clearwater Bay 1st and 2nd, Silverstrand, Campers', Trio (Hebe Haven), Pak Sha Chau, Kiu Tsui and Hap Mun Bay.

In the summer swimming season, the grading of the water *vis a vis* pollution and whether it is safe to swim is published fortnightly. The Hong Kong Tourist Association has excellent literature on how to reach the beaches, particularly by public transport.

Temples The most picturesque include: Chuk Lam Sim, the Bamboo Forest Monastery with three statues of Buddha; Ching Chung Koon Taoist Temple near Tuen Mun, famous for its huge temple building and cast iron bell; Min Fat Buddhist Monastery near Tuen Mun, more renowned as a place to get a good vegetarian lunch while *en route* elsewhere than for its architecture; Temple of Ten Thousand Buddhas in Shatin, one of the most famous of all the temples in the territory; situated atop some 500 steps and reportedly misnamed because there are actually 13,000 gilted clay statues. (If you are particularly interested in temples, *This is Hong Kong -Temples* by Joyce Savidge and *Welcome to Hong Kong Temples* by RF Cooper should be welcome additions to any tour.)

Other Highlights

Lau Fau Shan A fishing village built on an oyster bed -- not those imported from Australia, New Zealand or the US, but much larger ones. Buy your seafood live and take it into a restaurant for cooking. Beware: the oyster beds, on which Lau Fau Shan built its reputation, have deteriorated in the polluted water around Hong Kong. Make certain they are well-cooked, or give them a miss. Near Yuen Long.

Luen Wo Market This traditional fresh food market in Fanling is one of the few left. The Hong Kong Tourist Association has an excellent 'Fact Sheet' on the subject.

Kam Tin Walled Village A seventeenth century walled village (the real name is Kut Hing Wei) belonging to the Tang family clan of the type that once dotted the landscape of the NT. Perhaps the New Territory's most famous landmark. Near Yuen Long. Very touristic — touts everywhere.

Lok Mau Chau Before China opened up to Western visitors, this hilltop lookout was the tourists' only chance to peer through the Bamboo Curtain. Still a lovely pastoral view.

Touring/Sightseeing If you decide to see the New Territories in style, you can hire a car and driver from most car hire companies. Avis charge $200-250 per hour (min 4 hours) which includes the car, driver and gas. Most cars can carry four passengers. Other car hire companies offer similar prices.

The HK Tourist Association itself runs an excellent 6-hour New Territories Tour called 'The Land Between' ($260 adults/$210 children). Call 801 7111 for information.

A suggested route for a self-drive tour, which could include stops at beaches and factories (for discount shopping), even golf courses, could be Castle Peak

Road, Route Twisk (which cuts inland over Tai Mo Shan, the highest mountain in the territory), Kam Tin, Lok Ma Chau, Yuen Long, Fan Ling, Taipo, Shatin.

On the eastern side, the Saikung Peninsula is mainly known for its beaches, marinas and country park.

Outlying Islands

The three main islands (of 235 in the territory), Lantau, Lamma and Cheung Chau, are favorites with urban dwellers trying to get away for a public holiday or weekend, so be prepared for crowds, and a bit of pushing and shoving, at the Outlying Districts Ferry Pier on Hong Kong Island. Tours, both water and land, are available, but it is not difficult to do it yourself. For general information, the Hong Kong Tourist Association's leaflet 'Outlying Islands'' is invaluable. They also have a current listing of ferry times and fares, which vary depending on the class of the voyage and the day of the week.

Lantau Twice the size of Hong Kong island with a population of only 16,000 (versus a million plus). Places of interest include excellent beaches (particularly Cheung Sha and Silvermine Bay); the Po Lin Monastery with its 34-meter high statue of Buddha (said to be the tallest in the world); Lantau Tea Garden with its BBQs and horse-riding; Trappist Monastery (go via Peng Chau Island or Discovery Bay); the Sung Dynasty Tung Chung Fort; holiday/weekend apartments; hiking trails and campsites. There are two modern residential enclaves that have their own boat services from Blake's Pier in Central — Discovery Bay and Sea Ranch. Near Sea Ranch is the popular Frog and Toad bar and restaurant, which holds an annual mud wrestling championship. There is a lot to do on Lantau so get familiar with it and do it gradually.

Lamma The ferries go to Yung Shue Wan (the main village) and Sok Kwu Wan, famous for its string of outdoor Chinese seafood restaurants — dubbed by local yachties 'the Lamma Hilton'. There are also excellent seafood restaurants in Yung Shue Wan. There are beaches and hiking trails.

Cheung Chau The most populated of the islands and most popular, it was once thought of by Westerners on local hire conditions as a Mediterranean - like artist's colony, while the Chinese residents thought of it as a combination fishing village and commuter borough. Overbuilding and overpopulation has put paid to romantic images, but it is still a very pleasant place to visit — temples, beaches, restaurants, even a genuine pirate's cave. Windsurfing championships are held here, and there is an international standard hotel (the Warwick).

Macau

Across the Pearl River estuary, some 40 miles away, lies the Portuguese-administered territory of Macau. Dating from 1557, it is the oldest European settlement on the China Coast. Though the only one ceded by the Peking government voluntarily, in return for the Portuguese destroying the pirate fleets that preyed on shipping, it too is being returned to mainland sovereignty — 2.5 years after Hong Kong, at midnight, December 20, 1999.

Despite some hectic building in recent years which has marred the skyline, Macau still provides a marvelous contrast to Hong Kong, particularly for those in need of a quick fix of tranquility. A slice of the Latin Orient, if you like, complete with pastel-colored buildings (`a la* Iberian Peninsula) and a slower pace.

For the millions of Hong Kong Chinese who visit Macau, its main *raison d'etre* is gambling — big time casino gambling, dog races, trotting track and *jai lai* (pelota) bets that are illegal in Hong Kong. To them everything else about the place is irrelevant.

If you'd like a bit more out of a destination, Macau certainly offers it — and it is compact enough to see it all in a couple of hours. The peninsula itself is only 2.1 square miles. If you add in the islands of Taipa (connected to Macau by a bridge) and Coloane (connected to Taipa by a causeway), it comes to six square miles.

Touring/Sightseeing Tours are available from Hong Kong, but it would be more fun to do-it-yourself. Tour guides meet every vessel and the going price is about $100 per head. (Before you descend the steps to the waiting area, stop in the Department of Tourism Office right at the top and pick up a free guide and various brochures).

If you feel like driving, rental cars and 'mini-mokes' (like a beach buggy) are available. You will need an International Driver's License, obtainable from the Hong Kong Transport Department (Murray Road Carpark in Central and other locations). You cannot drive on your Hong Kong license. Contact: Macau Mokes, Shop 305, Shun Tak Centre, Hong Kong, Tel 543 4190 or Macau Ferry Terminal Bldg, 1/F, Macau, Tel 78851.

Whichever way you go, the ruins of St Paul's, dating from 1602 and seventeenth century Monte Fort which overlooks it, are musts, as is the Temple of Kun Lam, famous for its fortune telling (try it) and the site of the signing of the first Sino-American trade treaty (1844). Good views are to be had from the Bishop's palace. The Temple of A-Ma, which pre-dates the Portuguese and from which Macau takes its name is interesting. There is much more of course.

Eating From a Western viewpoint, one of the most interesting aspects of Macau is its restaurants, with Macanese and Portuguese cuisine. Don't rush it though. Leave plenty of time for a long, leisurely lunch washed down with inexpensive Portuguese green wine (*Vinho Verde*).

Macau/China Tours, Golf Tours It is possible to combine a trip to Macau with a jaunt through the ornate, 19th century Portes do Circo (Border Gate) into southern China. You can go on a day tour, overnight, or just to play golf (See Leisure Activities).

Macau Resorts The Hyatt-Regency's Taipa Island Resort and Macau Oriental offer a resort package for those who want to get away for a brief time, play a bit of tennis or squash, swim and sunbathe. Just the thing to recharge the batteries. Older than both is Pousada de Coloane, set on a small black sand beach - also known for its Sunday Portuguese food buffets.

Macau Grand Prix Held on the third or fourth weekend each November, it is not the time of the year to come for that aforementioned quiet weekend as some 50,000 motor-racing *aficionados* converge on the tiny territory for two solid days of Formula Three, production car, classic car, and motorcycle races through the streets of Macau. (Most old hands reckon any Macau taxi driver could hold his own on the 3.1 mile Guia Circuit).

Visas If you are a resident of Hong Kong, you'll get an automatic 3-day visa upon arrival. If you are from the US, Canada, Australia, New Zealand, the UK (plus other countries) you do not need a visa.

Currency Macau currency (the pataca) is divided into 100 avos. The pataca is worth 1-2% less than the Hong Kong dollar, but the Hong Kong dollar is fully negotiable and most people never bother to change money for short stays. The reverse is not true. Patacas are not circulated in Hong Kong and must be exchanged like any other currency — at a bad rate. Credit card purchases, hotel stays and the like are all in Hong Kong dollars.

Transportation Full details of the jetfoils, hydrofoils, jet-cats, high-speed ferries are noted in the Transportation chapter.

Warning: Macau is packed at the weekends and public holidays (esp long ones like Chinese New Year and Easter), as well as the week prior to and including Grand Prix Weekend. Round trip ferry tickets should be in hand before your departure, to avoid panic dealing with scalpers in Macau. Hotel, car, even restaurant reservations, should also be obtained before you leave Hong Kong.

Excellent leaflets and guides can be obtained in Hong Kong from:

Macau Government Tourist Office
Buffer Hall (just after customs), Kai Tak Airport
Tel 769-7970

Macau Tourist Information Bureau
Room 305, Shun Tak Centre, 3/F
200 Connaught Road Central
Tel 540 8180
(This building houses the Macau Ferry Terminal.)

In Macau:

Macau Government Tourist Office
Travessa do Paiva
Macau
Tel 77218

Macau Ferry Terminal, 1/F
Tel 510104

Trips Farther Afield — Southeast And North Asia, PRC

Have a map of Asia? Check it and you find that Hong Kong is wonderfully located to explore the region. Hong Kong is so close to Guangzhou (formerly Canton) and Taipei (each about an hour's flight time away from Hong Kong), Manila (1.5 hours) and Shanghai (1.75 hours), that it takes as long to work your way through Kai Tak as it does to fly there, to say nothing of the time it takes you to drive to the airport. Bangkok and Seoul are less than three hours, Tokyo, Beijing, Penang, or Singapore less than four.

There is a thriving outbound travel business here and you can get anything from cheap bucket-shop type tickets to very up-market posh all-in tours. Both the *South China Morning Post* and the *Hong Kong Standard* have comprehensive ads listing the prices of the day. In June 1991, you could have purchased single trip tickets to Manila, Taipei or Bangkok, the territory's three favorite shorthaul destinations for under $1,000. Incidentally, courier trips within Asia are even cheaper ($1,400 return to Singapore, $1,500 to Tokyo).

It is also worth noting that if you belong to a frequent flyer's club, particularly the American ones, you can use the tickets in Asia. At press time, United and Northwest fly into Hong Kong.

Cathay Pacific Airways offers Discovery Tours to 23 cities and resorts outside China. These are very popular with residents who are leery of dealing with agents they do not know. Don't let the word 'tour' throw you. They are sold to individuals and families, and if you do not want the included tour, you can stay put by the pool or beach for your entire stay. Like the seats, the tours come in Economy, Business and First Class. You can also choose your hotel. CPA's China Tours are run differently — you do not have a choice of hotels or class. Dragonair, Hong Kong's second airline, specializes in cheap charter routes to locations like Kathmandu in Nepal or Pattaya beach resort in Thailand.

China

China is particularly accessible for Westerners living in Hong Kong. Dozens and dozens of all-in tours are available — from one day visits to Shenzhen, the Special Economic Zone adjacent to Hong Kong (or you can take a bus on your own, see Transportation) and weekends in Guangzhou to 2-3 week marathons to most major cities.

From Macau, there are day trips across the border or to the Special Economic Zone of Zhuhai or bus trips all the way to Canton.

What is not generally known is that you can easily go on your own. As long as you have a visa, you can hop a train or boat and head for the Middle Kingdom. Yes, it is almost that easy. There is a catch though — once you leave the main cities and hotels, you'd better have that Mandarin phrase book handy because language is a problem. Also, check with China Travel Service or your consulate where you can go and cannot go. Some 200 cities are officially open to foreigners, enough to keep most tourists going.

Books like the *Survival Guide to China,* part of the Lonely Planet series, *China On Your Own* by Russell and Penny Jennings and *China Off the Beaten Track* by Brian Schwartz are particularly useful in this respect. Many other guidebooks on China are available.

Chapter 14
LEAVING

PHOTO BY JOHN LANGFORD

F ew announcements can equal the impact on a household of the statement, 'We're moving'. Moving can bring on all sorts of traumas in some families. Now, however, there is help for these families from the experts. Modern moving companies have done considerable research into the problems of moving and can provide brochures and personalized advice. (You can find them listed in the Yellow Pages under 'Mover and Storage Service'.) Leaving is somewhat like arriving, only in reverse. Thus, in the chapter 'Moving to Hong Kong', there is a checklist that you might find useful in planning your departure -- or you may wish to make your own list of things to remember.

So the two most important considerations when a family is contemplating a move is their selection of a reliable moving company and their determination to keep meticulous lists. Allow as much time as possible and do not leave arrangements to the last minute.

Moving your household effects from Hong Kong is a relatively simple procedure since there are no export customs or duties. Your main concern will be the import regulations of the country to which you are planning to move your household goods and personal effects.

Customs duties and the problems attendant on returning to one's home country at the end of a foreign assignment are so varied as to be an impossible subject for generalizations. Check with the consulate or commission of the country to which you are moving.

English-language lists of the contents of each of the numbered cartons or carts should be made by you or by the packing crew supervisor. This inventory will be required for customs clearance at the destination of the shipment as well as for insurance purposes, and it should be kept in a safe place. Perhaps several copies should be made.

Most movers will accept little or no liability for breakage, scratches, or lost items. Therefore, it is highly advisable that proper insurance arrangements to cover your goods are made before you move. It pays to be sure.

US citizens may obtain brief and comprehensive pamphlets from the United States Customs Service, 11/F, St John's Bldg, 33 Garden Road, Hong Kong (521 4552 or 841 2244). The following comments are general considerations for Americans returning to the United States.

If you have left the US for purposes of employment, schooling, or travel, you are considered a 'returning resident', and all articles acquired abroad —

whether purchased or received as gifts — are subject to applicable duty. There are some exemptions. Household effects: furniture, paintings, carpets, tableware, etc, acquired abroad may be imported duty free if they are not intended for another person or for sale, and if they have been used by you for at least one year. (Jewelry, stereo components, cameras, boats, and clothing cannot be passed free of duty as household effects.)

Check the latest regulations on Treasury licenses, which may be required for articles from a few specified countries. nearly all articles of Chinese origin, once prohibited, may now be brought or shipped into the United States.

Your household goods must clear customs at the first port of arrival to another port of entry for customs clearance.

Customs Form 3299 can usually be obtained prior to departure from your moving company or their customhouse broker at the port of entry. Household and personal effects cannot be cleared without this declaration.

All arrangements for customs clearance and forwarding in bond must be made by you. Your moving company can usually handle all the necessary arrangements, including clearance through customs in the United States by a customhouse broker.

You may also have an agent effect the customs clearance of single noncommercial shipment for you if it is not possible for you personally to secure the release of the goods. You must authorize and empower that agent in writing to execute the customs declaration and the entry for you. The written authorization of the agent should be addressed to the 'Officer in Charge of Customs' at the port of entry.

Shipments that arrive before you return (without prior arrangements for acceptance) will be placed in storage by customs after five days, at the expense and risk of the owner. If not claimed within one year, the items will be sold.

Your Identity Card must be surrendered when you leave Hong Kong for the last time. The health regulations of the country to which you are going should be checked to determine if you need innoculations of any sort.

Electrical appliances that may not work in other countries, and household furniture you do not wish to take can be sold through newspaper advertisements or supermarket bulletin boards. Make arrangements to use up or give away your stock of wines and liquor. It is not recommended to include liquor in household shipments to the States. Certain harbors — among them, Houston, New Orleans, Norfolk, Boston, Savannah, Miami and all the West Coast ports — do not permit any wine or alcohol, even with a bona fide declaration. If the liquor is declared, it will be confiscated and destroyed. If it is not declared, it will be seized and destroyed, and the owner will be fined and be charged the duties and taxes. If the fine is not paid, there is the risk that the whole shipment will be seized and sold at auction after one year.

In addition, certain states are dry, and even if the harbor permits entry of alcohol with a declaration, customs will not authorize forwarding to a dry state. Finally, all US airports forbid liquor in household shipments.

Again, for American citizens, the US Customs Service is extremely informative about regulations regarding entry into the States. They can provide a variety of brochures, such as travelers' tips on what you can or can't bring in, duty-free states, etc. If you give them enough time, they can even research specific questions which are not answered in their publications.

When you're considering other things to pack, you should also remember that there are many dangerous items in the cabinets of the average kitchen and bathroom. Regardless of your destination, you must dispose of all your flammables and other hazardous materials before your move. You should, therefore, discard or give away bottles containing liquids in glass, or any item that could cause fires.

If your household employees have served you well, you may wish to help them locate new employers. Letters of reference are valuable as well. And don't forget that custom dictates 'severance pay'.

APPENDICES

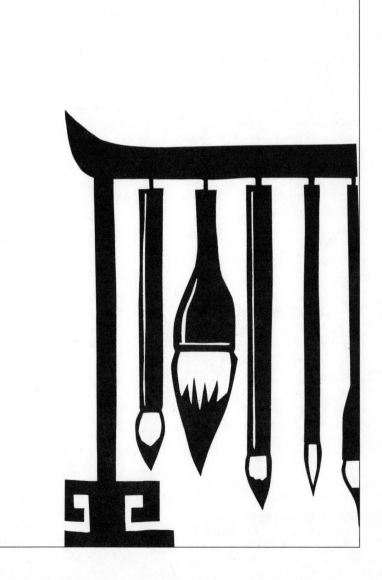

Emergency Numbers

Police, Fire or Ambulance   999

- To obtain prompt action, when the operator answers,
  say 'Police', 'Fire' or 'Ambulance' (as applicable).

St John's Ambulance Brigade (free service)

- *Hong Kong*   576 6555
- *Kowloon*   713 5555

Electricity

China Light & Power Co Ltd   097 1122
- serves Kowloon, New Territories, Lantau Island
  and Cheung Chau

The Hongkong Electric Co Ltd   555 4000
- serves Hong Kong Island and Lamma Island

Gas

Hong Kong & China Gas Co Ltd   334 5345

Telephone

Hong Kong Telecom
- Directory Inquiries (English)   1081
- Telephone Repair   109

Water

Water Supplies Department
- Kowloon & New Territories   396 0210
- Hong Kong & Outlying Islands   880 2500

Hospitals

Other information on private and government hospitals can also be found in 'Living and Health'. In addition, the Business Telephone directory has complete hospital listings.

Most Westerners requiring hospital care seem to prefer admission to any of the hospitals listed below. Your choice, of course, will be made in consultation with your physician, since - except in the case of emergency - you must have his or her referral in order to gain admission.

Hong Kong Island

Canossa Hospital   *522 2181*
1 Old Peak Rd
Maternity and surgical services, etc. Nursing supervised by Canossian Roman Catholic nuns. The present building was opened in 1960s, rooms are air conditioned, some have harbor views. A private room costs $1,100 per day; semi-private, $600; wards, $250 (general and maternity).

Central Hospital   *522 3141*
1B Lower Albert Rd
Central
Private hospital. Private room $800-1,100, semi-private $350-600 and general $200.

Hong Kong Sanatorium
& Hospital   *572 0211*
2 Village Rd
Happy Valley
Private hospital. Private room costs $1,050; semi-private $690 and general $190 - 300.

Hong Kong Adventist Hospital   *574 6211*
40 Stubbs Rd
A general hospital with specialty and maternity service. Emphasizing preventive medicine, the hospital offers classes year round on smoking cessation, CPR, childbirth preparedness, cancer prevention, stress control and management, and others. Personal counseling services on a number of subjects are also available. All   rooms in this modern building have air-conditioning and

pleasant views. Cost: $1,525 per day for a private room; $895 per day for a semi-private room; and $395 per day for a ward (three to five beds). Twenty-four-hour emergency services. Dental and medical out-patient clinics (which will expect immediate payment).

Matilda & War Memorial Hospital   *849 6301*
41 Mount Kellett Rd
The Peak
British nurses, specialty and maternity wards. Charges are $1,375 per day for a private room, $850 per day for 'second class', and $500 (first day; $350 each additional day) for general wards - some with verandahs - in a peaceful, quiet location. Out-patient clinic.

Queen Mary Hospital   *581 9211*
Pokfulam Rd
Pokfulam
Government hospital with 24-hour emergency service.

Kowloon

Baptist Hospital   *837 4141*
222 Waterloo Rd
Kowloon Tong
A private hospital. Costs: $800 per day for a private room, $400 semi-private. $140 for general ward (10 patients per ward).

New Territories

Prince of Wales Hospital   *636 2211*
30 Ngan Shing Street
Shatin
A government hospital. Private room costs $1,570; semi-private $1,045; general ward $34.

Romanized Chinese Names of Streets and Buildings

This list does not use a standard romanization and the Cantonese tones are not indicated. Some translations are 'Street slang' terms that are easily understood by taxi drivers. We include the Chinese character names with the suggestion you photocopy these pages to show taxi drivers.

Central Business District	**Jung wan seung yip kui**	中環商業區
Cat Street	Mo lo gaai	摩羅街
Chater Road	Je da do	遮打道
Connaught Road	Kwon Nook dow jung	干諾道中
D'Aguilar Street	Da gay la gaai	德已立街
Des Voeux Road	Da foo do	德輔道中
Duddell Street	Do dell lay gaai	都爹利街
Hollywood Road	Ho-lay-wood do	荷里活道
Ice House Street	Sut chong gaai	雪廠街
Ladder Street	Lo tai gaai	樓梯街
Pedder Street	Peda gaai	畢打街
Pottinger Street	Boot dean ja gaai	砵甸乍街
Queen's Road, Central	Wong ho dai do jung	皇后大道中
Wellington Street	Well-ing-don gaai	威靈頓街
Wyndham Street	Wan hum gaai	雲咸街
Admiralty Centre	Gum chung lon	海富中心
Alexandra House	Alexandai dai ha	歷山大廈
Bank of China	Chung kwok nan hong	中國銀行
Bond Centre	Bun dah chung sum	奔達中心
Central Building	Jung geen dai ha	中建大廈
Exchange Square	Gau yik gong chang	交易廣場
Jardine House	Yee wo dai ha	怡和大廈
King's Theatre	Yu-loc hay yuen	娛樂戲院
Pacific Place	Tai koo gong chang	太古廣場
Prince's Building	Tie-ji hong	太子行
Queen's Theatre	Wong-hau hay yuen	皇后戲院
Shun Tak Center	Shun tak chung sum	信德中心
St George's Building	Saint Georgey dai ha	聖佐治行
Swire House	Tai koo dai ha	太古大廈
The Landmark	Chi dai gong chang	置地廣場
Wheelock House	Wei duc fon dai ha	匯德豐大廈
Worldwide Plaza	Wan kau dai ha	環球大廈

Mid-Levels	**Boon-san**	半山
Bowen Road	Bo-wan do	寶雲道
Conduit Road	Con-duc do	干德道
Kennedy Road	Gen-ne-dy do	堅尼地道
Kotewall Road	Yuet-wah di	旭龢道
MacDonnell Road	Mac-donnal Do	麥當勞道
Magazine Gap Road	Ma-gay-sen hap do	馬己仙峽道
May Road	Mui do	梅道
Old Peak Road	Gau san-deng do	舊山頂道
Stubbs Road	See-tu-but do	司徒拔道
Adventist Hospital	Kwong on yee yuen	港安醫院
Canossa Hospital	Sun-ga-la-sa yee yuen	聖嘉諾撒醫院
The Peak	**San deng**	山頂
Barker Road	Ba-ga do	白加道
Coombe Road	Gum do	甘道
Peak Road	San-deng do	山頂道
Matilda Hospital	Ming-duk yee yuen	明德醫院
Upper Peak Tram Station	San-deng lam che zarm	山頂纜車站
Repulse Bay	**Cheen sui wan**	淺水灣
South Bay Road	Nam Wan do	南灣道
Deepwater Bay	Sum sui wan	深水灣
Island Road	Heung-doe do	香島道
Aberdeen	**Heung gong jai**	香港仔
Stanley	**Chet-chee**	赤柱
Happy Valley	**Pau ma day**	跑馬地
Race Course	Pau ma cheung	跑馬場
Causeway Bay	**Tung lo wan**	銅鑼灣
Daimaru Department Store	Dai yue kun see	大丸公司
Sogo Department Store	Sung gong kun see	崇光公司
Windsor House	Wun sa dai ha	溫莎大廈

Wanchai	Wan jai	灣仔
Hennessy Road	Heen-lay-see do	軒尼詩道
Lockhart Road	Lock-huk do	洛克道
Academy of Performing Arts	Yeng ngai hoc yuen	演藝學院
Arts Centre	Ai se chung sum	藝術中心
Asian House	Hay shun lau	熙信樓
China Resources Building	Wah yun dai ha	華潤大廈
Great Eagle Centre	Ying gwon chung sum	鷹君中心
Lee Theatre	Lay-mo toi	利舞台
Sincere Insurance Bldg	Sin-cee bo-heem dai-ha	先施保險大廈
Exhibition & Convention Centre	Wai yee jea lam chung sum	會議展覽中心

Hotels (Hong Kong)	Jau deem (Heung gong)	酒店（香港）
Conrad	Hoi wig jau deem	海域酒店
Excelsior	Yee dong jau deem	怡東酒店
Furama	Fu lai wah jau deem	富麗華酒店
Grand Hyatt	Kwan yuet jau deem	君悅酒店
Hilton	Hei yee dun jau deem	希爾頓酒店
Hotel Victoria	Hoi gong jau deem	海港酒店
Holiday Inn Harbor View	Hoi Kwong ga yat jau deem	海港假日酒店
Hyatt Regency	Hi Yuet jau deem	凱悅酒店
JW Marriott	Man ho jau deem	萬豪酒店
Kowloon	Gao lung jau deem	九龍酒店
Mandarin Oriental	Man wa jau deem	文華酒店
Miramar	May lay wah jau deem	美麗華酒店
New World Harbour View	Hoi King ga yat jau deem	海景假日酒店
Nikko	Yat hong jau deem	日航酒店
Omni Hong Kong	Heung gong jau deem	香港酒店
Omni Marco Polo	Ma hau be law jau deem	馬可孛羅酒店
Omni Prince	Tai Tsi jau deem	太子酒店
Park Lane Radisson	Pak leng jau deem	柏寧酒店
Peninsula	Boa dou jau deem	半島酒店
Ramada Renaissance	Wah mei dah lai sun jau deem	華美達麗新酒店
Regal Airport	Gay cheung jau deem	機場酒店
Regal Meridien	Fu ho jau deem	富豪酒店
Regent	Lai jing jau deem	麗晶酒店
Ritz Carlton	Lai ka jau deem	麗嘉酒店
Royal Garden	Dei yuen jau deem	帝苑酒店
Shangri-la	Heung ga lay lie jau deem	香格里拉酒店

Pier	Ma tau	碼頭
Star Ferry Pier	Tin sing ma tau	天星碼頭
Blake Pier	Bok kung ma tau	卜公碼頭
Macau Ferry Pier	Gong-o ma tau	港澳碼頭
Outlying Island Ferry Pier	Gong oi se ma tau	港外線碼頭

Kowloon	**Gao lung**	九龍
Argyle Street	Ah-ga-lo gaai	亞皆老街
Austin Road	Or-se-din do	柯士甸道
Carnavon Road	Ga-na-fun do	加拿芬道
Cross harbour Tunnel	Hui die sui do	海底隧道
Granville Road	Ga-lee-wooi-lo do	加連威老道
Hankow Road	Hon hau do	漢口道
Jordan Road	Jo-dan do	佐敦道
Kai Tak Airport	Kai-duk gay cheung	啓德機場
Kimberley Road	Kun-ba-lay do	金巴利道
Mody Road	Mo-day do	麼地道
Nathan Road	Na-tan do	彌敦道
Prince Edward Road	Tai-je do	太子道
Ocean Terminal	Hoi-wun dai ha	海運大廈
Salisbury Road	Sa-lay-see-ba-lai do	梳利士巴利道
Star Ferry Pier	Tin sing ma tau	天星碼頭
Star House	Sing-kwong hong	星光行
Waterloo Road	Wo-ta-lo do	窩打老道
Queen Elizabeth Hospital	Yee lay sa barh yee yuen	伊利莎佰醫院

New Territories	**Sun-guy**	新界
Castle Peak Road	Ching-san do	靑山道
Clearwater Bay	Ching-sui wan	淸水灣
Sai Kung	Sai Kun	西頁

Clothing Sizes

British, American, and European

Be aware when buying clothing in Asia that Asian sizes are not necessarily the same as European sizes. For example, an Asian size 10 will have shorter arms, tighter wrist bands and tighter neck bands than the same European size 10. It is usually best to buy one size larger than you normally take.

| | *Women* | | | | | *Men* | | |
	UK	USA	Euro			UK	USA	Euro
Dresses,	10	8	38	*Suits*		34	34	44
Coats &	12	10	40			35	35	46
Suits	14	12	42			36	36	48
	16	14	44			37	37	49.5
	18	16	46			38	38	51
	20	18	48			39	39	52.5
						40	40	54
						41	41	55.5
						42	42	57
Cardigans,	32	10	38	*Shirts*		13	13	33
Sweaters &	34	10	40			14	14	35-36
Blouses	36	12	42			15	15	38
	38	14	44			16	16	40-41
	40	16	46			17	17	43
	42	18	48			17.5	17.5	44
Shoes	3.5	5	3.5	*Shoes*		6	7	39.5
	4	5.5	36			7	8	41
	5	6.5	37			8	9	42
	6	7.5	38.5			9	10	43
	7	8.5	40			10	11	44.5
	7.5	9	40.5			11	12	46
	8	9.5	41			12	13	47
	8.5	10	42					

Chinese Measurements

Chinese Mass

10 fan	= 1 tsin (mace)
	= 58.3333 grains
	= 3.77994 grams

10 tsin	= 1 leung (tael)
	= 1.3333 ounces
	= 37.7994 grams

12 leung = 1 pound

16 leung	= 1 kan (catty)
	= 1.3333 pounds
	= 0.604790 kilograms

100 gan	= 1 tam (picul)
	= 1.19048 cwt (hundred weight)
	= 60.4790 kilograms

Chinese Length

10 fan	= 1 tsun (Chinese inch)
	= 1.4625 inches
	= 37.1475 millimeters

10 tsun	= 1 chek (Chinese foot)
	= 1.21875 feet

2.4 chek = 1 yard

Weights and Measures

Conversions to Metric Measures

Symbol	When You Know	Multiply By	To Find	Symbol
Length				
in	inches	2.5	centimeters	cm
ft	feet	30	centimeters	cm
yd	yards	0.9	meters	m
mi	miles	1.6	kilometers	km
Area				
in^2	square inches	6.5	square centimeters	cm^2
ft^2	square feet	0.09	square meters	m^2
yd^2	square yards	0.8	square meters	m^2
mi^2	square miles	2.6	square kilometers	km^2
	acres	0.4	hectares	ha

Mass (Weight)

oz	ounces	28	grams	g
lb	pounds	0.45	kilograms	kg
	short tons 2,000 (lb)	0.9	tonnes	t

Volume

tsp	teaspoons	5	milliliters	ml
tbsp	tablespoons	15	milliliters	ml
fl oz	fluid ounces	30	milliliters	ml
c	cups	0.24	liters	l
pt	pints	0.47	liters	l
qt	quarts	0.95	liters	l
gal	gallons	3.8	liters	l
ft^3	cubic feet	0.03	cubic meters	m^3
yd^3	cubic yards	0.76	cubic meters	m^3

Conversions to US Measures

Length

mm	millimeter	0.04	inches	in
cm	centimeters	0.4	inches	in
m	meters	3.3	feet	ft
m	meters	1.1	yards	yd
km	kilometer	0.6	miles	mi

Area

cm^2	square centimeter	0.16	square inches	in^2
m^2	square meters	1.2	square yards	yd^2
km^2	square kilometers	0.4	square miles	mi^2
ha	hectares(10,000m)	2.5	acres	

Mass

g	grams	0.035	ounces	oz
kg	kilograms	2.2	pounds	lb
t	tonnes (1000kg)	1.1	short tons	

Volume

ml	milliliters	0.03	fluid ounces	fl oz
l	liters	2.1	pints	pt
l	liters	1.06	quarts	qt
l	liters	0.26	gallons	gal
m	cubic meters	35	cubic feet	ft^3
m	cubic meters	1.3	cubic yards	yd^3

Temperature

C	Celsius	1.8	Fahrenheit	F
		(then add 32)		

Private Clubs

Although there are a number of beaches, swimming pools, and public sporting faci
in new apartment complexes with some facilities included (swimming pool, squa
of private clubs with sporting facilities.

Costs for most clubs, especially those on Hong Kong Island and in the Kowloon
a result, families posted to Hong Kong for short periods (two to four years) spend th
for use by the company's employee and family. Some clubs allow transfer of de

Club	Location(s)	Badminton	Basketball	Beach (Private)	Boat Mooring	Bowling	Bridge	Children's Playground	Cricket	Football	Games Room	Golf	Health/Fitness	Hockey	Horse Riding	Lawn Bowls	Library	Mini Golf	Rowing	Rugby	Sauna	Snooker (Billiards)	Soccer	Squash	Swimming Pool(s)	Table Tennis	Video Club	Water Sports
(1) Aberdeen Boat Club — Tel 553 3032	1			*				*			*											*	*	*				*
(2) Aberdeen Marina Club — Tel 555 8321	1							*	*		*				*		*				*	*	*	*	*			*
(3) American Club — Tel 8427400	2										*				*						*			*	*	*		
(4) Clearwater Bay Golf and Country Club — Tel 719 1595	1	*						*				*	*								*	*	*		*			*
(5) Craigengower Cricket Club — Tel 577 8331	1	*							*							*									*			
(6) Discovery Bay Golf Club — Tel 987 7273	1											*													*	*		
(7) Gordon Hard Boat Club — Tel 4507336	1		*																							*		*
(8) Hebe Haven Yacht Club — Tel 719 9682	1		*	*																								*
(9) Hilltop Country Club — Tel 412 0201	3	*								*	*										*	*	*	*	*			
(10) Hong Kong Country Club — Tel 552 4165	1			*	*	*					*										*		*	*	*	*		

Kong, most are overcrowded. particularly on weekends. Some families seek refuge
ough for most (particularly expatriates) refuge is sought in the increasing number

because of the cost of viable land sites. Most clubs have long waiting lists, and as
ment with corporate debentures, where the company buys a permanent membership
hip. Check the classified section of the newspaper for debenture sales.

ATE	COST CORPORATE/ DEBENTURE	WAITNG LIST/ QUALIFICATIONS
month	Individual $60,000 Corporate $110,000	Yes
month	$450,000 - $470,000	None at present
ership $100,000 month	$1.25 million	No
ct secretary 595	$216,000 - $1.5 million	Membership for golf club suspended
00 entrance month	250,000 for 2 nominees	Closed temporarily
- $750/month	$600,000 - $800,000	
ry: $700/year n: $1,700/year	None	military given first priority, civilian membership limited number
0/entrance month	None	0-6 months depending on whether you sail
00 entrance month	$200,000 - $360,000 for 4 and 8 nominees $940 - $1,880/month	No
00 entrance month	$1 million	Debenture:none Private: 2-3 years

Private Clubs

Club	Location(s)	Badminton	Basketball	Beach (Private)	Boat Mooring	Bowling	Bridge	Children's Playground	Cricket	Football	Games Room	Golf	Health/Fitness	Hockey	Horse Riding	Lawn Bowls	Library	Mini Golf	Rowing	Rugby	Sauna	Snooker (Billiards)	Soccer	Squash	Swimming Pool(s)	Table Tennis	Video Club
(11) Hong Kong Cricket Club Tel 574 6266	1								*+ (junior)					*								*		*	*	*	
(12) Hong Kong Football Club Tel 576 2808	1										*		*	*						*+ (junior)		*	*	*+ (junior)	*	*	*
(13) Hong Kong Marina Tel 792 1436	1				*																						
(14) Indian Recreation Club Tel 576 1673	1	*					*						*	*												*	
(15) Kowloon Bowling Green Club Tel 368 7733	1															*						*		*			
(16) Kowloon Cricket Club Tel 367 4141	1										*		*	*		*						*		*	*	*	
(17) Ladies Recreation Club Tel 522 0151	1	*					*	*			*		*			*+ (junior)						*		*	*+ (junior)	*	*
(18) Royal Hong Kong Golf Club Tel 670 1211	2											2 (location)												*	*		
(19) Royal Hong Kong Jockey Club Tel 837 8111	3										*													*	*		
(20) Royal Hong Kong Yacht Club Tel 832 2817 8120365	3	*	*	*	*						*		*	*	*	*			*		*		*				
(21) Shek-O Country Club Tel 522 6022	1										*					*								*	*		
(22) United Services Recreation Club Tel 367 0672	1	*	*																					*	*		

Note: Information on costs, waiting lists and qualifications is valid as of December, 1991. The information may vary slightly or dramatically, always contact the club or relevant membership secretary for current information.

† M = Men; W = Women; C = Couples

ATE	COST CORPORATE/ DEBENTURE	WAITING LIST/ QUALIFICATIONS
•00 entrance ⁄month	$300,000	Approx. 1-2 years
•0 (W) •00 (M) entrance - $375/month	$300,000/debenture	3-5 years
•00 entrance ⁄month	None	None
ese $10,000; 100/month n $1,500; 100/month		
•00 entrance ⁄month	None	1-2 months
⁵00 entrance ⁄month	$200,000	2 years
•00 (W) •00 (M) entrance - $640/month	$400,000	over 2 years
.ct secretary	$5.4 million	Yes (16 years)
•00 entrance ⁄month	None	None
•00 (W)/ $15,000 (M)/ •00 entrance ⁄$370/$460/month	$500,000	No (3-4 months processing)
,000 entrance ⁄month	None	Yes (10 years)
•00 entrance ⁄month	None	1-2 months

Further Reading

Major publication centers:

Hong Kong Government Publications Centre. Located on the ground floor of the General Post Office, beside the Star Ferry terminal in Central. There are government books and pamphlets on virtually all aspects of Hong Kong, maps for hikers and boaters and all of the gazetted laws and regulations of the territory as well as some locally published books on Hong Kong (including some from AmCham).

Hong Kong Tourist Association. In the basement and the 35th floor of Jardine's House, across the road from the GPO and Star Ferry Terminal. HKTA produces a free monthly 'Official Guidebook' plus excellent pamphlets and maps on museums, nightlife, restaurants, walks, shopping districts, arts and crafts, Chinese festivals, golf outings, etc.

Urban Council Publications Centre. Located in the foyer of the Concert Hall at City Hall ('Low Block'). Publications include catalogs from exhibitions in the several museums run under Urbco auspices and others on various local topics of interest produced by Government or local publishers.

Commercial Bookstores. Most general bookstores have Hong Kong and China sections which will likely include the titles listed below. Major English language bookstores are Swindon (Tsim Sha Tsui) and its subsidiaries, Hong Kong Book Centre (Central), and Kelly & Walsh (Pacific Place). There are several SCMP Family Bookshops on the Island and in Kowloon, Times Book Centre (HK and Kowloon), Wanderlust (specializing in travel titles), Bloomsbury (specializing in law and business books) and several Bookazine and Jumbo Grade A stores which sell popular paperbacks as well as a large selection of magazines. Mainland Chinese bookstores selling English-language books include Chung Wah Bookshop (Nathan Road), Commercial Press (Central) and Joint Publishing Company Readers' Service Centre (Central).

Major local publishers:

Hong Kong Government and the Urban Council of Hong Kong produce many books of interest, and at very reasonable prices. Chinese and Hong Kong universities have their own presses, and it is worth calling for their catalogs (HKU also has a Centre For East Asian Studies which produces both books and scholarly monographs). Both Oxford University Press, Longman Group (Far East) and Heinemann Asia have extensive lists. There are a few small, independent publishers in English — mostly in travel or business books (China Guides Publishers, Hong Kong Publishing, Formasia, American Chamber of Commerce). Mainland China controlled companies with bookstores here also publish in English (eg Commercial Press, Joint Publishing Co).

Travel Books

American Express Pocket Guide to Hong Kong and Taiwan by Fred S Armentrout and Ann Wilson (Mitchell Beazley, late 1992)
Insight Guide to Hong Kong (Apa Productions, 1991)
Insider's Guide to Hong Kong by Derek Maitland
Hong Kong, Macau & Canton (Lonely Planet)
A Visitor's Guide to Historic Hong Kong by Sally Rockwell

History

Myself a Mandarin: Memoirs of a Special Magistrate by Austin Coates (Heinemann Asia)
Historic Postcards of Hong Kong (Stock House)
History Around Us (Urban Council, 1982)
Hong Kong 100 Years Ago (Urban Council, 1970)

Maps and Recreation Guides

Hong Kong's 100 Best Restaurants (Hong Kong Tatler, annual)
Hong Kong Guide, Streets & Places (Hong Kong Government)
Magic Walks (vols I & II) by Kaarlo Schepel
Another Hong Kong — An Explorer's Guide (Emphasis, 1990)

Government & Politics

Civil Liberties in Hong Kong (Oxford University Press, 1988)

The Government and Politics of Hong Kong (Oxford University Press, 1991)
Hong Kong: Borrowed Place, Borrowed Time by Richard Hughes (Far Eastern Economic Review, 1975)
Hong Kong — Epilogue to an Empire by Jan Morris (Penguin, 1988)
Hong Kong 1991 (Government yearbook, annual)
The Other Hong Kong Report (The Chinese University Press, annual)
The Future of the Law in Hong Kong (Oxford University Press)

Useful Listings

Associations & Societies in Hong Kong (HKTA, annual)
Consular Posts, Officially Recognized Representatives and Bodies Established Under the Sino-British Joint Declaration (Government Printer, annual)
List of Registered Medical and Surgical Practitioners 1991 (Government Printer, annual)
Dentist List (Government Printer, annual)
Hong Kong Government Telephone Directory (Government Printer, annual)
Names of Buildings (Hong Kong Government, 1990)

Social Life

The Making of Hong Kong Society (Oxford University Press)
Promoting Prosperity — The Hong Kong Way of Social Policy (Chinese University Press)
Crack in the Wall — The Life and Death of Kowloon Walled City by Jackie Pullinger (Hodder & Stoughton, 1984)

In Search of the Great Hong Kong Novel

The World of Suzie Wong, by Richard Mason (Wm Collins Sons, 1957). Not everyone's choice, no doubt. Do I hear mutterings about cliches, racial stereotypes, the whore-with-a-heart-of-gold syndrome? But Mason wrote with much sensitivity of Suzie and her milieu and with insight into the nature of European society of the time. Wit and wistfulness, sadness and hope are honestly presented in a manner devoid of cant. He captures, I think, the ambivalence and determination of the Chinese community in Hong Kong: Suzie's immense pride despite her choice of career, her courage, the circumspection with which she loves the foreign artist longing to take her away. Although I confess to liking the film, it is a less satisfying achievement than the books.

Love Is A Many Splendoured Thing, by Han Suyin. A truly awful movie, this time, and the book impresses most by its author's capacity to use a great many words to say not very much. I heard Han Suyin speak at a Marco Polo Club dinner in the mid-1970s and I marvelled at her arrogance; since then I've not been able to read any of her books, and her ideological flexibility, exposed by the likes of Derek Davies and Simon Leys, has not encouraged me to change my attitude towards her. Nevertheless the love story, told from the woman's perspective, is compelling, and inferentially we learn something about colonial life in the early post-war period which is not available elsewhere.

The Brave White Flag, by James Allen Ford. Recently reprinted, this seems to be the only fictional account of the battle for Hong Kong against the invading Japanese. It is certainly more readable than most of the dozens of non-fiction books dealing with the same events. Ford's writing is assured: factual accuracy mixed with genuine passion (the author was a POW in Sham Shui Po and his brother was tortured and executed by the Japanese) gives a sharp sense of the futility and horror of the British defence. This is a version seen through the eyes of lowly participants and is a useful supplement to official history.

The Road, by Austin Coates. Nothing Coates has written matches *Myself a Mandarin*, and his Macao novel (*City of Broken Promises*) is more entertaining than The Road. But it is a well-crafted book, eschewing sensationalism for introspection and portraying the trials of a minor colonial official with lightness and sympathy.

The Monkey King, by Timothy Mo. A comic tale, told with gentle irony and bringing a fresh perspective to bear upon Hong Kong society. I had greater pleasure from this book than from *An Insular Possession* (1986), a mature and ambitious work which excites more admiration than enjoyment. The Monkey King gives ample evidence of burgeoning talent yet stands on its own as a gratifying piece of light literature.

Years of the Hungry Tiger, by John Gordon Davies. A macho manner and self-conscious striving for literary style somehow combine effectively, at least if one perseveres through the first fifty pages or so. Ignore the cocklofts on the rooftops, which never existed anyway. Three is a relentless rhythm to the narrative which suits the subject-matter and convincingly conveys the pace of Hong Kong. The sequel, *Typhoon* (1978), sustains the author's cash-flow rather than the energy of the original tale.

These are my six of the best. I had intended to list the top ten, but I can find no others to recommend with complete confidence. Alexander Cordell's first-person account of a young Tanka girl from Fo Tan coping with culture shock (*The Sinews of Love, 1965*), Preston Schoyer's *The Typhoon Edge (1959)*, rather dated but agreeably written, and Tin Tai-yi's *Kampoon Street (1964)* are the best of the rest. Keith Colquhuon doesn't say much about Hong Kong in *Filthy Rich (1982)* except "They may want to fly a QC from London -- the local chaps are so incompetent". James Clavell's *Noble House (1981)* is so tedious that I have lost confidence in *Taipan (1966)*, a book I liked when I first came to Hong Kong but would probably find dismaying to read again. I could not finish *Dynasty (1977)* by Robert Elegant, though I tried manfully.

Some good novels use Hong Kong only as a setting for one or two episodes in stories whose main themes are irrelevant to the colony; in this category I place John Le Carre, *The Honourable Schoolboy (1977)*, and Andrew Osmond and Douglas Hurd, *The Smile on the Face of the Tiger (1969)* (The theme of this one is actually very relevant but it is more a diplomatic thriller than a Hong Kong novel). Martin Booth's *Hiroshima Joe (1985)* is simply too depressing to think about. *The Painted Veil* by Somerset Maugham (1925) and *The Conquerors* by Andre Malraux (1928), sometimes said to be about Hong Kong, have little to say about it and are set in China.

It is tempting, but resistible, to include Patrick Acheson, *Flagrant Harbour (1983)* for its crudity and irreverent humour; Leslie Thomas, *Onward Virgin Soldiers (1971)*, ditto; Amanda Blake, *The Colony Club (1989)* for its hilarious insight into the rich sexual fantasies of local gweipos; Christopher New, *The Chinese Box (1975)*, a disjointed work struggling to live up to its dust-jacket's description as "a brilliant study of people whose destinies are shaped not only by each other but also by the strange, anachronistic, yet fascinating society in which they live"; and Lee Ding Fai's *Running Dog (1980)*, which a good editor might have made something of. I'm afraid I could not bring myself even to begin Dolly Oliver's *Paul the Pretender (A Romance of Hong Kong)* (1912, the earliest local novel of which I am aware).

There is a whole genre of potboilers, thrillers, or action novels involving triads, bargirls, Kowloon Walled City, corrupt police and typhoons. They present comic-strip sequences of Hong Kong life. *Candle in the Wind* by Peter Essex (1989) is probably the most recent, but there are many other examples, such as *Triad* by Derek Lambert (1987), *The Wind and the Water* by Stuart Mason-Parker (1988), *Chasing the Dragon* by Sandy Gall (1981), *Pangolin* by Peter Driscoll (1980), *Bastion* by Anthony Esler (1980), *The Mahjong Spies* by John Trenhaile (1986), *A Web of Dragons* by Michael Hartmann (1987), *The Peking Payoff* by Ian Stewart (1978) ("the future of Hong Kong lies in the hands of one sick and beautiful woman ..."), and *The Sanctuary* by Anthony G Cooper (1984). Denis Way's *Fire Horse* (1988) is better than most but goes somewhat over the top in its plot construction. Quiller gets to Hong Kong (*The Mandarin Cypher (1975)*); so do Quinn Leland (*Secret: Hong Kong (1962)*), Killmaster (*Dragon Flame (1966)*), Crown (*Bamboo Shoot-Out (1975)*) and Mrs Polifax (*...and the Hong Kong Buddha (1985)*); James Hadley Chase (*A Coffin from Hong Kong (1964)*) and Robert Ludlum (*The Bourne Supremacy (1986)*) have included us in their itineraries. William Marshall has now published at least ten Yellowthread Street mysteries.

My collection sadly boasts only one bodice-ripper, Denise Emery's *Sunrise in Hong Kong (1981)*. Jonathan Gash, *Jade Woman (1988)* is clever and ludicrous; Margaret Pemberton, *A Multitude of Sins* is a more sophisticated Colony Club; the less said about Lily Chan's *The Struggle of a Hong Kong Girl* the better. Elizabeth Darrell's *The Jade Alliance (1979)* earns points for originality (the travails of a Russian aristocratic family in Hong Kong in 1906) but loses them for its quaint notions of local culture. None of these could even pretend to be a novel which in some way attempts a genuine understanding of Hong Kong; they are simply adventure yarns, mystery stories or romances in an exotic setting.

Mason-Parker, John Gordon Davis, Hartmann and Cooper are or were Hong Kong civil servants (the first three from the Attorney General's Chambers); New is at HKU, Way is in local business, and journalists Stewart and Acheson lived here for a while. Several other local expats have produced novels of awesome banality: for example, James Simon, *How to Kill a Gweilo (1983)*, Geoffrey Thursby, *Miller (1983)* and Bill Lowe, *Conspiracy of Amateurs (1985)*. These must be real collectors' items now. Lowe writes much better short stories (*Twist in the Tale (1988)*) but he does not set them in Hong Kong.

It may be that the best hope for the great Hong Kong novel lies in translated works. Have local authors writing in Chinese produced anything which might quality? Will the recent Cantonese cultural renaissance in the territory inspire and nurture a serious novel about the unsettled society of Hong Kong? Or are serious novelists too busy preparing to emigrate?

- Reprinted with permission from Bloomsbury Book Guide, In search of the Great Hong Kong Novel by Peter Wesley-Smith, July/August 1989.

INDEX

Fanling, 135
fans, 160
Far Eastern Economic Review, 83
fast-food outlets, 143
fast food, 17, 147
fax machines, 161
Feast of Hungry Ghost (Yue Lan), 21
fencing, 178
festivals, 17, 19, 21
field hockey, 178
Filipino Club, 190
Filipinos, 8
Film Clubs, 186
Financial Women's Assn, 191
Fine Arts Society, 184
First Opium War, 3
First Registration Tax , 34, 129
fish, 144
fishing, 178
Flagstaff House, 187
flea collar, 159
floating clinics, 69
floor mats, 151
floor polishers, 61
florists, 134
flower market, shops, stalls, 18, 161, 162, 195, 196
flying, 178
food, 15, 16, 32, 65
food hall, 143, 163
food hygiene, 6
food imports, 7
food speciality shops, 147, 163
football (American Gridiron), 178
foreign earned income, 107
foreign investor, 109
foreign nationals, 40
foreign ownership, 109

foreign prescriptions, 67
Fortress, 149
fortune tellers, 23, 203
free trade zones, 112
French International School, 120
frequent flyer's club, 206
fresh food markets, 66
fresh fruit, 144
Friends of the Art Gallery of the Chinese University of Hong Kong, 184
Friends of the Cultural Centre, 184
Fringe Club, 185
Frog & Toad Pub, 137, 202
Fung Pin Shan Museum, 187
fung shui, 150
funicular railway, 128
furniture, 29, 32, 142, 164
futons, 168

gambling, 203
gang warfare, 74
garden, 161
gardening tools, 162
gas, 52
gas appliances, 148
gazetted laws, 226
GCSE exams, 118, 122
Gemmological Assn of Hong Kong, 189
German Swiss International School, 56, 119
Gilman home appliances, 149
ginseng, 157
Giordano, 158
Girls' Brigade, 198
Glenealy Junior School, 123
go-karting, 195
Goethe Institute, 85, 186, 190
gold, 101, 164
Golden Center, 159